Critical Theories in International Relations

Critical Theories in International Relations

Identity and Security Dilemma

Edited by Tayyar Arı

LEXINGTON BOOKS
Lanham • Boulder • New York • London

Published by Lexington Books
An imprint of The Rowman & Littlefield Publishing Group, Inc.
4501 Forbes Boulevard, Suite 200, Lanham, Maryland 20706
www.rowman.com

86-90 Paul Street, London EC2A 4NE

British Library Cataloguing in Publication Information Available

Library of Congress Cataloging-in-Publication Data

Names: Arı, Tayyar, 1960- editor.
  Title: Critical theories in international relations : identity and security
    dilemma / Edited by Tayyar Ari.
  Description: Lanham, MD : Lexington Books, [2023] | Includes
    bibliographical references and index. | Summary: "The book analyzes the
    critical theories in international relations that have become
    increasingly popular in the post-Cold War era. The book will analyze
    critical theory, Frankfurt School, constructivism, post-colonialism,
    feminism, critical geopolitics, political economy, Copenhagen School,
    Aberystwyth School, Paris School and Ontological security"-- Provided by
    publisher.
  Identifiers: LCCN 2022055541 (print) | LCCN 2022055542 (ebook) | ISBN
    9781666915525 (cloth) | ISBN 9781666915532 (epub)
  Subjects: LCSH: International relations--History--20th century. | Identity
    politics--History--20th century. | Security,
    International--History--20th century.
  Classification: LCC JZ1305 .C74 2023 (print) | LCC JZ1305 (ebook) | DDC
    327.109/04--dc23/eng/20221220
  LC record available at https://lccn.loc.gov/2022055541
  LC ebook record available at https://lccn.loc.gov/2022055542

Contents

Acknowledgments

The book analyzes the critical theories in international relations that have become increasingly popular in the post–Cold War era. The study will reveal the intellectual foundations of critical thinking by benefiting the contributions of some philosophers and sociologists such as Kant, Marx, Foucault, Derrida, and Bourdieu. The book will discuss Critical theory, Frankfurt School, constructivism, postcolonial theory, feminist theory, critical geopolitics, critical political economy, Copenhagen School, Aberystwyth School, Paris School, and Ontological security theory. Most of the authors are senior professors in this field, studying the theories of international relations. The book was written for undergraduate, graduate, and postgraduate IR students and other researchers studying critical theories.

I am indebted to all my colleagues who contributed to the book and others who made revisions and contributions with valuable criticisms. I also wish to express our heartfelt thanks to my family for their endless love and encouragement, which gave me the needed strength to complete this study. Finally, great appreciation for the Lexington Books/Rowman & Littlefield Publishing Group, but in particular, thanks to Joseph Parry.

Prof. Dr. Tayyar Arı
Editor

Introduction

Critical and Post-modern Challenge to International Relations

Tayyar Arı

The inability of mainstream theories to explain the new developments that emerged after the Cold War made critical theories more popular and attractive. Traditional mainstream theories looking at problems from the state's perspective and having similar methodological and ontological concerns have opened up space for critical theories. Mainstream theories can be expressed by different names. In other words, they can be expressed as conventional theories, material theories, rational theories, empirical theories, positivist theories, classical theories, American-based theories, status quo theories, explanatory theories, problem-solving theories (Cox distinction), and objectivist theories. On the other hand, post-positivist theories, which are generally expressed as critical theories, are also named anti-rational theories, reflexive theories, constitutive theories, post-structuralist theories, post-empirical theories, subjective theories, social theories, constructivist theories, anti-realist theories, anti-state theories, and normative theories. While these expressions generally reflect the common features of this group of theories, they also point to the big difference between traditional and critical theories.

The main features of traditional mainstream theories are that they have scientific and objective concerns and think that generalizations can be made based on regularities in international relations. They argue that it is necessary to focus mainly on the material and observable due to scientific concerns. They ignore the change in facts to make experiments and observations. In this respect, the most common feature of critical theories based on subjective and social ontology, which are against objective and material ontology, is that they have a critical stance unlike mainstream theories that seek general truths and base science on assumptions that can be verified or falsified. Another common feature of critical theories is that they include issues that

1

mainstream theories ignore. Critical approaches (influenced to some extent by the Frankfurt School and the Marxist tradition) speak of subjective rather than general truths. Emancipation, human security, environment, gender studies, and social issues have become priority areas. They focus on the subjective truths produced by each circumstance rather than the generally accepted truths.

They look at historical events and current developments within the framework of power relations to which they are exposed. In this context, critical theories deconstruct the analyses and explanations put forward by mainstream theories. However, the discussion of realist and anti-realist theories has been the central axis for debate since the 1940s, especially when it comes to theory discussion. At the same time, the theories of international relations are being classified. Theoretically, realism and, methodologically, positivism have been the target of critical and post-modern theories, including neo-idealism and neo-liberalism. Therefore, the realism–anti-realism debate is a debate that started before the positivism–post-positivism debate and is still ongoing. As long as we talk about security in international relations, it should not be expected that realism, which assumes that the main actors are sovereign states and that the main agenda is security, will go out of fashion. While anti-realist theories criticize realism, which approaches all problems based on state and national security and with an objectivist understanding of security, each has a different focus and priority.

In this context, the Frankfurt School, which inspired the critical tradition and is based on the works that started in the 1920s, made essential contributions to the field with Horkheimer, Gramsci, Habermas, Cox, and Linklater. Although they did not have a fully post-positivist and post-modernist view, they undeniably influenced the emergence of later critical and post-modern theories with their anti-modernist, anti-positivist, and anti-state stances. The Frankfurt School can be regarded as the first representative of a critical approach, both theoretically and methodologically. Undoubtedly, although Marx philosophically inspires these approaches, it is seen that they also represent a new Kantian vein due to their emphasis on the individual. In particular, both the criticism of modernity and the criticism of positivism have been a source of inspiration for later generations. The concept of emancipation introduced by the Frankfurt School impacted the Welsh School's approach to security in the future significantly.

On the other hand, post-structuralism or constructivism, built on the philosophical foundation of Foucault and Derrida, and that impacted David Campbell, Richard Ashley, and Der Derian, revealed the problematic nature of the pregiven conventional reality and explained how subjective reality was constructed. The post-structuralist reading, which pursues subjective reality instead of general principles and general truths, has deconstructed concepts such as foreign policy, sovereignty, anarchy, and security in international relations.

Constructivism has subjected the relationship between identity, security, and foreign policy to a new reading with Nicholas Onuf and Alexander Wendt, bringing it to the field as a new theory in international relations. The Constructivist theory approaches identity with a reflexive point of view, unlike the mainstream theories that adopt a unilateral linear perspective, and focuses on the truths produced by social structure and intersubjective interactions. It focuses on the identity within the context of relationship and interaction in the social structure and the state, rather than being a fixed and given phenomenon, and draws attention to its nature that affects interests and perception of the state.

The Post-colonial theory, which is one of the theories that carry the critical tradition and which has a greater awareness due to its social context, to different fields, draws attention to the fact that the mental structure remaining from the colonial period continues in the former colonies, especially despite the post-colonial period. The Post-colonial theory, which draws attention to the ethnocentric approach of the West, emphasizes that most of the societies that are the other of the West, even if they did not have a colonial relationship with the West or did not have a colonial past, were left underdeveloped because they were ready to accept the Western preeminence and could not develop their unique values.

On the other hand, the Green theory, which develops an eco-centric understanding, unlike the traditional environmentalist narrative, points out that the international community should increase its sensitivity and gain a new consciousness on this issue rather than waiting for the solution of environmental problems from the state. It is skeptical of international cooperation processes, claiming that the state that causes environmental problems cannot be willing and sincere to solve them. In this context, the Green theory has been very influential on the perspective of traditional environmental approaches, which have an anthropocentric perspective even though they have ecological consciousness. It has played a significant role in changing the conventional understanding that looks at everything regarding human and state benefits.

The Aberystwyth School, which represents the first radical change in the perspective of critical theory in the field of security and among whose pioneers are Richard Wyn Jones and Ken Booth, reflects the Frankfurt School's perspective on security. In addition, it has enabled the traditional security understanding to expand on the basis of the subject and deepen on the basis of actors. In this context, the Welsh school, which enriches the field with studies focusing on human security, argues that the individual will not be secure unless he gets rid of the conditions surrounding him. In this context, the theory focuses on the concept of emancipation inspired by the Frankfurt school and its relation to security. According to the school, security is political.

The contribution of the Copenhagen School to security is that it emphasizes the subjectivity of security as an alternative to the objectivist perspective of the traditional approach. The Copenhagen school, which argues that security is a produced phenomenon rather than a pregiven situation, points out that security reflects a subjective situation rather than an objective one since the securitizing actor decides what and who is to be encoded as a security threat. In this context, security for the Copenhagen School is subjective, and the securitizing actor decides it.

The Paris School, or the theory of insecurity, on the other hand, states that while producing security, insecurity is also produced and draws attention to the fact that the concept of security and insecurity is similar to the Mobius strip. The Paris school, which is identical to the Copenhagen school by focusing on the subjectivity of security, draws attention to the fact that many institutions and actors can take part in this process, starting with the concept of security professionals, unlike the Copenhagen school. Instead, it relies on the state as the securitizing actor. While drawing attention to the importance of language in constructing security/insecurity, it emphasizes that other tools are also used. It also points out that it may not be unusual to use the example of Frontex, and securitization/desecuritization can be done routinely. It also argues that what is inside and outside is now unclear, and therefore national and international are intertwined.

On the other hand, Ontological security focuses more on the security of the self. The ontological theory, which associates insecurity with the disruption of routine, emphasizes that biographical narratives are about the continuity of the self and that ontological security is achieved through these narratives. The theory focuses on anxiety instead of the concept of fear, preferred by traditional approaches. In this context, it draws attention to the fact that not only physical security but non-physical security, identity, and self-confidence are prioritized. Ontological Security theory, which analyzes individual and state levels, points out that security is defined through the other.

This edited book is composed of four major parts and eleven chapters.

Chapter 1 argues that there is an interaction between economics and politics and that this interaction leads to behavioral changes on both sides. In a sense, IPE is concerned with how political forces such as states, individual actors, and institutions influence and are influenced by global and national economic interactions. In this context, IPE's main field of study is quite broad. In the early years, IPE researchers focused on debates in the discipline of International Relations (IR), but in later years they have addressed a wide range of issues from environmental studies to women's studies. On the other hand, we believe that IPE should be included among critical theories due to its critical stance of the Marxist approach, its inspiration for critical theories, and the influence of neo-Marxist theories on the development of the critical school. In this context, the study will first focus on the origins and emergence of the IPE approach, followed by the classical theories' approach to IPE, the Marxist IPE tradition, and finally the current IPE debates.

Chapter 2 presents an analysis and evaluation of critical theory, along with its relationship with the discipline of international relations. The chapter is composed of four sections. The first section provides a briefing about the meanings and basics of critical theory. The second talks about the birth of the Frankfurt School and the evolution of the classical critical theory within that School. The third focuses on the basic pillars of critical theory, addressing and discussing them as epistemology, ontology, and praxeology, in that order. The fourth and final section, lastly, touches upon the relationship between critical theory and international relations, mainly by referring to the works of Robert Cox and Andrew Linklater. Some of the weak points of critical theory that call for further research are also addressed in concluding the study.

Chapter 3 discusses the tragedy, international ethics, and normative international relations theory. This chapter focuses on whether and how the concept of tragedy provides valuable insights into global ethics and how it may facilitate a transformation of social practices and institutions in the contemporary world order. Tragedy offers valuable insights into the modern International Relations theory and the practice of avoiding tragic international political outcomes. International relations are most often based on different tragedies explained by classical realists and other theorists. The consequences of many tragedies were reflected in creating new international orders based on international norms, rules, law, and power relationships. The modern international order has been designed to prevent the recurrence of such tragedies as world wars, genocide, mass destruction, environmental catastrophes, etc. Whereas realist approaches argue that tragic perspectives help us to gain a deeper understanding of realpolitik and the selfish nature of human beings, the normative international theory asserts that the concept of tragedy "enables us to see ethical dilemmas clearly" and thus, allows us to transform the practice of international relations for the better.

Chapter 4 analyzes the main tenets of Constructivism in International Relations. After summarizing the main arguments of Realism/Neorealism, the chapter presents its criticisms toward Neorealism at two points: the structure of the international system and identity/interests formation. As opposed to Neorealism, which views the structure as material, Constructivism argues that the structure is social. According to Constructivism, ideas, norms, knowledge, and culture have structural characteristics and play important roles in international relations. Secondly, Constructivism holds that states' identities are not given; they are formed through systemic interaction and they determine state interests. Finally, the chapter gives a detailed explanation of Unit-Level, Systemic, and Holistic Constructivism.

Chapter 5 will analyze the Critical Security Studies and the Aberystwyth School, which started to develop within the Critical Security Studies Master's Program of the International Politics Department of the University of Wales. In this context, the development process of the Aberystwyth School and security as a derivative concept will be examined. In particular, the emancipatory goal of the school and concepts of identity and self/other will be discussed. CSS and the Aberystwyth School question the narrow, militarized, positivist, and theoretically realist security conception. In the framework of this critical attitude, the Aberystwyth School emerged to revisit the security concept.

Chapter 6 focuses on the works and conceptualizations of the Copenhagen School on the security concept. By considering the empirical and theoretical motivations for understanding the security realm since the ending process of the Cold War, the members of the Copenhagen School have made remarkable contributions to Security Studies. In this respect, conceptualizations of security sectors, regional security complex, and securitization have been extensively considered by scholars of Security Studies in their works for the assessment of international security. While they reflect both the broadening and deepening process of the security concept, the Copenhagen School maintains a linkage with the traditional security conception by giving attention to the state and its security.

Chapter 7 explains the Paris School or theory of insecurity and, in this context, its similarities to and differences from other critical security approaches; and that is why for the Paris school, (in)securitization is not just a speech act that legitimizes the extraordinary and the exception, and why many different instruments are being used. The chapter also discusses important concepts such as speech act, surveillance, ban-opticon, governmentality, dispositive, Mobius strip, and internal-external security. And the relation between the migration problem and (in)security in Europe is also analyzed because according to Didier Bigo, the issue of migration is generally perceived as a security problem.

Chapter 8, discussing the main arguments of ontological security, contains information about the place and scope of ontological security within critical security studies. Moreover, the differences between ontological security and physical security and the reflections of ontological security at the individual and the state level are analyzed regarding the scope of internal existence/ self/identity discussions. At the same time, the chapter evaluates the reflections of subjective security in the context of positioning "self" and "other." It is discussed how the concepts of routine, biographical narrative, stability, ontological insecurity, anxiety, and shame are used as the main concepts of ontological security theory in foreign policy processes and crisis resolutions.

Chapter 9 is structured to achieve four aims. The first is to reveal the long process of the emergence of postcolonial theory, with its humanitarian, religious, economic, and political justifications from the "invention" of the Americas until the present. The second is to discuss its theoretical interactions with non-traditional, non-constructive, critical, post-modern, post-structuralist, and feminist perspectives. The third is to outline major strands such as colonial discourse theory, Orientalism, Eurocentrism, identity and hybridity, and subaltern studies. Postcolonial theory is not exempt from criticism. Some scholars regard it as the reconstruction of the West's domination over the former colonies and criticize the theory as a new expression of the West's historical power and alleged superiority over the rest of the world. In this respect, such criticism is also discussed in this article.

Chapter 10 discusses whether feminist and gendered approaches have a different language in women's studies, the reasons for this different concept use, and the analysis of their crossing points. Considering the origin of the concepts primarily, their employment in the academic literature, and their emphases/evaluations by these concepts in the discipline of international relations, particularly in women's studies, the study addresses a set of their interrelationships in the framework of this analysis. Feminist approaches have made intensive contributions to international relations, especially since the early 2000s, although their development began in the late 1980s. In addition to the contributions of feminists to the field, they have developed and deepened theoretically, epistemologically, ontologically, methodologically, and ethically through critical-based discussions among themselves. This transformation, which takes place within the framework of feminist approaches in international relations, is based on intensive discussions that focus on epistemological foundations of feminist knowledge, gender ontology, and strong foundations of ethical positions in a highly unequal world. Especially in today's world, where diversity comes to the fore and multi-dimensional identity discussions are held intensively, feminist thoughts become more visible by introducing future and innovative perspectives. However, while feminism is considered a theoretical approach in women's studies in international relations, studies are performed under gender analysis instead of feminism, especially in recent times.

Chapter 11 examines critical geopolitics by delving into its intellectual history, theoretical assumptions within the context of post-structural IR theories, and methodological orientations. The opening section problematizes the historical transformation of classical geopolitics as a subfield of political geography and international relations. The following section investigates the theoretical assumptions of critical geopolitics by focusing on three major traditions in the history of critical geopolitics. In the final section, I shed light on the main methodological framework of critical geopolitics to make sense of global politics from a critical perspective.

PART I

Political Economy and Critical Tradition

Chapter 1

International Political Economy

Critical Approaches

Veysel Ayhan

INTRODUCTION

Academic discussions on the IPE discipline started in the 1970s. The inadequacy of classical theories in explaining economic and political crises at global and national levels contributed to the emergence of this discipline. Prior to the political economy debates, classical economists analyzed the impact of politics on the economy at a limited level, while political scientists assessed the impact of economic relations and actors on politics at a secondary level. On the other hand, approaches that argue that there is an interaction between economics and politics and that this interaction leads to behavioral changes on both sides led to the birth of the discipline of political economy. However, the criticisms of the international economic and political order, especially by Marxist authors, have paved the way for a wider discussion of IPE. In this context, the main field of study of IPE is quite broad. In the early years, IPE researchers mainly included critiques of Marxist authors, while in later years they addressed a wide range of topics from environmental studies to women's studies. In a sense, IPE developed a critical approach to grand theories in international relations. As a matter of fact, this study will examine the origins of IPE and then examine the IPE approaches in grand theories.

THE ORIGINS OF INTERNATIONAL
POLITICAL ECONOMY

The influence of international relations writers on the emergence of IPE as a discipline is significant. However, the contribution of economists to the emergence of the political economy approach cannot be denied. Moreover, it is known that the first authors to write about the change in the relationship between economics and politics were those with a background in economics. The concept of Political Economy was originally used for the first time in a book entitled *Traite de I èconomie Politique* written by economist Antoine de Montchètien in 1615. The work analyzed the social distribution of production and wealth, increasing the welfare of the nation, and how economics and politics are interrelated. Although Montchètien was the first to use the concept in the title of a work, it is known that the concept found a place in scientific studies before him. In this context, in 1611, the economist Louis de Mayerne-Turquet included the concept of "political economy" in his work and used the concept as the duties of the sovereign power (government) towards the citizens who established the state.[1]

In this regard, the concept was originally introduced in the world of economics in the first half of the 1600s.[2] On the other hand, Sir James Steuart (1712–1780) was the first person in English literature to use the term "political economy" in the title of a book. For Sir Steuart, the discipline of political economy was the science of teaching a nation how to get rich.[3] In 1948, Jacob Viner drew attention to the relationship between power and the pursuit of wealth in foreign policy. In 1968, Richard Cooper in his book *The Economics of Interdependence* underlined the political challenges posed by the growing interconnections between national economies. In 1970, Charles Kindleberger in his book *Power and Money* emphasized the growing tension between economic and political activities, which were becoming increasingly interdependent at the global level. In 1971, Raymond Vernon pointed out that multinational corporations were important political actors at the global level in his book *Purchased Sovereignty*.

In the late 1960s and early 1970s, the influence of economists in the field was limited when authors with a background in IR began to work on IPE, and the field almost became a sub-discipline of IR. In this context, Canadian Robert Cox, Briton Susan Strange, and Americans Robert Gilpin, Charles Kindleberger, Steven Krasner, Peter Katzenstein, Joseph Nye, and Robert Keohane were among the founders of IPE.[4] On the other hand, Robert Cox associates the rise of political economy in the 1970s with Susan Strange's article "International Economics and International Relations: A Case of Mutual Neglect, 1970."[5] The author points out the importance of the fact that after this date, economists and policy makers realized that they needed to benefit from each other. In a sense, IPE has become a separate field of interest for scholars from different disciplines trying to understand social dynamics. IPE has become a common interest for scholars from different fields such as women's studies and environmental, culture, and civilization studies.

THEORIES AND APPROACHES OF POLITICAL ECONOMICS AND INTERNATIONAL RELATIONS

The origin of the IPE discipline at the academic level was formulated and rapidly popularized by IR authors in response to the inadequacy of existing IR theories to explain the political economy developments that emerged in the 1970s.[6] Increasing economic interdependence and the growth of foreign direct investment, especially with the formation of the European Common Market and the increase in direct trade and capital relations within and outside Europe, have led to both the emergence and widespread academic discussion of IPE. There were also other developments during this period that triggered the emergence and development of IPE. In particular, the process that began in 1971 with the US devaluation of the dollar, the end of the gold standard era and the collapse of the Bretton Woods international monetary regime (the dollar being the sole means of payment), and the stagflation (inflationary stagnation) of developed industrial countries in 1973 when OPEC countries increased oil prices several times over coincided with the Third World countries' demands for a New International Economic Order (NIEO).[7]

In "Critical Political Economy," Robert Cox suggests that the interaction between the state and the market must be considered together in order to understand the international system. Cox claims that there is an interaction between international economic relations and international politics and that this interaction cannot be ignored given its consequences.[8] Among the most important representatives of the discipline of political economy in international relations, Susan Strange defines political economy as the study of the interactive interaction between the state and markets.[9] When Susan Strange published her IPE study *States and Market* in the 1980s, she was criticized by many international relations writers for ignoring power and reality.[10] Arguing that the state and markets should be synthesized, Strange believes that the distinction between economics and politics is unrealistic and often arbitrary.[11] Along with Strange, Polanyi and Sally published at the *Review of International Political Economy* and *New Political Economy*, and the thesis that politics-economics or the state and markets influence each other in international relations began to be recognized as a separate discipline.[12] So by the

2000s, the basic assumption of political economy theory was that there was a direct interaction between economics and politics.

In the context of political economy studies, international relations scholars such as Strange, R. Cox, R. Gilpin, Spero, and Sally began to examine state-market interaction in terms of the role of actors and problems such as economic institutions, multinational corporations, monetary policies, energy crises, etc. Some of the authors have tried to develop an alternative IPE approach to the realist paradigm that somehow emphasizes power and power politics and explains the whole field with these concepts, and to the globalist and Marxist theories that place the economy at the center of the whole system.[13] In this regard, the focus of criticism was that the traditional paradigm failed to develop parameters to explain the relationship between politics and economics, despite the fact that international politics is increasingly influenced by international economic relations. Standing out as a critical approach to traditional paradigms in international relations, the IPE discipline has put forward the thesis that the interaction between global economic relations and politics should be analyzed at sociological, cultural, legal, moral, and institutional levels. One of the most prominent figures in this regard was Joseph Schumpeter.[14]

However, the discipline of IPE, which did not find much place in the Western literature during the Cold War, was a popular trend in the Soviet scientific community in the same years.[15] Soviet researchers analyzed international economic order and relations within the framework of Marxist or Structuralist/Radical/Globalist literature.

We see that authors influenced by the above paradigms have developed different explanations of structural change and transformation. In general terms, political economists from the Marxist and Globalist/Structuralist traditions argue that the economic mode of production and economic relations influence the political process and the behavior of actors. National economists, on the other hand, adopting the basic assumptions of the mercantilist and realist paradigm, have analyzed the relationship between economics and politics in the context of national principles, values, security, and national interest and criticized the relationship between economics and politics as leading to the erosion of these values. According to national economists proposing a protectionist trade policy, economic relations and free trade constrain the independence and sovereignty of the national state over time. Analyzing the relationship between economics and politics in the context of concepts such as market, mutual exchange, mutual interest, freedom, free trade, etc., liberal IPEers suggest that economic relations and global economic relations lead to the prosperity and peace of states and societies. In this framework, the different view of the political economy relationship and interaction between these three different schools has also led to the emergence of three different political economy approaches.[16]

Indeed, David N. Balaam and Michael Veseth in their *Introduction to International Political Economy* argue that the IPE perspective has to be analyzed at the Marxist/radical, mercantilist/realist, and liberal levels mentioned above. Robert Gilpin also analyzed the IPE perspective at the level of liberalism, structuralism, and realism. In addition, Theodore H. Cohn, in his work *Global Political Economy*, analyzed international political economy at the level of realist perspective, liberal perspective, and historical structural perspective.[17] Therefore, it would be useful to examine the interaction between politics and economics at all three levels. It is worth noting that the relationship between economics and politics is interpreted differently by the three paradigms.

Liberal IPE Approach

Liberal philosophy historically represents a tradition of political thought with specific goals and ideals. Adam Smith, one of the pioneers of classical liberalism, argued for minimizing the role of governments in the economic order. The state would protect the mechanisms that ensure national defense and the continuation of the free market, undertake the tasks of legal regulations and infrastructure, but would not be directly involved in the market as a productive force or as a force intervening in the economic functioning (production, prices, etc.). Challenging the mercantilist understanding of the state at the time, Smith argued that the best mechanism to prevent the misuse of state power was the expansion of individual freedoms under free market conditions.[18] This approach, which considers the limitation of the state in national terms together with the removal of borders on the international economy, asserts that the removal of state barriers to international trade will increase production and prosperity in the world. Accordingly, free international trade was in the interest of all states and that national wealth would increase through this trade.[19]

However, it is important to underline that there are important differences between the IPE perspective and classical liberal economists or liberal economists. Whereas Adam Smith and his successors focused primarily on the economic relations of production and the benefits of mutual exchange, IPE cares about how economic developments and economic relations affect the distribution of wealth internationally and, in particular, political processes. However, IPE authors argue that the discipline of political economy cannot be understood without analyzing the institutional and processual links between these institutions and regimes and the domestic and foreign policies of the state.[20]

On the other hand, Keynes differed from the classical economists and advocated state intervention in the economy to overcome the crisis.[21] When the policies put forward by the Keynesian economists, who had gained great power after the 1940s, proved insufficient to overcome the general economic crisis that occurred after the 1970s, the American Milton Friedman and the Austrian Friedrich A. Hayek brought back to the agenda the notion of free market, free economy, and individual freedom proposed by Adam Smith.[22] Friedman and Hayek argued that the 1960s were quite different from Adam Smith's time, but that Smith's methodology and rhetoric could be used to overcome contemporary problems.[23]

As a result, Karl Polanyi, one of the pioneers of the political economy perspective, argued that the strengthening of the neoliberal trend has seriously affected the state-market interaction at the international system level. Analyzing 19th- and 20th- century capitalism, Polanyi suggested that capitalism affected the position of the state in the economy in two complementary stages. Starting the first stage with classical liberalism's attempts to limit the state, Polanyi argues that these attempts to reduce the state's control over the economy by adhering to the natural law of the functioning of the economic order were abandoned after the 1930s. However, according to Polanyi, this process came to the agenda again with neoliberal policies and the neoliberal trend forced the state to articulate the national economy to the global economy. Processes such as privatization, legal regulations to support foreign investments, international law, and the acceptance of some special practices (such as arbitration) have limited the power of the nation-state to intervene in the economic process. In this framework, we can define the neoliberal movement as the process by which national markets are freed from state and public intervention and become part of the global economy.[24]

IPE and Realism

According to Robert Gilpin, one of the pioneers of the state-centered approach to political economy, *"there would be no political economy (discipline) without the state and markets. Ignoring the state and assuming that the price mechanism and market forces alone determine economic activity would be the realm of pure economists. . . . Likewise, ignoring markets and assuming that the state takes over the allocation and distribution of economic resources would be the realm of pure political scientists."*[25] Gilpin argues that the political economy approach is a discipline that unifies these two fields under one umbrella of study by revealing the relationship between politics and economics. For Morgenthau, one of the most important representatives of the realist tradition, which assumes that nation-states are the most fundamental actors in understanding international relations, the field of international politics is the relations between sovereign states within the framework of interests defined as power.[26] According to Morgenthau, who argues that politics has its own principles and functioning, "historical data point to the primacy of politics over economics." In other words, he suggests that politics has always played a decisive role over economics. Neorealist K. Waltz also notes that international politics has a decisive influence on economic, social, and all other domains.[27]

Machiavelli, one of the important predecessors of the realist tradition, argued that "gold alone does not make a good soldier, but a good soldier always makes gold," suggesting that military power acquisition policies would bring commercial advantages as well as security to the state. Machiavelli also suggested that the prince establish control over the economy, capital, and money.[28] On the other hand, according to Thucydides, who wrote about the wars between the Greek city-states in his work *The History of Peloponnesian War*, the reason for the wars between the Greek city-states was that many economic conditions changed and this change increased suspicion and mistrust among the states. Unlike the traditional realists, Thucydides stated that money was as important as soldiers in war. *"War is a problem not only when there are not enough troops, but also when there is not enough money,"* he said, emphasizing the importance of economic power as much as military capacity.[29]

The American Alexander Hamilton (1755–1804) and the German Friedrich List (1789–1846) were the leading advocates of mercantilist policies. Before that, the most important contributors to mercantilist thought were Thomas Mun and Bernard Mandeville.[30] Hamilton advocated the idea of limiting foreign trade to protect the nascent American industry. The 19th-century German political economist List was one of the leading advocates of mercantilist policies in Europe. According to List, who stated that the state should protect the national economy against foreign competition, *"the power of production was incomparably more important than wealth itself."*[31]

The mercantilist approach is based on the basic assumption that all states seek to acquire power and wealth in order to preserve and maintain their independence and security. This approach, which was further developed within realism in later years, legitimizes the use of military force to achieve unilateral policies that bring commercial gains.

Structuralist/Radical IPE Approach

Another approach that influenced political economy is the structuralist/radical paradigm, also known as Dependency Theory, Center-Periphery Approach, Marxist Theories, and World System Approach. The paradigm, shaped largely by writers influenced by Marxist analyses, is called globalism

or structuralism because non-Marxists have also made a significant contribution to its development. The common problem area that these authors
focus on is "why Third World countries in Asia, Africa and Latin America
are not developing."[32] In other words, the problematic of why some states
in the international system develop while others do not is discussed in the
structuralist approach. An important part of the structuralists, which has an
important place in the IPE approach, treats the economy as a substructure,
while all other activities, including foreign policy, are treated as superstructures formed by economic relations and mode of production. The power and
influence of the structuralist approach to political economy stems from the
fact that it attaches such a large role to the economy.

According to structuralists who argue that economics and politics cannot
be separated from each other in international relations, the process of globalization has led to the establishment of globally dependent relations in economics and politics. Structuralists argue that there are certain economic-based
patterns of behavior that influence and encompass the structure of international politics and the international system. In order to understand politics and
political behavior, it is first necessary to establish how the economic system
works. In other words, in the international system shaped by economically
based relations, economic interests are the phenomenon guiding the behavior
of states.[33] However, at this point, it should be noted that authors of Marxist
origin see states as an instrument of political control of the ruling class. Marx
and Engels regarded the state as an artificial institution that protects the interests of the ruling class (in the capitalist system, the bourgeoisie) and is under
its political control. The state, which is formed on the basis of maintaining
the relationship between the exploiter and the exploited, is considered as an
organization that protects the interests of the exploiter classes and extends
this to overseas territories when necessary. However, this assumption was
revised and reinterpreted by structuralist Marxists, especially after states took
some social decisions. Structuralist Marxists believe that the assumption that
the state is directly under the control of socio-economic actors does not fully
reflect reality. States sometimes make decisions that protect the interests of all
groups, including the working class. However, despite this, they are far from
considering the state and politics as an autonomous sphere like structuralists
or realists.[34]

Structuralists also argue that historical analyses are necessary to understand
the international system. Its characteristics, which have led some authors to
call it the "historical structuralist perspective," are generally adopted by both
Marxist and non-Marxist structuralists. According to structuralist authors
who treat history as a process of struggle between classes, the classes that
have taken over the means of production have always exploited other classes
in order to maintain their superiority. According to Marxist authors who state

that the relationship of exploitation emerged with the transition from classless society to class society, after the capitalist system, this relationship of exploitation was formed between the exploited working class and the exploiting bourgeoisie.[35]

In analyzing events and phenomena in the international arena, it is more accurate to speak of a modern discipline of political economy rather than a modern discipline of international relations within the framework of the structuralist perspective, which asserts the inseparability of the political and economic.[36] Because for structuralists, the history of international relations is a history shaped by political economy relations.

While dependency theorists divide states into center-periphery countries, structuralists of Marxist origin view the state as an artificial institution created by the bourgeois class to protect its economic interests. However, both argue that in order to understand political actors and international politics, one must first look at the structure of the economic system. Particularly considering the relationship between the industrialized countries of the North (North America, Europe, and Japan) and the poor, underdeveloped, and non-industrialized countries in South America, Africa, and Asia, there appears to be a political and economic system that exists between these states and encompasses the entire international system. The proponents of the Dependency Theory argue that underdevelopment is the result of a political and economic order based on the exploitation of peripheral and semi-peripheral countries by a group of advanced capitalists. The basic assumption is that the underdeveloped countries' failure to develop is not due to their inability to implement the capitalist system, but to their dependency relations with the developed countries within the global capitalist system. They contend that for centuries, all hegemonic powers have tried to shape economic conditions in accordance with their specific aims and interests. At this point, a society fails to develop due to the combined action of internal and external factors. In other words, the international bourgeoisie, either directly or through their financial institutions, establishes links with the national bourgeoisie of a country and secures its economic interests through them. In this way, the relationship established between the international bourgeoisie and the national bourgeoisie increases the pressure of the external structure, but also deepens the relationship between these two classes.[37] Economic links play a very important role in the establishment and sustaining of this relationship. Finally, a significant number of structuralist authors do not believe in the possibility of a fair redistribution of power and wealth within the capitalist system. Those of Marxist origin go even further and argue that the relationship of exploitation will only disappear with the transition to socialism.[38]

Radical Political Economy Approach:
Marxist-Leninist Perspective

Karl Marx has a very important place in the radical political economy perspective. While Karl Marx did not carry out a systematic study of international relations, his thesis of class conflict and his theory of capitalism constitute the basic framework of structural IPE perspectives. Based on historical class conflict, Marxist theory's class conflict thesis and critique of capitalism were written under conditions when the economic, cultural, and political structure of 19th-century Europe was being formed. Marx interpreted the political economy quite differently from the liberal or mercantilist perspective. Instead of proposing a set of suggestions on how the market should function within a state, he proposed an alternative paradigm, targeting the system as a whole. The second title of *Capital* written by Marx was *A Critique of Political Economy.*[39] For Marx, who claimed to transform political economy into a real science, this could only be possible with a model that could grasp the real totality of the relations of production in bourgeois society, as opposed to an understanding of economics that is content with appearances. In this regard, Marx called the relations of exchange and distribution of material goods between people in the production process as relations of production or economic relations. The Marxist approach argued that the economic system, which it called capitalism, brought about a structural change in the whole of society. In *The Communist Manifesto* written by Marx and Lenin, this structural change was expressed as follows: *"The bourgeoisie, wherever it has got the upper hand, has put an end to all feudal, patriarchal, idyllic relations. It has pitilessly torn asunder the motley feudal ties that bound man to his 'natural superiors,' and has left remaining no other nexus between man and man than naked self-interest, than callous 'cash payment.'"*[40] Analyzing the issue from a political economy perspective based on Marx's approaches, Buchholz suggests that *"every system of production gives rise to an order and a ruling class. In Roman times, those who owned slaves claimed to have rights over what they produced. In the feudal period, lords claimed a right over what serfs produced. Under capitalism, too, those who own the means of production and land claim a right to what paid workers produce."*[41]

In his analyses of political economy, Marx argued that economic production is the main determinant of the formation of the relationship between people and its structural change. According to Marx, the state existed to defend and protect the interests of the ruling class, the capitalist bourgeoisie, while market actors directed class exploitation.[42] *"The executive of the modern state is but a committee for managing the common affairs of the bourgeoisie,"* Marx argued, adding that the class that owns the means of production (the bourgeoisie) has, since the establishment of modern industry and the world market, taken political sovereignty in the modern era. The critical meaning that the Marxist tradition attributed to the concept of political economy once again explained why Alfred Marshall and M. P. Marshall preferred to use the term "economics" instead of "political economy," as mentioned above. Marxists believed that the ruling class of the bourgeoisie, backed by the monopoly of the modern state on the use of force, was constantly increasing its gains at the expense of other segments of society, especially the working class.

According to Marx, who emphasized the accumulative character of the capitalist system, the bourgeoisie is forced to spread to the four corners of the earth by the need for an ever-expanding market for its products. The fact that the capitalist has to spread out with the motive of finding new markets for what he produces is an important feature that distinguishes the capitalist system from other systems. In order to sell his goods and to become richer, a capitalist has to establish himself everywhere, to settle everywhere, to establish contacts everywhere. The Marxist political economy perspective argues that existing economic relations are of such a nature that they have cultural, economic, sociological, political, etc. structural consequences for the whole world.[43] Marxist theory thus argued that the change and transformation that started in the economic production system in a country was not only an event affecting the cultural, political, and social conditions in that country, but also had a dimension that affected the whole world. Structural changes in the system are often the result of initiatives by external factors. According to the Marxist understanding of political economy, raw material resources are among the most important factors affecting the profit margin for developed countries acting with the profit motivation. Marx wrote that "the rate of profit is inversely proportional to the rise and fall of raw material resources. This demonstrates how important the price of low raw material resources is for developed countries."[44] The pursuit of an imperialist policy (military occupation or dependent economies) by capitalist countries seeking to increase their profit margins leads to the reshaping of the political and social structure in raw material–rich underdeveloped countries.

Expressing that capitalists had to expand internationally, Marx did not directly develop a theory of imperialism. The theory of imperialism, which has an important place in structural IPE, was put forward by Hilferding, Bukharin, and Lenin. The theory of imperialism is often associated with Marxist economics, but many theories were developed by non-Marxists. John A. Hobson was not a Marxist, but his influence on later Marxist writers was so great that he cannot be ignored in a study of Marxist theories. Hobson (1858–1840) suggested that under-consumption is an important element in the theory of imperialism. When saving exceeds the scope for domestic investment, owners of capital look for investment opportunities abroad. Asserting that the policy of imperialism resulting from overproduction and

underconsumption within the country could be prevented by some inter-
ventionist policies, Hobson argued that the problem did not stem from the
nature of the capitalist system as stated by Marxists. *"Imperialism, he said,
is bad business, a line of argument which goes back to the classical economists (at least). He backed the case up with other arguments; imperialism
was bad for democracy (because of the side effects of militarism), bad for
the peoples subjected to foreign rule (whatever the claims of the imperialists), bad for Britain's reputation, and so on."*[45] Despite Hobson's detailed
work, the most important authors on the theory of imperialism are of Marxist
origin. Between 1900 and 1920, the concept of imperialism was introduced
into Marxist theory, and a definite theory of imperialism was constructed,
by three writers: Rudolf Hilferding, Nicolai Bukharin, and Vladimir Ilych
Lenin.[46] Among them, Lenin's pamphlet, "Imperialism, the Highest Stage of
Capitalism," is the most famous Marxist work on imperialism.

V. I. Lenin (1870–1924) characterized imperialism as the monopoly stage
of capitalism. According to Lenin, one must give a definition of imperialism
that will include the following five of its basic features: *"(1) the concentration of production and capital has developed to such a high stage that it has
created monopolies which play a decisive role in economic life; (2) the merg-
ing of bank capital with industrial capital, and the creation, on the basis of
this 'finance capital,' of a financial oligarchy; (3) the export of capital as distinguished from the export of commodities acquires exceptional importance;
(4) the formation of international monopolist capitalist associations which
share the world among themselves; and (5) the territorial division of the
whole world among the biggest capitalist powers is completed. Imperialism
is capitalism at that stage of development at which the dominance of monopolies and finance capital is established; in which the export of capital has
acquired pronounced importance; in which the division of the world among
the international trusts has begun, in which the division of all territories of
the globe among the biggest capitalist powers has been completed."*[47]

Considering Lenin's approach, international economic relations cannot be
separated from the search for markets for the goods and capital of capitalists
seeking to increase their accumulation and their attempts to provide cheap
raw materials. For Lenin, capitalists share the international market among
themselves by creating monopolies, just as they do domestically. Lenin also
believes that this process would continue until it results in the division of the
whole world among capitalists.[48]

To sum up, the Marxist-Leninist literature argues that the economic mode
of production is the determining force of national and international politics.
The Marxist tradition, which explains all events in terms of economic mode
of production and relations, has a very important place in IPE theory. In
particular, Lenin's theory of imperialism was accepted and developed by the

dependency theorists who emerged in later years. Dependency theorists, who treat global international economic relations differently from liberals, considered international trade under different headings such as center-periphery, capitalist world system; however, they studied international trade as a system based on exploitation in essence.

Dependency Theories and IPE

Dependency theories emerged in the 1960s when a group of Latin American authors criticized liberal theories of modernization and saw developed countries as responsible for the failure of other countries to develop. Dependency theory developed mainly under the influence of two different theoretical traditions. The first one, and the one that occupies a dominant place in the theory, is the Marxist tradition. The other is Latin American structuralism. Marxist-based dependency theorists have been influenced by Marx and Lenin's analysis of capitalism, class conflict, capitalist mode of production, and imperialism. While a significant number of Latin American structuralists have also been influenced by these perspectives, they have focused more on the problem of why so-called Third World countries have failed to develop. In other words, the most important feature that distinguishes dependency theorists from Marxists is that they have worked on the problems between North and South.[49] In particular, the Argentine political economy theorists Cardoso and Faletto's *Dependency and Development in Latin America*, published in 1979, was one of the most controversial works on the political and social process in Latin America. Cardoso and Faletto proposed that if capitalist societies could look at and understand Latin American countries from a non-materialist perspective, then there would be no need to evaluate capitalist countries from a Marxist perspective.[50]

Scholars of dependency theory conduct comparative research in many fields, including sociological, anthropological, political, and economic, in order to answer the question of why the countries of the South have failed to develop. While Latin American dependency theorists, who work epistemologically differently from traditional theories, mainly acknowledge the impact of endogenous and exogenous factors on underdevelopment, the majority of them attribute the emergence of these factors to the deliberate political economy practices implemented by developed countries. Dependency theory criticizes the capitalist development process and argues that the system leads to the establishment of mechanisms that lead to the further development of developed countries.[51]

In this framework, dependency theory sees "*the world capitalist system as divided into a centre and a periphery (terminology varies; metropolis and satellite, or core and periphery, are alternatives). The normal processes of the system cause the gap between centre and periphery to widen, as the centre develops at the expense of the periphery, while the periphery is reduced to a state of dependence. Imperialism, in the usual sense of political and military dominance, plays a secondary role in dependency theories, which were intended to explain what was seen as a continued failure of development in the Third World, in the era of decolonization."*[52]

As we have emphasized above, these criticisms constitute the main framework of the theoretical analyses brought by dependency theorists on why underdeveloped countries failed to develop. In this context, authors such as Frank, Galtung, and Wallerstein have made important observations on the center-periphery relationship and turned the approach into an important theory. It would be useful to look at these in more detail.

Frank coined the term "undevelopment" for the state of affairs before capitalist penetration: *"The 'development of underdevelopment' occurs because the world capitalist system is characterized by a metropolis-satellite structure. The metropolis exploits the satellite, surplus is concentrated in the metropolis, and the satellite is cut off from potential investment funds, so its growth is slowed down. More important, the satellite is reduced to a state of dependence which creates a local ruling class with an interest in perpetuating underdevelopment, a 'lumpenbourgeoisie' which follows a 'policy of underdevelopment.'"*[53] Given this approach, trade between the Center and the Periphery is always a relationship between unequals in power.

On the other hand, P. Sweezy and H. Magdoff contend that multinational corporations are not multinational in the sense that their operations, management, or employees are from different nationalities. In their view, a multinational corporation is a multinational corporation in the sense that it operates in many countries and its purpose is to increase the profits of the corporation as a whole, not to increase the profits of any individual unit at the country level. In this sense, some of the most important features of national companies seem to be reflected in multinational companies. These are the centralization of ownership and control. These two authors argue that these two characteristics show that multinational companies are not as multinational as they are thought to be. The fact that companies, which produce for a wide market in a competitive environment and are constantly driven to increase their profit margins, shift their production to a different country and create subsidiaries there, either to reduce costs or to control new markets on their own, does not lead to serious changes in the structure of multinational corporations. The nationality of the capital is not in the hands of the country where it is located, but in the hands of the nation-state that controls it.[54] Therefore, according to this conception outlined by Sweezy and Magdoff and generally accepted by center-periphery theorists, multinational corporations are nothing but the structuralization of the exploitation relationship that exists between the center and the periphery, and even more so between classes. In particular, as will be discussed below, according to authors such as Galtung and Wallerstein, all these relations and the companies and institutions created (such as the IMF, the WTO) are merely instruments for the continuation of the exploitation relations of the Central states over the so-called Periphery states.

While explaining underdevelopment, Galtung, a dependency theorist, suggested that underdevelopment was caused by the exploitation of undeveloped nations, called the Periphery, by developed countries, which he characterized as the Center. Drawing on Lenin's theory of imperialism, Galtung opposes the distinction between domestic and foreign policy and argues that imperialism is an important perspective for understanding the institutional and structural link between domestic and foreign policy. Galtung states that center countries also have a center and a periphery. The same division also exists in the periphery countries. For Galtung, the structural relationship between two countries is formed when the center of the center country establishes a relationship with the center of the periphery country within the framework of the principle of common interest. Galtung believes that the power of the parties has a significant impact on the establishment of the relationship between the two sectors, and through this relationship, income is transferred from the periphery to the center.[55]

On the other hand, Wallerstein argues that the distinctive feature of the modern world system is its capitalist structure based on accumulation. The capitalist world economy/system emerged primarily in Europe and parts of the American continent in the 16th century. Wallerstein asserts that the ever-expanding system became universal after the second half of the 19th century when regions that had not yet been integrated into the capitalist world economy were economically and politically integrated into the system. Suggesting that the capitalist world system is determined by the international economy, Wallerstein also notes that the political structures, social structures, cultures, and relations of countries with other states are also determined by the capitalist world economy.[56]

Wallerstein saw the formation of the capitalist world system as a product of the world economy rather than the nation-state. For Wallerstein, the concentration of military power in the countries of the capitalist center gave them unequal power vis-à-vis others, and these countries used their power as an important element in making other regions part of the capitalist world system. The capitalist system based on accumulation, which by its very nature necessitated an imperialist expansion, led to the integration of other parts of the world into the capitalist world economy. On the other hand, the capitalist world system is divided into three tiers of states, those of the core, the semi-periphery, and the periphery. The "semi-periphery" is a sort of labor aristocracy of states or geographical areas. Without it, a world system becomes polarized and liable to revolt, while an intermediate tier diffuses antagonisms.[57]

Thus, Wallerstein added "semi-periphery" states to Galtung's center-periphery approach within the capitalist world economy. The semi-periphery countries play a special role in the smooth functioning of the capitalist world economy. While the semi-periphery countries, which possess partial characteristics of both the center (high income, high wages, advanced technology, high profits, high production of industrial goods, etc.) and the periphery (low income, old technology, low wages, low profits, etc.), were receiving their shares from the exploitation of the periphery, the classes around the center were receiving the same from the exploitation of the semi-periphery and the periphery countries.[58]

The capitalist world economy is the process by which local economies in a region are transformed into national economies as a result of the initiatives of the bourgeoisie who want to increase capital accumulation, and national economies are transformed into international economies through the initia-tives of capitalists. In this structure, political authorities fulfill the role of permanent civil servants of the capitalists. The capitalist world economy is a political superstructure and consists of sovereign states. Sovereignty here, of course, does not mean having absolute authority over decisions. Especially in the center countries, the state apparatus was strengthened to protect and promote the interests of the bourgeoisie. Capital accumulators use the state apparatus to realize their interests. According to Wallerstein, the capitalist world economy is a historical phenomenon which will eventually disappear. The capitalist world economy refers to the social relationship between labor and capital. Surplus value is transferred from the proletariat to the capitalist as a result of this relationship. Drawing on the dialectical discourses of Marxist doctrine, Wallerstein argues that the capitalist world system is an afterthought and will soon disappear.[59]

NEW DEBATES IN INTERNATIONAL
POLITICAL ECONOMY

In the new millennium, critical approaches to the field and nature of IPE have emerged and the discipline has been reformulated. In this context, critical IPE authors such as Benjamin Cohen and John Hobson have criticized the failure of traditionalist IPEs to explore the "Big Questions" of the contemporary era in their book *IPE and the Review of the New Political Economy*. In a sense, the authors pioneer new debates about the global system and where the world is evolving and how we can influence it. They also argue that the differences between the American and British schools of IPE have diminished and are weak in the face of contemporary challenges. Hobson points out that IPE has a Western-centered perspective and that the main arguments and research topics of the discipline are influenced by this. Emphasizing that Marxist approaches are also Western-centered, Hobson gives Marx's approach to the spread of British Imperialism to India as an example to support his thesis. On the other hand, there is a lack of critical research on capital and labor markets. In this context, according to the new IPEers who emphasize the increasing working poverty in the world, a significant portion of the world's 3 billion working people live in poverty or within the poverty line. It should also be taken into account that the national and global resistances that have developed with demands for the eradication of poverty and a fairer and more equal distribution of income have an impact on the global system. In addition to income inequality, increasing poverty is also threatening the existence of the global system. One in three workers worldwide lives on less than US$2 a day. On the other hand, until 2013, the 85 richest people in the world had a wealth equal to half of the world's population. Therefore, it is important to understand the contradiction between capital and labor and to reveal the power relationship between them. The authors emphasize that the national and global system of the 21st century, marked by deepening income inequality, has exacerbated this imbalance.

In this regard, Usman W. Chohan has tried to bring a new perspective to the theory by arguing that the impact of political economy will be much wider, especially during and after the coronavirus period. In his work "A Post-Coronavirus World: 7 Points of Discussion for a New Political Economy," he drew attention to the post-coronavirus economics and possible crises in the economy. In his article, Chohan emphasizes that issues such as economic growth, debt burdens, collapsing public services, and sanctions had significant effects on the political sphere, and this situation paved the way for a new debate on the need to examine changes within the scope of the new political economy.[60]

On the other hand, Feminist approaches have an important place in current IPE debates. According to some Feminist authors who argue that traditional IPE studies have a state-centered approach, it is crucial to acknowledge gender inequalities in the functioning of the global political economy. In this context, the authors argue that the global system, capital-labor relations, and political processes cannot be seen as a gender-neutral arena. Critical IPEers, who state that the gender phenomenon cannot be ignored in labor-capital relations, assert that there are class and gender differences in the formation of labor exploitation and even in the emergence of the exploitative relationship. The mobilization of low-cost women's labor supply in the global economic system and production areas ensures the institutionalization and globalization of hierarchical exploitation. From multinational corporations to small firms, it is pointed out that this leads to the reproduction of a gendered labor-capital and exploitation order and that the liberal view of global economic integration does not focus on the mechanism of gendered exploitation. Feminist IPE authors argue that the relationship between labor and resource allocation at the micro level and capitalist accumulation at the macro level leads to the institutionalization of gender discrimination. These authors also draw attention to the transformation of cheap migrant women's labor into a means of exploitation, which has recently become more visible, the emergence of gendered approaches at the sectoral level, and the existence of labor markets defined as women's work or men's work. They point to the need to prioritize the kind of research that foregrounds the construction of gendered, racialized identity while examining capital-labor relations, production, and markets.

In this context, the impact of the economic measures taken by the states on women workers, especially in the period between 2019 and 2022, because of the coronavirus, has also drawn the attention of feminist political economy writers. In her work "Coronavirus Fiscal Policy in the United States: Lessons from Feminist Political Economy," Katherine A. Moos emphasizes that the economic measures and supports taken by the US had limited impact on women workers and housewives.[61] As a matter of fact, although states supported the society with large budgets at the public level during the coronavirus outbreak, there was a rise in unemployment among women, especially in shrinking markets. Deniz Beyazbulut, a researcher at DISK's Research Department, who stands out with her trade union research, told DW that during the fight against the virus, men's participation in the labor force also declined, but this trend was faster for women. According to the report prepared by DİSK, in the first year of the virus, there was a 6.5 percent decrease in women's employment, while this rate remained at 2.7 percent for men. Likewise, data shows that women have become the target group for unpaid leave and uninsured labor.[62]

One of the current IPE debates is the impact of the relationship between politics and economics on nature and environmental problems. Asserting that environmental problems cannot be evaluated independently of production relations, inter-state relations, and global markets, environmentalist movements promote international cooperation for a more livable world. Until the early 2000s, IPE addressed environmental issues or "green" worldviews. Mainstream authors of IPE have been reluctant and insensitive to include the environment much in their analysis of IPE. However, the emergence of multiple environmental problems in the world since the early 2000s, ranging from resource scarcity to environmental degradation, exacerbated as a result of broad trends in the global economy, highlighted the need for international cooperation. The efforts of IPE authors drawing attention to environmental issues have created a strong awareness of the emerging global environmental policy and measures, both individually and at the national and international level. The Montreal Protocol on the protection of the ozone layer in 1987 and the UN Framework Convention on Climate Change, which was opened for signature at the United Nations (UN) Conference on Environment and Development in Rio de Janeiro in 1992, have led to the further prominence of critical IPE for the protection of the environment. Indeed, many of the environmental IPE pioneers initially drew heavily on regime theory to analyze global environmental politics. With its focus on principles, rules, norms, and decision-making procedures, regime theory proved to be an attractive framework. Thus, they contributed to the emergence of environmental agreements and institutions at the international level. Today, it is noteworthy that environmentalist movements are expanding their influence in the global economy and politics.[63]

Another phenomenon drawing attention in the field of political economy, especially in the post-coronavirus period, is food security and its impact on the domestic and foreign policies of countries. Increasing food prices due to the Russia-Ukraine crisis have made the problem of access to food in less developed countries a top agenda item. The decisive role of Ukraine and Russia in grain and sunflower oil production, as well as the problems in energy, led to an increase in food and energy prices. While this has led to disruptions in the export and import balances of countries, it has also led to the expansion of the poor masses in underdeveloped countries that are lacking in food and energy. The war in Ukraine accelerated the impoverishment of the masses even more than the economic contraction caused by COVID-19. Climate change and the war in parallel with the global pandemic in the same period hastened the contraction of the world economy. On the other hand, it is argued that the impact of the war on food security will be higher than expected. The Russian Federation and Ukraine played an important role in food security as the world's food depots. Together they supplied about 30 percent of the world's wheat and barley, 50 percent of sunflower oil, and one-fifth of maize. At the same time, neighboring Belarus and the Russian Federation rank fifth in the world supply of fertilizer. It is obvious that the cessation of fertilizer supply will have a negative impact on food production. According to the April 2022 United Nations Food and Agriculture Organization (FAO) report, world food prices have risen 30 percent higher and continue to rise. Between 2019 and 2022, the number of people suffering from hunger increased by 46 million in Africa, 57 million in Asia, and 14 million in Latin America and the Caribbean. Seventy-seven million people have been driven into extreme poverty.[64] According to the UN report, in addition to global cooperation in dealing with new crises, income transfers from developed countries to developing countries are also required.

CONCLUSION

Although the birth of the IPE discipline at the academic level dates back to the 1970s, it is noteworthy that publications analyzing the interaction between economics and politics have included the concept of political economy since the 1600s. The energy crises after the 1960s, the troubles in the international monetary system, and the North-South debates inevitably led to a vigorous academic discussion of the relationship between economics and politics. In the same period, developments such as increasing economic interdependence and the expansion of foreign direct investments due to the impact of globalization, especially the formation of the European Common Market and the increase in direct trade and capital relations within and outside Europe, led to both the emergence and widespread academic discussion of IPE. There were also other developments during this period that triggered the emergence and development of IPE. In particular, the process that started with the US devaluation of the dollar in 1971, the end of the gold standard era, and the collapse of the Bretton Woods international monetary regime (the dollar being the sole means of payment), and the stagflation (inflationary stagnation) of the developed industrial countries in 1973 when OPEC countries increased oil prices several times over coincided with the Third World countries' demands for a New International Economic Order (NIEO). The theoretical analysis of economic relations and modes of production at the national and global level by authors with Marxist roots has contributed to the development of critical political economy at the academic level.

In conclusion, in the context of recent debates, it is obvious that political economy provides a basis for discussions beyond being a unit of explanation in the context of liberalism, Marxism, and realism only at the theoretical level. It is noteworthy that critical political economy tries to provide more explanatory approaches on many issues such as increasing impoverishment, inequality in income distribution among countries, changes in policies towards women and minority groups within countries, and the effects of climate change on migrant mobility and employment.

REFERENCES

Abbott, Jason P., and Worth, Owen. "Introduction: The 'Many Worlds' of Critical International Political Economy." In *Critical Perspectives on International Political Economy,* edited by Jason Abbott and Owen Worth, 1–13. New York: Palgrave Macmillan Press, 2002.

Arı, Tayyar. *Uluslararası İlişkiler Teorileri.* 10. Baskı. Bursa: Aktüel, 2021.

Arı, Tayyar. *Postmodern Uluslararası İlişkiler Teorileri 2, Uluslararası İlişkilerde Eleştirel Yaklaşımlar.* Bursa: Dora, 2014.

Aydınlı, Halil İ. and Ayhan, Veysel. "The Discussion on the Limitation of Power from the Perspective of the Historical Development of the Concept of Sovereignty." *Cumhuriyet University, Journal of the Faculty of Economics and Administrative Sciences* 5 (2004): 67–84.

Ayhan, Veysel. *İmparatorluk Yolu: Petrol Savaşlarının Odağında Orta Doğu.* Ankara: Nobel Yayıncılık, 2006.

Balaam, D. N., and Veseth, Michael. *Introduction to International Political Economy,* Second Edition. New Jersey: Prentice Hall, 2001.

Brewer, Anthony. *Marxist Theories of Imperialism: A Critical Survey, Second Edition.* London; New York: Taylor & Francis e-Library, 2001.

Burch, Kurt. "Constituting IPE and Modernity." In *Constituting International Political Economy,* edited by Kurt Burch and Robert A. Denemark, 21–40. Boulder: Lynne Rienner Publishers, 1997.

Chohan, Usman W. "A Post-Coronavirus World: 7 Points of Discussion for a New Political Economy" (March 20, 2020). *CASS Working Papers on Economics & National Affairs* No. EC015UC, March 2020, Available at SSRN: https://ssrn.com /abstract=3557738 or http://dx.doi.org/10.2139/ssrn.3557738

Clapp, Jennifer, and Helleiner, Eric. "International political economy and the environment: Back to the basics?" *International Affairs* 88, no. 3 (2012): 485–501.

Cohn, Theodore H. *Global Political Economy: Theory and Practice,* 2nd Ed. New York: Longman Pub., 2003.

Cox, Robert W. "Critical Political Economy." In *International Political Economy: Understanding Global Disorder,* edited by Björn Hettne, 31–45. London; New Jersey: Zed Books Press, 1995.

Deutsche Welle. "Salgın Neden en çok Kadınları Vurdu." Accessed March 7, 2021, https://www.dw.com/tr/salg%C4%B1n-neden-en-%C3%A7ok-kad%C4%B1nlar %C4%B1-vurdu/a-56787185

Farrands, Christopher. "Being Critical About Being 'Critical' in IPE: Negotiating Emancipatory Strategies." In *Critical Perspectives on International Political Economy,* edited by Jason Abbott and Owen Worth, 14–33. New York: Palgrave Macmillan, 2002.

Galtung, Johan. "A Structural Theory of Imperialism." *Journal of Peace Research* 8, no. 2 (1971): 81–117.

Garaudy, Roger. "Marx ve Ekonomi Politik." In *Sosyo-Ekonomik Perspektif,* trans. Hakan Bahçeci, edited by Uğur Dolgun, 238–244. Bursa: Asa Kitapevi, 2001.

Gilpin, Robert. "Three Models of the Future." *International Organization* 29, no. 1 (Winter, 1975): 37–60.

Gilpin, Robert. *Global Political Economy: Understanding the International Economic Order.* Princeton; Oxford: Princeton University Press, 2001.

Hettne, Björn. "Introduction: International Political Economy of Transformation." In *International Political Economy: Understanding Global Disorder,* edited by Björn Hettne, 3–30. London; New Jersey: Zed Books Press, 1995.

King, James E. "The Origin of the Term 'Political Economy.'" *The Journal of Modern History* 20, no. 3 (Sept. 1948): 230–231.

Lenin, V. I. "Imperialism, the Highest Stage of Capitalism." In *A Compilation on International Relations and Political Theory*, edited by Howard Williams, Moorhead Wright, and Tony Evans; trans. Ebru Eralp. Ankara: Siyasal Kitabevi, 1996.

Lenin, V. I. *Imperialism, the Highest Stage of Capitalism* (Petrograd, April 26, 1917), 78, https://www.files.ethz.ch/isn/125485/6000_Imperialism_Highest_Stage_Capitalism.pdf 78

Machiavelli, Niccolo. *The Prince*, trans. Harvey C. Mansfield. Chicago: University of Chicago Press, 2010.

Marx, Karl. *Capital: A Critique of Political Economy*, trans. Samuel Moore and Edward Aveling. Moscow: Progress Publishers. Accessed March 3, 2022, https://www.marxists.org/archive/marx/works/download/pdf/Capital-Volume-I.pdf

Marx, Karl, and Engels, Friedrich. *Manifesto of the Communist Party*. Moscow: Progress Publishers, 1969, chap. 1, https://www.marxists.org/archive/marx/works/1848/communist-manifesto/ch01.htm

Marx, Karl and Engels, Friedrich. *Komünist Manifesto ve Türkiye'deki Öyküsü*. 8. Baskı. Çev. Gaybiköylü. Ankara: Bilim ve Sosyalizm Yay., 1997.

Moos, K. A. "Coronavirus Fiscal Policy in the United States: Lessons from Feminist Political Economy." *Feminist Economics* 27, no. 1–2 (2021): 419–435.

Oktay, Tanrısever F. "The Problem of Method: Traditionalism-Behaviorism Debate." In *State, System and Identity*, edited by Atilla Eralp. Istanbul: İletişim Yayınları, 1996.

Papp, Daniel S. "Marxism-Leninism and Natural Resources: The Soviet Outlook." *Resources Policy* 3, no. 2 (June 1977): 134–148.

Ravenhill, John. "International Political Economy." In *The Oxford Handbook of International Relations*, edited by Christian Reus-Smit and Duncan Snidal, 539–557. Oxford University Press, 2008.

Ravenhill, John. "The Study of Global Political Economy." In *Global Political Economy*, edited by John Ravenhill, 3–28. Oxford: Oxford University Press, 2017.

Seyidoğlu, Halil. *Uluslararası İktisat: Teori, Politika ve Uygulama*. 13. Baskı. İstanbul: Kurtiş Matbaası, 1999.

Sievers, A. M. "Schumpeter'e Göre Kapitalist Uygarlık," Çev-Der: Uğur Dolgun. *Sosyo-Ekonomik Perspektif*. Bursa: Asa Kitapevi, 2001.

Sönmezoğlu, Faruk. *Uluslararası Politika ve Dış Politika Analizi*. İstanbul: Filiz Kitapevi, 1995.

Strange, Susan. "International Economics and International Relations: A Case of Mutual Neglect." *International Affairs* 46, no. 2 (1970): 304–315.

Sweezy, P., Baran, P., and Magdoff, H. *Çağdaş Kapitalizmin Bunalımı*, trans. Yıldırım Koç. Ankara: Bilgi Yayınları, 1975.

Tanrısever, F. Oktay, "Yöntem Sorunu: Gelenekselcilik-Davranışsalcılık Tartışması." Der.: *Atilla Eralp. Devlet, Sistem ve Kimlik*. 2. Baskı. İstanbul: İletişim Yay. 1996.

Tansey, Richard, and Hyman, R. Michael. "Dependency Theory and the Effects of Advertising by Foreign-Based Multinational Corporations in Latin America." *Journal of Advertising* 23 (March 1994): 27–42.

Thèma Larousse: Tematik Ansiklopedi, 464–465. Milliyet Yayıncılık, 1993–1994.

Tkachenko, S. L. "The Study of International Political Economy in Russia." *Communist and Post-Communist Studies* 37 (2004): 111–120.

Uche, L. Uka, "Some Reflections on the Dependency Theory." *Africa Media Review* 8, no. 2 (1994): 23–49.

UN News. "Global impact of war in Ukraine on food, energy and finance systems." Brief no. 1, accessed April 1, 2022, https://news.un.org/pages/wp-content/uploads /2022/04/UN-GCRG-Brief-1.pdf

Viotti, Paul R., and Kauppi, Mark V. *International Relations Theory: Realism, Pluralism, Globalism*, 2nd Edition. New York: Macmillan Publishing, 1993.

Wallerstein, Immanuel. "Dependence in an Interdependent World: The Limited Possibilities of Transformation within the Capitalist World Economy." *African Studies Review* 17, no. 1 (April 1974): 1–26.

Wallerstein, Immanuel. "Semi-Peripheral Countries and the Contemporary World Crisis." *Theory and Society* 3 (1976): 461–483.

Wallerstein, Immanuel. *Jeopolitik ve Jeokültür*, trans. Mustafa Özel. İstanbul: İz Yayıncılık, 1993.

Watson, Matthew. "Theoretical Traditions in Global Political Economy." *Global Political Economy*, 2nd Ed., edited by John Ravenhill, 29–66. Oxford: Oxford University Press, 2008.

NOTES

1. James E. King, "The Origin of the Term 'Political Economy,'" *The Journal of Modern History* 20, no. 3 (1948): 230.

2. King, "The Origin," 230.

3. Robert Gilpin, *Global Political Economy: Understanding the International Economic Order* (Princeton; Oxford: Princeton University Press, 2001), 25.

4. Veysel Ayhan, *İmparatorluk Yolu: Petrol Savaşlarının Odağında Orta Doğu* (Ankara: Nobel Yay., 2006), 9–80.

5. Susan Strange, "International Economics and International Relations: A Case of Mutual Neglect," *International Affairs* 46, no. 2 (1970): 304–315.

6. For extensive theoretical discussions on this issue, see Tayyar Arı, *Uluslararası İlişkiler Teorileri 2, Uluslararası İlişkilerde Eleştirel Yaklaşımlar* (Bursa: MKM Yayınları, 2014); Tayyar Arı, *Uluslararası İlişkiler Teorileri*, 10. Baskı (Bursa: Aktüel Yayınları, 2018).

7. John Ravenhill, "The Study of Global Political Economy," in *Global Political Economy*, ed. John Ravenhill (Oxford: Oxford University Press, 2008), 18–19. For more information see John Ravenhill, "International Political Economy," in *The Oxford Handbook of International Relations*, ed. Christian Reus-Smit and Duncan Snidal (Oxford: Oxford University Press, 2008).

8. Robert W. Cox, "Critical Political Economy," in *International Political Economy: Understanding Global Disorder*, ed. Björn Hettne (London; New Jersey: Zed Books Press, 1995), 32.

9. According to Strange, the distinction between economics and politics is often arbitrary. See: Björn Hettne, "Introduction: International Political Economy of Transformation," in *International Political Economy: Understanding Global Disorder,* ed. Björn Hettne (London; New Jersey: Zed Books Press, 1995), 3.

10. Christopher Farrands, "Being Critical About Being 'Critical' in IPE: Negotiating Emancipatory Strategies," in *Critical Perspectives on International Political Economy,* ed. Jason Abbott and Owen Worth (New York: Palgrave Macmillan, 2002), 18.

11. Hettne, "Introduction," 3.

12. Farrands, "Being Critical," 18.

13. Farrands, "Being Critical," 17.

14. For Schumpeter's contribution to the field, see: Jason P.Abbott and Owen Worth, "Introduction: The 'Many Worlds' of Critical International Political Economy," in *Critical Perspectives on International Political Economy,* ed. Jason Abbott and Owen Worth (New York: Palgrave Macmillan, 2002), 5. On Schumpeter's understanding of Capitalism, see Allen M. Sievers, "Schumpeter'e Göre Kapitalist Uygarlık," Çev-Der: Uğur Dolgun, *Sosyo-Ekonomik Perspektif* (Bursa: Asa Kitapevi, 2001), 265–286.

15. The IPE discipline in the Soviet Union remained under the influence of Marxist-Leninist literature; see, Stanislav L. Tkachenko, "The Study of International Political Economy in Russia," *Communist and Post-Communist Studies* 37 (2004): 111–120.

16. On this subject, see David N. Balaam and Michael Veseth, *Introduction to International Political Economy,* Second Edition (New Jersey: Prentice Hall, 2001), 5–23.

17. Theodore H. Cohn, *Global Political Economy: Theory and Practice,* 2nd Edition (New York: Longman Pub., 2003). Also see: Robert Gilpin, "Three Models of the Future," *International Organization* 29, no. 1 (Winter, 1975): 38.

18. Balaam and Veseth, *Introduction to International,* 46.

19. Gilpin, "Three Models," 37; Halil Seyidoğlu, *Uluslararası İktisat: Teori, Politika ve Uygulama,* 13. Baskı (İstanbul: Kurtiş Matbaası, 1999), 15–16.

20. Gilpin, "Three Models," 77.

21. Balaam and Veseth, *Introduction to International,* 58–59.

22. *Thèma Larousse: Tematik Ansiklopedi,* Milliyet Yay, 1993–1994, pp. 464–465.

23. Balaam and Veseth, *Introduction to International,* 61.

24. Cox, "Critical Political," 39.

25. Hettne, "Introduction," 2–3.

26. F. Oktay Tanrısever, "Yöntem Sorunu: Gelenekselcilik-Davranışsalcılık Tartışması," Der.: Atilla Eralp, *Devlet, Sistem ve Kimlik,* 2. Baskı, (İstanbul: İletişim Yay. 1996), 114.

27. Kurt Burch, "Constituting IPE and Modernity," in *Constituting International Political Economy,* ed. Kurt Burch and Robert A. Denemark (Boulder: Lynne Rienner Pub., 1997), 25.

28. Cohn, *Global Political,* 69; for Machiavelli's views, see Niccolo Machiavelli, *The Prince,* trans. Harvey C. Mansfield (Chicago: University of Chicago Press,

2010); Halil İ. Aydınlı and Veysel Ayhan, "The Discussion on the Limitation of Power from the Perspective of the Historical Development of the Concept of Sovereignty," *Cumhuriyet University, Journal of the Faculty of Economics and Administrative Sciences* 5, no. 1 (2004): 72–73.

29. Cohn, *Global Political*, 70.

30. Matthew Watson, "Theoretical Traditions in Global Political Economy," in *Global Political Economy*, 2nd Edition, ed. John Ravenhill (Oxford University Press, 2008), 34.

31. Balaam and Veseth, *Introduction to International*, 30–31.

32. Balaam and Veseth, *Introduction to International*, 450.

33. Paul R. Viotti and Mark V. Kauppi, *International Relations Theory: Realism, Pluralism, Globalism*, 2nd Edition (New York: Macmillan Publishing Co., 1993), 456–459.

34. Cohn, *Global Political*, 120–122.

35. Cohn, *Global Political*, 120.

36. Faruk Sönmezoğlu, *Uluslararası Politika ve Dış Politika Analizi*, 2. Baskı. (İstanbul: Filiz Kitapevi, 1995), 110.

37. Arı, *Uluslararası İlişkiler Teorileri*, 271–277; Viotti and Kauppi, *International Relations*, 458.

38. Cohn, *Global Political*, 120–121.

39. Karl Marx, *Capital: A Critique of Political Economy*, trans. Samuel Moore and Edward Aveling (Moskov: Progress Publishers), vol. 1, https://www.marxists.org/archive/marx/works/download/pdf/Capital-Volume-I.pdf

40. Karl Marx and Friedrich Engels, *Manifesto of the Communist Party* (Moscow: Progress Publishers, 1969), chap. 1, https://www.marxists.org/archive/marx/works/1848/communist-manifesto/ch01.htm; Karl Marx and Friedrich Engels, *The Communist Manifesto*, 8th edition, trans. Gaybiköylü (Ankara: Science and Socialism Pub., 1997), 13.

41. Balaam and Veseth, *Introduction to International*, 71.

42. Balaam and Veseth, *Introduction to International*, 74.

43. Balaam and Veseth, *Introduction to International*, 70; Cohn, *Global Political*, 122–123.

44. In his writings, Marx often uses the concept of raw material rather than raw material sources. See Daniel S. Papp, "Marxism-Leninism and Natural Resources: The Soviet Outlook," *Resources Policy* 3, no. 2 (June 1977): 136.

45. Anthony Brewer, *Marxist Theories of Imperialism: A Critical Survey, Second Edition* (London; New York: Taylor & Francis e-Library, 2001), 74.

46. Brewer, *Marxist Theories*, 88.

47. V. I. Lenin, *Imperialism, the Highest Stage of Capitalism* (Petrograd, April 26, 1917), 78, https://www.files.ethz.ch/isn/125485/6000_Imperialism_Highest_Stage_Capitalism.pdf

48. V. I. Lenin, "Emperyalizm: Kapitalizmin En Üst Seviyesi," in *Uluslararası İlişkiler ve Siyaset Teorisi Üzerine Bir Derleme*, ed. Howard Williams, Moorhead Wright, and Tony Evans; trans. Ebru Eralp (Ankara: Siyasal Kitabevi, 1966), 243–244.

49. Cohn, *Global Political,* 126.

50. Richard Tansey and Michael R. Hyman, "Dependency Theory and the Effects of Advertising by Foreign-Based Multinational Corporations in Latin America," *Journal of Advertising* 23 (March 1994): 27–42.

51. Luke Uka Uche, "Some Reflections on the Dependency Theory," *Africa Media Review* 8, no. 2 (1994): 43–45.

52. Brewer, *Marxist Theories,* 161–162.

53. Brewer, *Marxist Theories,* 164.

54. Paul Sweezy, Paul Baran, and Harry Magdoff, *Çağdaş Kapitalizmin Bunalımı,* trans. Yıldırım Koç (Ankara: Bilgi Yay., 1975), 292–299.

55. Johan Galtung, "A Structural Theory of Imperialism," *Journal of Peace Research* 8, no. 2 (1971): 81.

56. Immanuel Wallerstein, "Semi-Peripheral Countries and the Contemporary World Crisis," *Theory and Society* 3 (1976): 461–463.

57. Brewer, *Marxist Theories,* 177.

58. Wallerstein, "Semi-Peripheral Countries," 462–463.

59. Immanuel Wallerstein, *Jeopolitik ve Jeokültür,* trans. Mustafa Özel (İstanbul: İz Yay., 1993), 142–163; for Wallerstein's views on the capitalist world economy, see also Immanuel Wallerstein, "Dependence in an Interdependent World: The Limited Possibilities of Transformation within the Capitalist World Economy," *African Studies Review* 17, no. 1 (Apr., 1974): 1–26.

60. Usman W. Chohan, "A Post-Coronavirus World: 7 Points of Discussion for a New Political Economy (March 20, 2020). *CASS Working Papers on Economics & National Affairs* No. EC015UC, March 2020. Available at SSRN: https://ssrn.com/abstract=3557738 or http://dx.doi.org/10.2139/ssrn.3557738

61. Katherine A. Moos, "Coronavirus Fiscal Policy in the United States: Lessons from Feminist Political Economy," *Feminist Economics* 27, no. 1–2 (2021): 419–435.

62. *Deutsche Welle,* "Salgın Neden en çok Kadınları Vurdu," accessed March 7, 2021, https://www.dw.com/tr/salg%C4%B1n-neden-en-%C3%A7ok-kad%C4%B1nlar%C4%B1-vurdu/a-56787185

63. Jennifer Clapp and Eric Helleiner, "International political economy and the environment: Back to the basics?" *International Affairs* 88, no. 3 (2012): 485–501.

64. *UN News,* "Global impact of war in Ukraine on food, energy and finance systems." Brief no. 1, accessed April 1, 2022, https://news.un.org/pages/wp-content/uploads/2022/04/UN-GCRG-Brief-1.pdf

Chapter 2

Critical Theory and International Relations

Muzaffer Ercan Yılmaz

INTRODUCTION

Critical theory can be understood in many ways, indeed. In its generic sense, it is a social theory oriented toward criticizing and changing society as a whole, in contrast to traditional theories that aim only to understand or explain it. It is an approach to social philosophy that focuses on reflective assessment and critique of society and culture to reveal and challenge power structures. To be more specific, it is a normative approach that is based on the judgment that domination is a problem, and that a domination-free society is needed. It wants to inform political struggles that want to establish such a society.

Critical theory actually has a broad and narrow meaning in the history of social sciences and international relations. In the broad sense, the theory covers a wide range of approaches focused on the idea of freeing people from the modern state and economic system. That is to say, a theory is critical insofar as it seeks to liberate human beings from the circumstances that enslave them.

The idea particularly originates from the work of Immanuel Kant and Karl Marx who, in the eighteenth and nineteenth centuries, advanced different revolutionary ideas of how the world could be reordered and transformed. Both Kant and Marx held a strong attachment to the Enlightenment theme of universalism, the view that there are social and political principles that are apparent to all people, everywhere. In the modern era, both philosophers became foundational figures for theorists seeking to replace the modern state system by promoting more just global political arrangements. In this respect, critical theory sets out to critique repressive social practices and institutions in today's world and advance emancipation by supporting ideas and practices

37

that meet the universal principles of justice. This kind of critique has a transformative dimension in the sense that it aims at changing national societies, international relations, and the emerging global society, starting from alternative ideas and practices lingering in the background of the historical process.[1]

Critical theory is primarily a European social theory. It emerged out of the Kantian/Marxist tradition, as it has just been said, but as a grand theory, it was particularly developed by a group of philosophers and social scientists, originally located at the Institute for Social Research (Institut für Sozialforschung, in German), an attached institute founded in 1923 at the Goethe University in Frankfurt, Germany. That is the reason critical theory, in the narrow sense, is commonly known for the works of the scholars of the so-called "Frankfurt School."

Over the years, the goals and tenets of critical theory have been adopted by many social scientists. We can recognize critical theory today in many feminist approaches to conducting social science, in critical race theory, cultural theory, gender and queer theory, and in media studies.

This chapter presents an analysis and evaluation of critical theory, along with its relationship with the discipline of international relations. The chapter is composed of four sections. The first section provides a briefing about the meanings and basics of critical theory. The second talks about the birth of the Frankfurt School and the evolution of the classical critical theory within that School. The third focuses on the basic pillars of critical theory, addressing and discussing them as epistemology, ontology, and praxeology, in that order. The fourth and final section, lastly, touches upon the relationship between critical theory and international relations, mainly by referring to the works of Robert Cox and Andrew Linklater. Some of the weak points of critical theory that call for further research are also addressed, in concluding the study.

ESSENTIALS OF CRITICAL THEORY

Critical theory has actually different meanings for different scholars. Very often the choice of approach reflects the scholar's own scientific background or preference. Unlike other theories, critical theorists are not unified by a common position, but draw their inspiration from related ideological assumptions. Such assumptions are centered on the emancipation of mankind as well as the social transformation of society. The focus here is not merely to recreate society, but also to understand how oppressive social structures can be eliminated and transformed.

As a pure critique, critical theory is usually regarded as a critique of modernity and by extension, a critique of the developments and institutions associated with modern society. It can also be a critique of particular schools of thought within social sciences, rejecting their domination. More recently, a large part of critical theory has been the critique of art and culture, in particular consumer culture, advertising, the media, and other forms of popular culture.

However it is defined or understood, the central argument is that all knowledge is broadly political in nature. Critical theorists argue that knowledge is shaped by human interests of different kinds, rather than standing "objectively" independent from these interests. Human interests are understood as multiple and sometimes even contradictory. Hence, knowledge itself is also seen as fundamentally pluralistic and incongruous, rather than unitary and monolithic. Critical theory thus seeks to establish the internal relationship that exists between knowledge and experience. In light of the above, the social construction of facts is perceived mainly as products of human activity, not merely as natural accidents.[2] Critical theory eschews the distinction between subject and object but lays emphasis on human needs and what matters as relevant knowledge. One of the outstanding achievements of critical theory is its ability to put forth and analyze the political nature of knowledge.[3] Critical theory is envisaged as political because it embraces the political nature of other theories and attempts to shape such knowledge into veritable frameworks that rationally explain phenomena. Knowledge, therefore, is not simply generated from the subject's uninvolved interaction with objective reality, but it echoes already existing social orders.

Critical theory is not only an academic approach but also an emancipatory thought committed to the formation of a more equal and just world. It seeks to explain the reasons why the realization of this goal is difficult to achieve. Therefore, what is crucial is not only the social explanation but also politically motivated action to achieve an alternative set of social relations based on justice and equality. Critical theory thus transcends the boundaries of academic critique to explain political interests in concrete situations.

Emancipation is an important theme that cuts across the works of critical theorists. The emancipatory intent is the key driving force of their thought. Consequently, critical theory as a body of thought finds its relevance in the possibility of its emancipatory potential. Critical theory thus draws its purpose and coherence from this possibility. The emancipatory potential of critical theory distinguishes it from the traditional theoretical assumptions.[4] Many poststructuralist scholars do not overtly subscribe to the concept of emancipation as upheld by critical theorists. This notwithstanding, post-structural scholars have continued to be inspired by emancipation, and notions of the concept have been visible in their works. A fair and accurate criticism of the present can only be achieved on the grounds that a better world is conceivable or possible.

Moreover, the emancipatory vision of such a theory expresses its practical intent to understand the world and equally transform it. According to Alway, the emancipatory vision of critical theory consists of two principal elements. These two elements include the possibility of a better world as well as the agents and actions necessary to bring about the realization of such a vision. Emancipation as a central theme in critical theory paints an image of what the world could be and how the conception of such a better world can be realized.[5] The practical intent of the emancipatory vision is to achieve a better world. The emancipatory vision equally entails the identification of critical agents and actions necessary for the realization of such change.

The practical intent of critical theory is to emancipate the individual to live above oppressive structures and transform society. Nevertheless, the emancipatory agenda of critical theorists have come under heavy criticism from Marxists who argue that critical theory is a theory with true practical intent. Critics of critical theory maintain that, unlike Marxism, critical theory failed to adequately include the proletariat as agents of the revolution that will radically transform society. The practical intents of critical theory have been called into question for not giving the proletariat a central role in its emancipatory agenda. Linklater, however, maintains that the emancipatory vision of the postmodern critical theory is exactly what distinguishes it from Marxist critical theory.[6]

Unlike Marxist scholars who criticize the emancipatory intent of the critical theory, feminist theorists on the other hand have been inspired by the emancipatory vision of critical theory to develop an international emancipatory feminist agenda that seeks to liberate them from certain structures of oppression and subordination.[7] Feminist theorists and practitioners have leveraged the emancipatory intent to achieve broad-based representation of women and gained rights in areas that were hitherto not open for discussions like issues of domestic violence and the right to vote. The UN Convention on the Elimination of All Forms of Discrimination Against Women is a visible manifestation of the extent to which feminists have expanded the emancipatory vision to transform society.[8] The emancipatory vision of critical theory provides feminist theorists and women a structure to understand oppression and how they can mobilize from the local levels to international platforms to advocate for their rights.

One of the leading scholars of critical theory, Max Horkheimer,[9] asserts, in his classic work Traditional and Critical Theory, that a critical theory must do two important things: it must account for the whole of society within a historical context, and it should seek to offer a robust and holistic critique by incorporating insights from all social sciences. Furthermore, Horkheimer states that a theory can only be considered a true critical theory if it is explanatory, practical, and normative. That means that the theory must adequately explain the social problems that exist, it must offer practical solutions for how to respond to them, and it must clearly abide by the norms of criticism established by the field. With this point of view, Horkheimer also condemns traditional theorists for producing works that fail to question power, domination, and the status quo, in general.[10]

The explanatory approach is a key feature of critical theory, which distinguishes it from other classical theoretical approaches. Traditional theoretical approaches focus their attention on problems but do not adequately seek an in-depth understanding and explanation of why and how these problems emanate.[11] While traditional approaches lay emphasis on reasons and problems, the explanatory potential of critical theory seeks to present a broader understanding of the social and political circumstances that caused the problems in the first place. Critical theorists rely on the explanation potential to theorize and explain the circumstances that hinder subjects from achieving self-actualization. The explanatory component as an approach to theorizing shows significant interest not just in the presentation of the problem, but in the emancipation of the subjects.[12] The explanatory approach is therefore a key feature of critical theory which relies on interpretative and reconstructive elements to generate objective and explanatory knowledge that is relevant for critical purposes.

The practical feature of critical theory focuses on issues of feasibility. Critical theory derives its practicality from the fact that it strives to achieve the specific aim of human emancipation. In other words, the practicality of the theory can be understood through the proposition of Horkheimer who among other things contends that critical theory seeks to "liberate human beings from all circumstances that enslave them."[13] The application of practical knowledge thus enables critical theorists to develop appropriate frameworks for interpreting and explaining freedom from oppressive societal circumstances. Critical theorists maintain that the combination of angles of explanation, structure, agency, and understanding distinguishes and projects the practicality of critical theory. In constructing social theories, critical theorists have established a link between explanatory knowledge and criticism. This has within time enhanced the normative and critical explanatory features of the theory.

The idea of both "suffering" and "happiness" takes place in Horkheimer's works. Horkheimer's thoughts on suffering owe a great deal to Marx's views on the capitalist system that enslaves people. On the other hand, the notion that human beings have an inner drive to overcome suffering is taken from the early libido theory of Sigmund Freud, an Austrian neurologist who developed psychoanalysis, as well as Erich Fromm, a German social psychologist and psychoanalyst, who was associated with the Frankfurt School in the 1930s.

Horkheimer argues that capitalism has created a situation wherein people are made to focus on their own individual welfare, without considering anything other than the conservation and multiplication of their own property.[14] Social needs are thus handled through various disorganized activities, ironically focused on individual needs, which, in turn, inadequately deal with the social basis of individual welfare, detracting from individual welfare, indeed. For emancipatory social change, Horkheimer believes that there are some forces of resistance left within humans and that the spirit of humanity is still alive, if not in the individual as a member of social groups, at least in the individual as far as he or she is left alone. Horkheimer is certainly aware of the structural constraints, but he does suggest that it is possible to engage in a kind of non-conformism at least (without much of a description of what it would be like), which comes through the spontaneity of the individual subject.[15]

The engagement of the classical Frankfurt School with the discipline of international relations has been made particularly by scholars like Robert Cox and Andrew Linklater. In this regard, Robert Cox defines critical theory in the context of his famous landmark distinction between problem-solving theories and critical theories. According to Cox, problem-solving theories are preoccupied with maintaining social power relationships and the reproduction of the existing system, attempting to ensure that existing relationships and institutions work smoothly.[16] Unlike historical problem-solving theories which serve the existing social arrangements and support the interests of the hegemonic social forces, critical theory, according to Cox, is self-reflexive, criticizes the existing system of domination, and identifies processes and forces that will create an alternative world order.[17]

Andrew Linklater, another well-known theorist in international relations, approaches critical theory as a post-Marxist theory that continues to evolve beyond the paradigm of production to a commitment to dialogic communities that are deeply sensitive about all forms of inclusion and exclusion, domestic, transnational, and international.[18] Prior to linking later, Anthony Giddens was contending that the essence of critical theory rests in its ability to be post-Marxist. This, therefore, involves the capability of critical theory to recognize the strength and weaknesses of Marxism.[19] Cognizant of the complexities of international relations, Giddens argues for multidimensional approaches that do not rely on any specific dominant logic to explain the international system.

Drawing inspiration from Giddens, Andrew Linklater equally raises concerns about the single logic explanations. Linklater maintains that the Marxist thesis on production and class differences addresses only one of the many issues of inclusion and exclusion. Other areas of inclusion and exclusion within the international system include gender, religion, and race. According to Linklater, critical theory finds its relevance in identifying various forms of exclusion and highlights possible means through which communities can be more politically inclusive.

Moreover, Andrew Linklater lays significant emphasis on the various forms of exclusion that animate the modern state, which by extension sustains the international system that hinders the advancement of peaceful world order.[20] He further argues that critical theory should question the design of contemporary sovereign states, because they have been constructed in ways that justify exclusionary practices. Instead of following the conceptualization of the state and sovereignty as propounded by mainstream international relations analysts, critical theorists should question the current nature of the state as an entity of exclusion.

The issue of inclusion and exclusion is universal because almost every community has practices and procedures which determine the right to belong. Many of these patterns of inclusion and exclusion are legacies of class-divided societies. Critical theory thus provides valid interpretations of contemporary social and political exclusion. The objective here is to remove such exclusionary barriers because the international system is increasingly interdependent in a way that exclusionary practices only serve to create more problems than solutions.

Many scholarly writings on international relations have predominantly focused on great power politics to explain events within the international system. The fact that international relations are viewed from the great power perspective is evidence enough to justify that such a view is what matters most. By privileging the great power view, international relations analysts have excluded or paid less attention to how states from the developing world contribute to or influence events in the international system. The issues of exclusion and inclusion have been a long debate that has characterized the relationship between the West and the developing world. The sustainability of a just international order can only be attained when the issues of inclusion and exclusion are adequately addressed. This explains why states from the developing world have persistently petitioned those of the West for the need to access political and economic resources which they have been deprived of. What remains puzzling is the fact that the states that participate in such exclusionary practices are themselves entities within an inclusive community of states governed collectively by international legal norms.

The focus on the issue of community and universalism in the global world, and the issues surrounding the morality of inclusion and exclusion, is based on three key aspects. These aspects as identified by Linklater include the philosophical-normative, the practical, and the sociological. The philosophical aspect lays emphasis on explaining the basis of moral inclusion and exclusion in society. It equally examines the doctrine of sovereignty which provides the basis for including citizens and excluding non-citizens.[21] The philosophical-normative aspect seeks to expand the analysis by connecting the principles of inclusion and exclusion with other global issues that have to do with gender, race, sexual preference, and class. This is a sociological dimension that focuses on the historical change patterns of moral inclusion and exclusion.

It is therefore imperative to note that any principle of inclusion that does not sufficiently connect with universalism is by default a vehicle of exclusion. Critical theorists argue that the construction of social systems is inherently tied to the complexities of inclusion and exclusion.[22] This assertion is evident in the organization of ethnic groups, political parties, military alliances, citizenship, and even in international organizations. The above analysis paints a clear picture of how the principles of inclusion and exclusion play out at the local as well as at the international level. It has been observed that world politics is dominated by structures of inclusion and exclusion. Contemporary state systems apply principles of inclusion and exclusion in distinguishing between citizens and non-citizens. While inclusion is relevant, critical theory pays significant attention to the exclusionary dimension because of the necessity to construct a social and international order that is fair and just.

Similar definitions of critical theory emphasize one or more of its aspects. Joan Alway defines critical theory as a theory with practical intent oriented to the emancipatory transformation of society.[23] According to Mark Neufeld, the defining feature of critical theory is its "negation of positivism" and "technical reason" dominant in mainstream international relations.[24] In line with these different definitions, a heterogeneous group of theories has been labeled as critical in international relations, including feminism, post-structuralism, critical geopolitics, critical security studies, critical international political economy, post-colonialism, and international historical sociology.[25]

Critical theory is also deeply concerned with the fate of modernity. It has offered systematic and comprehensive theories of the trajectory of modernity, combined with critical diagnoses of some of the latter's limitations, pathologies, and destructive effects while providing defenses of some of its progressive elements.[26]

According to Douglas Kellner, critical theory has generally been committed to the idea of modernity and progress, while, at the same time, noting the ways that features of modernity can create problems for individuals and society.[27] In some ways, even Max Weber's theory of rationalization of modern society can be regarded as a critical theory. Weber argued that rationalization was a force that increasingly dominated Western and other societies, limiting creativity and the human spirit as a result.[28] Various critical theorists have relied heavily on the Weberian critique, and indeed, much of critical theory is a combination of the Marxian and Weberian traditions.

Overall, critical theorists focus essentially on ideology and cultural forces as facilitators of domination and barriers to true freedom. The contemporary politics and economic structures greatly influenced their thoughts and writings, as they existed within the rise of national socialism, state capitalism, and the spread of mass-produced culture.

It should be also noted that critical theory actually differs from post-modern theories, though it may resemble them, at first glance, in terms of its criticizing character. However, post-modern theories tend to argue that modernity has ended or that modernity must be rejected completely. Post-modernists may even reject the social theory and political practice, whereas critical theorists tend to theorize extensively and some argue that politics can be used to pursue progress. Critical theorists generally tend to have a comprehensive and overall social theory and an idea of progress for the better, even if they are unable to find ways of getting there. In contrast, a post-modern approach is more likely to be associated with the rejection of the comprehensive, universal theory.

THE FRANKFURT SCHOOL AND AFTERWARDS

The birth of critical theory is greatly inspired by Karl Marx's theoretical formulation of the relationship between economic base and ideological superstructure. The approach of Marx tends to focus on how power and domination operate, in particular, in the realm of the superstructure.[29] Marxism views the economy as a well-established infrastructure from which all other aspects of society derive their reality. Such aspects of society like religion, law, art, and philosophy collectively make up what is described as the superstructure. However, those who hold sway over production relations do everything to stay in power by intentionally manipulating and distorting reality. The Marxist tradition describes this as ideology. Such capitalist societies that are sustained by bourgeois superstructures tend to dominate and exploit the proletariat, who are viewed by Marx as the oppressed. Marx posits that the relationship between the owners of the factors of production and the proletariat constitutes an economic base on which the political, legal, and ideological superstructure is built.

Karl Marx focused his attention on political economy to generate discourse on unequal power relations that define and characterize the class structure within capitalist societies. Antonio Gramsci later elaborated on Marx's superstructure theory and developed the post-Marxist theory of hegemony.[30] Hegemony was simply the dominance of the ruling class over subjugated groups or classes. The economic superstructure facilitated the acceptance of such dominance.

The above analysis from a Marxist standpoint demonstrates the sources of power and the predictability of its pattern within the larger economic super-structure. It goes without saying that power rests predominantly with those who hold and manage strategic positions within the broader system of production. Power, therefore, becomes a tool through which economic interests are protected and an instrument of domination in class-structured capitalist economies.

Following Marx's critical steps, Georg Lukacs and Antonio Gramsci developed theories that explored the cultural and ideological sides of power and domination. Both Lukacs and Gramsci focused their critique on the social forces that prevent people from seeing and understanding the forms of power and domination that exist in society.

Shortly after the period when Lukacs and Gramsci developed and published their ideas, the Institute for Social Research[31] was founded where most critical theorists, called the Frankfurt School, began to show up.

The first officially appointed director of the Institute was Carl Grunberg, a Marxist professor at the University of Vienna. In 1930, Max Horkheimer succeeded him. While continuing under Marxist inspiration, Horkheimer interpreted the Institute's mission to be more directed towards an interdisciplinary integration of social sciences. It was under Horkheimer's leadership that members of the Institute were able to address a wide variety of economic, social, political, and aesthetic topics, ranging from empirical analysis to philosophical theorization.

The consideration of psychoanalysis by the Frankfurt School was also due to Horkheimer's encouragement. It was Eric Fromm, nevertheless, who achieved a significant advancement in the discipline. His central aim was to provide, through a synthesis of Marxism and psychoanalysis, "the missing link" between the ideological superstructure and socio-economic base.[32]

In 1933, because of the Nazi takeover, the Institute was temporarily transferred, first to Geneva and then in 1935 to Columbia University, New York. Two years later, Horkheimer published the ideological manifesto of the School in his Traditional and Critical Theory (1937) where he readdressed some of the previously introduced topics concerning the practical and critical turn of the theory.

A radical shift though occurred in the late 1930s, when Theodor W. Adorno joined the School and Fromm decided, for personal reasons, to leave. Nevertheless, the School's interest in psychoanalysis, particularly in Sigmund Freud's instinct theory, remained unchanged.

The School's interest in psychoanalysis coincided with the marginalization of Marxism. A growing interest began to show up with respect to the interrelation between psychoanalysis and social change, along with Fromm's insight into the psychic role of the family. This interest became crucial in empirical studies of the 1940s that led, eventually, to Adorno's co-authored work The Authoritarian Personality in 1950. The goal of this work was to explore a "new anthropological type," that is, the authoritarian personality. Such a character was found to have specific traits, like compliance with conventional values, non-critical thinking, as well as the absence of introspectiveness.[33]

In 1956, Jurgen Habermas joined the Institute as Adorno's assistant. Young Habermas contributed to the construction of a critical self-awareness of the socialist student groups around the country. It was in this context that Habermas reacted to the extremism of Rudi Dutschke, the radical leader of the students' association, who criticized him for defending a non-effective emancipatory view. It was principally against Dutschke's positions that Habermas, during a public assembly, labeled such positions the epitome of "left-wing fascism."

In 1971, Habermas left Frankfurt and returned there some ten years later, having completed The Theory of Communicative Action (1984). This decade was crucial for the definition of the School's research objectives. In The Theory of Communicative Action, Habermas provided a model for social complexities and action coordination based upon the original interpretation of classical social theorists, as well as the philosophy of John L. Austin and John Searle's "*s*peech acts" theory. Within this work, it also became evident how the large amount of empirical analysis conducted by Habermas' research team on topics concerning pathologies of society, moral development, and so on was elevated to a functionalistic model of society oriented to an emancipatory purpose. The assumption was that language itself possessed a normative force capable of realizing action coordination within society.[34]

Habermas described discourse theory as relying on three types of validity claims raised by communicative action. He claimed that it was only when the conditions of truth, rightness, and sincerity were raised by speech acts that social coordination could be obtained.[35] As noticed in the opening sections, differently from the first generation of Frankfurt School intellectuals, Habermas contributed greatly to bridging the continental and analytical traditions, integrating, thus, aspects belonging to American pragmatism and critical social theory.

Just one year before Habermas' retirement in 1994, the directorship of the Institute for Social Research was assumed by Axel Honneth. This inaugurated a new phase of research in critical theory. Honneth, indeed, revisited the Hegelian notion of recognition in terms of a new prolific paradigm in social and political inquiry.[36] His communitarian turn has also been paralleled by the work of some of his fellow scholars. Hauke Brunkhorst, for example, in his Solidarity: From Civic Friendship to a Global Legal Community (2002) reveals a line of thought springing from the French

Revolution to contemporary times: the notion of fraternity. By the use of historical conceptual reconstruction and normative speculation, Brunkhorst presents the pathologies of the contemporary globalized world and the function that solidarity would play.[37]

The confrontation with American debate, initiated systematically by the work of Habermas, soon became an obsolete issue in the third generation of critical theorists. The work of Rainer Forst testifies, indeed, to the synthesis between analytical methodological rigor and classical themes of the Frankfurt School.[38] Thanks to Habermas' intellectual opening, the third generation of critical theorists engaged in dialogue with French post-modern philosophers like Jacques Derrida, Jean Baudrillard, Jean F. Lyotard, and so forth, which are the contemporary interpreters of some central aspects of the Frankfurt School.

THREE PILLARS OF CRITICAL THEORY

There are basically three pillars of critical theory. The first concerns its epistemology, the second its ontology, and the third its praxeology.

Epistemology

Epistemology, in a generic sense, is a theory of knowledge. It deals with how the very concepts that constitute a theory are constituted and organized.

In his writing "Traditional and Critical Theory," Horkheimer argues that human and social sciences colonized the scientific approach of natural sciences and applied their empiricist epistemology and positivist methods to the study of the social world. Therefore, the "phenomenologically oriented sociologist" relied on the collection of social data as the basis for building theory and unveiling social laws. This had a significant impact on the social sciences since it was underpinned by a unitary conception of science prescribing the inadequacy of subjects, such as history or philosophy as theoretical tools for studying the social world.[39]

In the same way, Habermas argues that our social and cultural factors influence our sensory experience, as cognition shapes reality through its prior cognitive principles. Hence, positivism's correspondence theory of truth is impossible. Indeed, there is an undeniable relationship between knowledge and interest, as human knowledge of external reality is through our imposition of object-constituting epistemological categories that derive from our fundamental interests.[40]

To Habermas, further, there are two forms of knowledge derived from specific human interests. The first is empirical analysis as science where human interest is derived through creative interplay with exerting control over the natural environment. The need for physical survival leads to the development of knowledge about and over the external environment. The second is historic hermeneutic science. This interest arises out of the need for interpersonal communication to establish understanding between the individual and the group. This is to facilitate the capture of the meanings of actions and communications. Once communications fail, the condition for human survival is disturbed. An additional third interest is in the form of an emancipatory interest where self-knowledge and understanding generated through self-reflection can free people from domination.[41]

So as opposed to the fixed and historical account of the social world, critical theory aims to provide an understanding of fluid and trans-historical processes. The assumption of neutrality in knowledge production is called into question since critical theory recognizes that all theories do have a perspective. Perspectives derive from a position in time and space, specifically social and political time, and space. There is, indeed, no such theory in itself, discovered from a standpoint in time and space.[42]

Then, the first step of critical theory is to have an understanding of itself and to be aware of social, cultural, and political issues through engagement in self-reflexive reasoning. From a critical standpoint, the theorist must acknowledge that theory is itself a social construction that must reflect upon itself and take a normative position on the world. This self-reflexive dimension is what allegedly enables critical theory to produce knowledge without reproducing and reinforcing the inequities of the status quo.

Overall, positivist epistemology is supported by the claims of a neutral, non-normative, and value-free production of knowledge. This intellectual project produces its research agenda by perceiving science as an aggregation of regularities that can be discovered, assembled, and generalized. Each "science" has its specific sphere of knowledge production where disciplinary boundaries preclude the overlapping of scientific objects. Within this positivist framework, the discipline of international relations is seen as a "science" dealing with an object with its distinctive nature, a static perspective of the world made of recurrence. Units and structures are related in a deterministic way that enables theorists to provide explanatory laws with universal application. Human agency is reduced to a minimum degree; hence, this intellectual framework is said to be unable to account for political change in international politics.

Ontology

Ontology is a theory of being, it deals with the question of how reality is organized and develops.

The critique of domination and exploitation constitutes critical theory's ontological dimension. Marx treated Kant's fundamental philosophical questions about human beings and their knowledge, activities, and hopes in the form of a critical political economy. Marx's reformulation of Kant's question was his categorical imperative, that is, the critique of domination and exploitation.

Yet critical theory holds the assumption that a person can be more than a class individual. The goal of critical theory is the transformation of society as a whole so that a just society with peace, wealth, freedom, and self-fulfillment for all can be achieved. A precondition for such a society is the abolition of exploitation and all forms of domination. In this respect, communication is embedded in manifold ways into domination and exploitation. Examples include that communication labor is in contemporary society an important form of surplus-generating labor, that communication is part of the organization of production, distribution, and consumption, that those communications have increasingly been turned from common goods into commodities, and that class and power relations are sustained and organized with the help of communication.[43]

Ideology critique constitutes critical theory's other ontological dimension. In dominative societies, domination tends to be masked by ideologies that present reality not as it is, but in mythologized, inverted, and distorted ways. Given that in antagonistic societies, political contradictions are expressed in speech acts. Therefore, it is possible to study ideologies that manifest themselves in such speeches. The linguistic and visual strategies that political actors use for presenting themselves and those whom they consider enemies or opponents can also be studied in this way. In this respect, some studies on enemy images reveal a positive relationship between political factors and the creation of enemies. It is shown that the idea of the enemy does not "just appear," but it is cultivated carefully by politicians and by those who are in power for interest-based reasons.[44]

Praxeology

Praxeology is the study of aspects of human action, especially political action and ethics. It is concerned with the conceptual analysis and logical implications of preference, choice, means, and so forth.

Critical ethics forms a praxeological aspect of critical theory. Critical theory certainly wants to increase and maximize human happiness. It uses the Hegelian method of comparing essence and existence, since, in class societies, an appearance is not automatically rational. This essence can be found in humans' positive capacities, such as striving for freedom, sociality, cooperation, and it has the ethical implication that universal conditions should be created that allows all humans to realize these capacities. For political communication studies, critical ethics matters, since it needs criteria for judging the positive and negative aspects of specific media.

Another praxeological dimension is the focus on struggles and political practice. Critical theory feels associated with actual and potential social struggles of exploited and oppressed groups. It maintains stress on the importance of a better world. Its philosophy is a reflection of realities, potentials, and limits of struggles. Critical political communication scholars understand themselves as public intellectuals who do not just write books and conduct analyses but connect their knowledge to political debates and struggles for the better.

CRITICAL THEORY IN INTERNATIONAL RELATIONS

Of course, neither the scholars of the Frankfurt School nor those prior to them were international relations theorists in the contemporary sense. They were essentially philosophers and sociologists. Yet there were two particular scholars who played a crucial role in connecting critical theory to international relations by influencing two significant scholars in the area. The first was Antonio Gramsci, who influenced Robert Cox, and the second was Jürgen Habermas from the Frankfurt School, who influenced Andrew Linklater. While Cox focuses on contemporary redistribution struggles, Linklater turns to questions of identity and community as more significant than economic relations in today's quest for emancipation.

What is special about Gramsci, as far as his contributions are concerned, is that he developed the concept of "cultural hegemony," through which the capitalist system perpetuates itself. Cultural hegemony is basically the dominant ideology of society that reflects the beliefs and interests of the ruling class. More specifically, the term refers to the ability of a group of people to hold power over social institutions, and thus, to strongly influence the values, norms, and worldview of the rest of society. According to Gramsci, cultural hegemony functions by achieving the consent of the masses to abide by social norms and the rules of law by framing the worldview of the ruling class. It is most strongly manifested when those ruled by the dominant group come to believe that the economic and social conditions are natural and inevitable, rather than created by people, with a vested interest in a particular capitalist order.[45]

In this respect, Cox challenges realism's assumptions, specifically the study of interstate relations in isolation from other social forces. He stresses the need to see global politics as a collective construction evolving through the complex interplay of state, sub-state, and trans-state forces in economic, cultural, and ideological spheres. His purpose is to pay attention to the whole range of spheres where change is needed in contemporary global politics. For instance, when realism focuses only on great powers and strategic stability, it ends up forcing a set of unjust global relations stemming from power and coercion. For this reason, Cox challenges the idea that "truth" is absolute, as in realism's assertion that there is a timeless logic to international relations or liberalism's assertion that the pursuit of global capitalism is positive. Instead, he argues that theory is always for someone and for some purpose.[46] Drawing on Gramsci, Cox comes up with a picture of the world political system brought by the hegemony and hierarchies of power manufactured in the economic arena. Therefore, power is understood in the context of a set of globalized relations of production demanding the transformation of the nation-state, and depends on the combination of material elements and ideas for acquiring legitimacy.[47] Cox explores the economic contradictions spurring change in power relations and guiding transitions towards fairer world order, though acknowledging that emancipation is not inevitable.

The critical project connecting Linklater to Cox sets out to uncover all sorts of hegemonic interests feeding the world order as a first step to overcoming global systems of exclusion and inequality. Linklater's critical project aims at reconstructing cosmopolitanism, drawing not from some abstract or utopian moral principles but from non-instrumental action and ideal speech (open and non-coercive communication), the assumptions actually developed by Habermas. Ideal speech is the critical tool used in the reconstruction of political communities, from local to global levels, through open dialogue and non-coercive communication, a process whereby all affected by political decisions put forward their claims and justify them on the basis of rational and universally-accepted principles of validity.[48]

Thus, emancipation is conceived not with reference to an abstract universal idea but based on a process of open discussion about who can be excluded legitimately from specific political arrangements and what kinds of particularities (gender, race, language) entitle people to special sets of rights. To Linklater, the historical development of citizenship attests to both the potential and the limitations of such a process of open discussion about rights within the context of the state system. Citizenship has been especially the critical concept and set of practices not only to permit the enjoyment of universal rights inside a community but also to protect vulnerable minorities by granting them particular rights so as to avoid or mitigate the effects of discrimination.[49] On the other hand, however, citizenship has divided humanity into national groupings, and it has, therefore, been a barrier to the universal fulfillment of human freedom.

According to Linklater, then, emancipation demands global interactions guided by open, inclusive, and non-coercive dialogue about the ties that bind communities together. This also extends to our obligations to strangers and how fair it is to restrict outsiders from the enjoyment of rights granted to insiders. For Linklater, the answer lies in the potential for a more universal concept of citizenship, refashioned through open dialogue among those affected by the global processes that are changing the world. These processes are issues like non-state forms of violence, such as terrorism, forced migration, climate change, and resource depletion. Therefore, critical theory can be seen as an instrument of the powerless to advance more equitable types of global relations. Furthermore, within international relations theories, it combats the traditional approaches, mainly liberalism and realism, and shines a light on how they feed the imbalances of an unjust global order by failing to question their foundational claims. Linklater's work is marked by the awareness that modernity is an unfinished project in its potential for accomplishing human freedom, namely through the transformation of the competitive system of separate states into a global community.[50]

Linklater admits that immediate security needs force people to set up bounded communities and to act according to national loyalties. Thus, he recognizes the limits to cosmopolitan politics. At the same time, however, Linklater underlines that there is a growing awareness that global interconnectedness and vulnerabilities impose their consequences on how communities define themselves and live side by side with others. Proximity to strangers prompts, for instance, a heightened sense of sharing a finite planet and finite resources and leads individuals to question exclusive obligations to the state in favor of a degree of cosmopolitan responsibility towards those who do not belong to one's national community.[51]

Accordingly, Linklater explores the moral tensions emerging between humanity and citizenship so as to devise practical possibilities for creating more inclusive communities, with a civilizing effect on the conduct of international relations. Linklater does not underestimate the historical movement towards the creation of bounded moral communities, that is, nation-states, but also sees the potential within the historical process to enhance the expansion of rights and duties beyond the state. The fact that it has been possible for states in the modern international system to agree upon the protection of human rights, for instance, is a sign of the relevance of these ideas.[52]

What unites Cox and Linklater, then, is a political inquiry with an explicit emancipatory purpose. It aims at uncovering the potential for a fairer system of global relations resulting from already existing principles, practices, and communities that expands human rights and prevents harm to strangers.

CONCLUSION

Overall, critical theory, perhaps more than other approaches, promises to go deeper in understanding human problems. From the critical perspective, there are only durable solutions to social and international issues when political actors embrace cosmopolitan criteria that balance the whole range of interests and respect the rights of everyone involved. Politics, knowledge, and global orders should be for people and they all should serve the purpose of freeing them from unnecessary harm and unfair or unbalanced globalized interactions. By extension, institutions and states must be assessed in terms of how they fare in overcoming various types of exclusion for insiders and outsiders.

In the same way, the conclusion drawing from critical theory with regard to contemporary international relations is that cosmopolitan in its character, critical theory refuses to see states as bounded moral communities by nature. Instead, it finds in them the potential to protect strangers in need and includes them in a broader notion of national interest. To critical theory, solutions to human problems, broadly defined, must be sought in open dialogue, resorting to rational arguments that take into consideration everyone's concerns and interests. Leaving solutions to national governments alone is not an option due to their rather strict positions on national interests. On the contrary, a more balanced position would result from the active involvement of civil society and local authorities.

However, it should be also noted that the fact that critical theory itself focuses on criticism creates an inherent unwillingness for its adherents to engage in self-criticism. While critical theorists certainly have a point in saying that all knowledge is historical and interest-based, they do not tell, at least in a satisfactory way, how to step out of this historicity. Similarly, they do not provide a reliable and realistic way out of the circumstances that, in their view, enslave people, except in general terms. These issues certainly beg for further research for the proponents of critical theory if the theory is to be a more widely-appreciated grand theory of philosophy and sociology, as well as international relations.

REFERENCES

Adorno, Theodor W. et al. The Authoritarian Personality. New York: Harper and Brothers, 1959.

Alway, Joan. *Critical Theory and Its Possibilities: Conceptions of Emancipatory Politics in the Works of Horkheimer, Adorno, Marcuse, and Habermas*. London: Greenwood Press, 1995.

Austin, John L. *How to Do Things with Words*. Cambridge, MA: Harvard University Press, 1975.

Broniak, Christopher. "What is Emancipation for Habermas?" *Philosophy Today* (1998): 195–200.

Brunkhorst, Hauke. Solidarity: From Civic Friendship to a Global Legal Community, trans. by J. Flynn. Cambridge, MA: MIT Press, 2002.

Cox, Robert W. "Social Forces, States, and World Orders: Beyond International Relations Theory." *Millennium: Journal of International Studies* 10, no. 2 (1981): 126–155.

Cox, Robert W., and Jacobson, Harold K. *The Anatomy of Influence: Decision Making in International Organization*. New Haven, CT: Yale University Press, 1974.

Ferreira F. "Introducing Critical Theory in International Relations." https://www.e-ir .info, 2018.

Forst, Rainer. The Right to Justification: Elements of a Constructivist Theory of Justice. New York, NY: Columbia University Press, 2014.

Gramsci, Antonio. *Selected Writings*, edited by David Forgacs. New York: Schocken Books, 1988.

Giddens, Anthony. *The Nation-State and Violence: Volume Two of A Contemporary Critique of Historical Materialism*. Cambridge: Polity Press, 1988.

Griffiths, Martin. *Encyclopedia of International Relations and Global Politics*. London: Routledge, 2005.

Habermas, Jürgen. Theory and Practice. Boston, MA: Beacon Press, 1973.

Habermas, Jürgen. The Theory of Communicative Action. Boston, MA: Beacon Press, 1984.

Honneth, Axel. Critique of Power: Reflective Stages in a Critical Social Theory, translated by Kenneth Baynes. Cambridge, MA: MIT Press, 1985.

Horkheimer, Max. "Materialism and Morality." Between Philosophy and Social Science: Selected Early Writings, edited by G. Hunter, M. Kramer, and J. Torpey, 1–14. Cambridge, MA: MIT Press, 1993.

Horkheimer, Max. "Traditional and Critical Theory." Critical Theory: Selected Essays, edited by M. O'Connell, 188–243. New York, NY: Continuum Press, 1937.

Horkheimer, Max, and Adorno, Theodor W. *Dialectic of Enlightenment*. Amsterdam: Querido Verlag, NV, 1947.

Islam, Md Saidul. *Development, Power, and the Environment: Neoliberal Paradox in the Age of Vulnerability*. New York: Routledge, 2013.

Jay, Martin. The Dialectical Imagination. Berkeley: University of California Press, 1973.

Jones, Richard Wyn. *Security, Strategy, and Critical Theory*. London: Lynne Rienner Publishers, 1999.

Kellner, Douglas. *Critical Theory, Marxism and Modernity*. Baltimore: The Johns Hopkins University Press, 1989.

Linklater, Andrew. *Men and Citizens in the Theory of International Relations*. Basingstoke: Palgrave Macmillan, 1982.

Linklater, Andrew. "The Problem of Community in International Relations." *Alternatives* (1988): 135–153.

Linklater, Andrew. "The Achievements of Critical Theory." *International Theory: Positivism and Beyond,* edited by S. Smith, K. Booth, and M. Zalewski. Cambridge: Cambridge University Press, 1996.

Linklater, Andrew. *The Transformation of Political Community.* Columbia, SC: University of South Carolina Press, 1988.

Linklater, Andrew. "The Changing Contours of Critical International Relations Theory." *Critical Theory and World Politics,* edited by R. Wyn Jones, 23–43 Boulder, CO: Lynne Rienner, 2001.

Linklater, Andrew. *Critical Theory and World Politics: Citizenship, Sovereignty, and Humanity.* New York, NY: Routledge, 2007.

Linklater, Andrew. "Cosmopolitan Citizenship." *Citizenship Studies* 2, no. 1 (2007): 23–41.

Linklater, Andrew. *The Power of Harm in World Politics.* Cambridge and New York: Cambridge University Press, 2011.

McCormack, Tara. *Critique, Security, and Power: The Political Limits to Emancipatory Approaches.* New York: Routledge, 2010.

Neufeld, Mark. *The Restructuring of International Relations Theory.* Cambridge, UK: Cambridge University Press, 1995.

Pensky, Max. *Globalizing Critical Theory.* Oxford: Rowman and Littlefield, 2005.

Persadie, Natalie Renée. *A Critical Analysis of the Effectiveness of Law as a Tool to Achieve Gender Equality.* New York: University Press of America, 2012.

Rush, Fred. *The Cambridge Companion to Critical Theory.* Cambridge: Cambridge University Press, 2004.

Strydom, Piet. *Contemporary Critical Theory and Methodology.* New York: Routledge, 2011.

Webber, Mark. *Inclusion, Exclusion and the Governance of European Security.* Manchester: Manchester University Press, 2007.

Weber, Max. *Economy and Society.* New York, NY: Bedminster Press, 1968.

Yalvaç, Faruk. "Critical Theory: International Relations' Engagement with the Frankfurt School and Marxism." *Oxford Research Encyclopedias.* At http:// oxfordre.com/internationalstudies/view, 2015.

Yılmaz, Muzaffer E. "Enemy Images and Conflict." *İstanbul Üniversitesi Siyasal Bilgiler Fakültesi Dergisi,* no. 32 (2005): 1–11. Online Reference.

.

NOTES

1. Marcos F. Ferreira, "Introducing Critical Theory in International Relations," at https://www.e-ir.info, date accessed 12.09.2018.

2. Fred Rush, *The Cambridge Companion to Critical Theory* (Cambridge: Cambridge University Press, 2004).

3. Andrew Linklater, *Critical Theory and World Politics: Citizenship, Sovereignty and Humanity* (New York, NY: Routledge, 2007).

4. Richard Wyn Jones, *Security, Strategy, and Critical Theory* (London: Lynne Rienner Publishers, 1999), 56–60.

5. Joan Alway, *Critical Theory and Its Possibilities: Conceptions of Emancipatory Politics in the Works of Horkheimer, Adorno, Marcuse, and Habermas* (London: Greenwood Press, 1995), 2–10

6. Andrew Linklater, "The Achievements of Critical Theory," *International Theory: Positivism and Beyond,* edited by S. Smith, K. Booth, and M. Zalewski (Cambridge: Cambridge University Press, 1996), 279.

7. Christopher Broniak, "What is Emancipation for Habermas?" *Philosophy Today* (1998): 195–200.

8. Natalie Renée Persadie, *A Critical Analysis of the Effectiveness of Law as a Tool to Achieve Gender Equality* (New York: University Press of America, 2012), 21–25.

9. Max Horkheimer (1895–1973) was one of the pioneers of the Frankfurt School, a group of social scientists associated with the Institute for Social Research in Frankfurt, Germany. Horkheimer was the director of the Institute from 1930 to 1933, and again from 1949 to 1958. In between those periods, he directed the Institute in exile, primarily in the United States. As a philosopher, he is best known for his work during the 1940s, including *Dialectic of Enlightenment* (1947), which was co-authored with Theodor W. Adorno. While deservedly influential, *Dialectic of Enlightenment,* as well as other works from that period on, should not be separated from the context of Horkheimer's works as a whole. Especially important, in this regard, are the writings from the 1930s onward, which were largely responsible for developing the epistemological and methodological orientation of the Frankfurt School critical theory.

10. Max Horkheimer, "Traditional and Critical Theory," Critical Theory: Selected Essays, edited by M. O'Connell (New York, NY: Continuum Press, 1937), 188–243.

11. Tara McCormack, *Critique, Security and Power: The Political Limits to Emancipatory Approaches* (New York: Routledge, 2010), 55.

12. Piet Strydom, *Contemporary Critical Theory and Methodology* (New York: Routledge, 2011), 110–115.

13. Max Pensky, *Globalizing Critical Theory* (Oxford: Rowman and Littlefield, 2005).

14. Max Horkheimer, "Materialism and Morality," Between Philosophy and Social Science: Selected Early Writings, edited by G. Hunter, M. Kramer, and J. Torpey (Cambridge, MA: MIT Press, 1993), 1–14.

15. Horkheimer, "Materialism and Morality," 99.

16. Robert W. Cox, "Social Forces, States and World Orders: Beyond International Relations Theory," *Millennium: Journal of International Studies* 10, no. 2 (1981): 129.

17. Cox, "Social Forces, States and World Orders," 129–130.

18. Andrew Linklater, "The Changing Contours of Critical International Relations Theory," *Critical Theory and World Politics,* edited by R. Wyn Jones (Boulder, CO: Lynne Rienner, 2001), 25.

19. Anthony Giddens, *The Nation State and Violence: Volume Two of A Contemporary Critique of Historical Materialism* (Cambridge: Polity Press, 1988), 336.

20. Martin Griffiths, *Encyclopedia of International Relations and Global Politics* (London: Routledge, 2005), 619–624.

21. Andrew Linklater, "The Problem of Community in International Relations," *Alternatives* (1988): 135–153.

22. Mark Webber, *Inclusion, Exclusion and the Governance of European Security* (Manchester: Manchester University Press, 2007), 2–15.

23. Joan Alway, *Critical Theory and Its Possibilities: Conceptions of Emancipatory Politics in the Works of Horkheimer, Adorno, Marcuse, and Habermas* (London: Greenwood Press, 1995).

24. Mark Neufeld, *The Restructuring of International Relations Theory* (Cambridge, UK: Cambridge University Press, 1995), 129–130.

25. Faruk Yalvaç, "Critical Theory: International Relations' Engagement with the Frankfurt School and Marxism," *Oxford Research Encyclopedias*, at http://oxfordre .com/internationalstudies/view, date accessed 02.09.2022.

26. Douglas Kellner, *Critical Theory, Marxism and Modernity* (Baltimore: The Johns Hopkins University Press, 1989), 3.

27. Kellner, *Critical Theory, Marxism and Modernity*, 4.

28. Max Weber, *Economy and Society* (New York, NY: Bedminster Press, 1968).

29. Base and superstructure are two linked theoretical concepts developed by Marx. In a generic sense, base refers to the forces and relations of economic production. Superstructure, on the other hand, refers to all other aspects of society. It includes politics, culture, ideology, values, norms, and expectations, in general. In Marxist philosophy, the superstructure grows out of the base. That is, economic base determines, at least influences to a great extent, the political and ideological superstructure.

30. Md. Saidul Islam, *Development, Power, and the Environment: Neoliberal Paradox in the Age of Vulnerability* (New York: Routledge, 2013), 109.

31. The Institute for Social Research (*Institut für Sozialforschung*) was the creation of Felix Weil, who was able to use money from his father's grain business to finance the Institute. Weil was a young Marxist, who had written his Ph.D. on the practical problems of implementing socialism and it was published by Karl Korsch. With the hope of bringing different trends of Marxism together, Weil organized a week-long symposium (the Erste Marxistische Arbeitswoche) in 1922 attended by Georg Lukacs, Karl Korsch, Karl August Wittfogel, Friedrich Pollock, and many others. This event was so successful that Weil set about erecting a building and funding salaries for a permanent institute, which led to establishment of the Institute for Social Research.

32. Martin Jay, The Dialectical Imagination (Berkeley: University of California Press, 1973), 92.

33. Theodor W. Adorno et al., The Authoritarian Personality (New York: Harper and Brothers, 1959).

34. Jürgen Habermas, The Theory of Communicative Action (Boston, MA: Beacon Press, 1984).

35. Habemas, The Theory of Communicative Action, 14–15.

36. Alex Honneth, Critique of Power: Reflective Stages in a Critical Social Theory, translated by Kenneth Baynes (Cambridge, MA: MIT Press, 1985).

37. Hauke Brunkhorst, Solidarity: From Civic Friendship to a Global Legal Community, trans. by J. Flynn (Cambridge, MA: MIT Press, 2002).

38. Rainer Forst, The Right to Justification: Elements of a Constructivist Theory of Justice (New York, NY: Columbia University Press, 2014).

39. Max Horkheimer, "Traditional and Critical Theory," Critical Theory: Selected Essays, edited by M. O'Connell (New York, NY: Continuum Press, 1937), 192.

40. Jürgen Habermas, Theory and Practice (Boston, MA: Beacon Press, 1973).

41. Habermas, Theory and Practice, 17.

42. Robert W. Cox, "Social Forces, States and World Orders: Beyond International Relations Theory," *Millennium: Journal of International Studies* 10, no. 2 (1981): 126–155.

43. https://plato.stanford.edu/entries/critical-theory, at https://www.e-ir.info, date accessed 12.09.2022.

44. Muzaffer E. Yılmaz, "Enemy Images and Conflict," *İstanbul Üniversitesi Siyasal Bilgiler Fakültesi Dergisi*, No. 32 (2005): 4–5.

45. Antonio Gramsci, *Selected Writings*, edited by David Forgacs (New York: Schocken Books, 1988).

46. Robert W. Cox, "Social Forces, States and World Orders: Beyond International Relations Theory," *Millennium: Journal of International Studies* 10, no. 2 (1981): 128.

47. Robert W. Cox and Harold K. Jacobson, *The Anatomy of Influence: Decision Making in International Organization* (New Haven, CT: Yale University Press, 1974).

48. Andrew Linklater, *Critical Theory and World Politics: Citizenship, Sovereignty and Humanity* (New York, NY: Routledge, 2007).

49. Andrew Linklater, *Men and Citizens in the Theory of International Relations* (Basingstoke, UK: Palgrave Macmillan, 1982); *The Transformation of Political Community* (Columbia, SC: University of South Carolina Press, 1988).

50. Andrew Linklater, "Cosmopolitan Citizenship," *Citizenship Studies* 2, no. 1 (2007): 23–41.

51. Linklater, "Cosmopolitan Citizenship," 33.

52. Andrew Linklater, *The Power of Harm in World Politics* (Cambridge and New York: Cambridge University Press, 2011).

PART II

Social Approaches and Critics of Conventional Theories

Via Media in IR

Chapter 3

Normative International Relations Theory Today

Ethical Dilemmas and Tragedy

Zerrin Ayşe Öztürk

INTRODUCTION

Normative International Relations Theory entered into the discipline of International Relations (IR) with the normative and critical turn of the 1980s and 1990s. Since then, the role of ethics in the theory and practice of international relations has been expanded and enriched through the emergence and development of several IR theories by adopting the critical theory–making in IR. Ethical arguments for and against any foreign policy decisions or actions are not actually new to the theory and practice of IR as international norms have been developing even throughout the bipolar order of the Cold War era. During the past three decades, the international norms in IR have expanded as a result of end of the Cold War and its repercussions—including the end of bipolarity, the acceleration of the globalization process, the emergence of new security threats and risks, and so on.

In this chapter, I will look at the *normative turn* in IR theory, firstly, by examining the role of *Normative Theory* within the discipline—reflecting upon its critical role to pave the way for *Post-positivist IR theories* as well as reopening the debate on the origins and ideals of the discipline itself. The *normative turn* in IR theory has led up to the methodological debate as well as the *Post-positivist IR theories'* engaging discussion on the role of ethics, norms, and values in world politics. Since then, a *normative critique* of international relations has been expanding in the discipline. Secondly, the chapter moves on to the ethical dimensions and ethical problems in the globalized world of

politics. Since everyday political interactions in global politics comprise hard
normative choices for both state actors and non-state actors, new ethical issues
or old issues with newly-acknowledged ethical dimensions require attentive
theoretical analysis. Thus, *normative dilemmas* and *tragedy* in contemporary
world politics will be examined accordingly. This chapter concludes that the
normative turn in IR theory has played a vital role in both the theoretical and
methodological development of IR theories since the mid-1980s. However,
international/global norms, normative dilemmas in foreign policy, and ethics
of politics require further theoretical reflections—particularly, if the IR theorists wish to remain faithful to the origins of the discipline.

IR THROUGH A MAGNIFYING GLASS: REFLECTING UPON NORMATIVE IR THEORY

The emergence and development of IR theories have been intertwined with
the development of the discipline itself, particularly through the *Great
Debates.* Coming to the 1980s, IR theorists criticized the scientific research
of *structural realism* and *neorealism*—questioning the methodological and
conceptual basis of these explanatory theories rejecting the role of norms,
values, and ideas on interactions among international actors. As Mervyn Frost
puts it, all "international interactions should be understood in ethical terms."[1]
Thus, this ethical discourse on what international/global norms ought to be
that are regulating these interactions among IR actors—developed through
the 1980s and 1990s—have highlighted the divide between *Rationalist/
Positivist IR theories* versus *Reflectivist/Post-positivist IR theories.*[2]

The so-called *Fourth Great Debate* in IR compares *explanatory* versus
critical IR theories reflecting upon Robert Cox's famous line that "theory
is always for someone and for some purpose."[3] Hence, the *Rationalist/
Positivist IR theories* have predominantly focused on explaining the empirical processes and international events, while the *Reflectivist/Post-positivist
IR theories* have been exploring normative bases of international actions to
understand reasons and consequences of and for interactions among international actors. The distinction here is not only about how to analyze and
separate facts from values, but it is also about the objectives and the ideals of
the discipline—that means what IR ought to be like.

Therefore, the birth of IR as a separate academic discipline has been
founded upon certain normative considerations for a desire not to repeat the
same catastrophic mistake of human suffering that occurred during the First
World War. Starting from the *First Great Debate,* the moral dimension of
the discipline was articulated by liberals by attempting to answer questions
like "Why do wars occur? / How to prevent such total wars in the future?"

To understand the problem of total warfare required facing hard international issues—particularly in foreign policy—which are full of normative aspects and value dilemmas. Therefore, as Burchill and Linklater assert, "the purpose of theory in the early years of the discipline was to change the world for the better by removing the blight of war. A close connection existed between theory and practice."[4] Accordingly, starting from the very first theoretical approach to international relations—namely, *Idealism*—IR theory, particularly the *Liberal Internationalists* who believed in the power of human reason and human action to change the world for the fulfillment of the human potential, actualized as *progress* in international politics.

Normative Theory in IR aims at exploring not simply what is done, but rather what ought to be done. Hence, *Normative IR Theory* addresses questions relating to standards of behavior, obligations, responsibilities, rights, and duties relating to not only states, but also individuals and the international state system itself. Accordingly, it engages with norms, rules, values, practices, and procedures in international relations. In fact, IR theorists are already taking normative positions while they are making research on international politics—simply starting from their choice of inquiry and the theory they choose to examine the interactions among international actors. Hence, even the *Rationalist IR theories* are already normative theories; yet, they simply do not admit that they are already base their major assumptions on normative concepts and normative explanations of international relations. Whereas they do not acknowledge how they are biased, their assumptions and central concepts are all based on major social values, and certain discourses of truth such as sovereignty, power, anarchy, structure, capability, national interest, and so on. As Molly Cochran puts it, "All theory in International Relations (IR) is normative theory."[5] Thus, *Normative IR Theory* suggests that IR scholars should openly and explicitly assert their normative positions if they want to keep their moral commitment to IR as an academic discipline.

The emergence and growing importance of *Normative Theory* in IR have been discussed by many IR scholars since the 1980s.[6] One of the most succinct definitions of *Normative IR Theory* is done by Chris Brown, as follows: "By normative international relations theory is meant that body of work which addresses the moral dimension of international relations and the wider questions of meaning and interpretation generated by the discipline. At its most basic it addresses the ethical nature of the relations between communities/states."[7] *Normative IR Theory* has provided two major contrasting approaches—*Communitarianism* and *Cosmopolitanism*—providing ethical foundations for debating international relations: "Communitarians in both political theory and normative IR theory hold that the individual's self-actualization is realized in the expression and pursuit of shared goods within a community."[8] Whereas *Communitarianism* advocates for the right of the state, *Cosmopolitans* argue for the duty of the state as the normative foundation for international practice in contemporary political and theoretical debates.[9] The *Communitarianism* and *Cosmopolitanism* divide provides a useful tool for analysis for examining three major topics of *Normative IR Theory*: the autonomy of the state; the ethics of the use of force or *Just War Theory*; and the issue of international justice. The two categories specifically help us to understand and evaluate the relationship between moral values and international obligations.

Since the 1950s, the idea of *international society* played a prominent role in IR theory based on a set of agreed rules, norms, and institutions as identified by the *English School* theorists. According to Hedley Bull, the *English School* views IR as fundamentally a normative field of study: "Values matter not just in terms of the relationship between the researcher and their subject but are central to the subject of IR."[10] Hence, Bull and his fellow scholars tried to answer the question of *"What shall we do, and how shall we live?"* and answered it by constructing and enhancing an *international society* based on the practice of order and justice. Whereas the *English School* scholars emphasized the importance of order rather than justice or prosperity during the Cold War era, they have started to take "a more explicitly normative stance on questions of poverty and human rights"[11] since the mid-1980s. During the post–Cold War era, the normative debate among the *English School* theorists continued around a *Pluralist-Solidarist* divide. Particularly, the exclusive rights of sovereign states have shifted towards recognizing the rights of all individuals that can be illustrated by the debates of protection of human rights, refugee issues, humanitarian crisis and intervention.

In the 1990s, *Social Constructivism* emerged as a crucial theoretical approach within the discipline—they argued for the importance of social, historical, and normative structures alongside the material ones.[12] *Constructivists* claimed that "these are thought to shape the social identities of political actors. Just as the institutionalized norms of the academy shape the identity of a professor, the norms of the international system condition the social identity of the sovereign state."[13] Thus, *Social Constructivism* has paved the way for the revival of normative theorizing in IR theory by legitimizing it "by demonstrating the possibility of ideas driven by international change; and . . . by clarifying the dynamics and mechanisms of such change."[14] Furthermore, *Constructivism* has not been engaged in the politics of ethics, but also the ethics of politics: accordingly, in the last two decades *Constructivist* IR scholars have researched on international society, world society, the role of international NGOs, transnational terrorism, international and global order, interconnections between culture (as inter-subjective meanings and practices) and international relations, redefinition of norms such as sovereignty, global governance, state power or violence in international relations, and so on.[15]

With the end of the Cold War, *Feminist IR theories* have joined the critical scholarship in IR as they "have introduced gender as a relevant empirical category and analytical tool for understanding global power relations as well as a normative position from which to construct alternative world orders."[16] *Feminism* has several normative goals: firstly, unveiling how social, political, and economic relations are gendered; secondly, addressing the complexity of international and global power processes and institutions in order to change the interlocking nature of oppressions of women for furthering women's agency; and thirdly, including women's experiences to create a more critical and universal theory of international relations.[17]

In the beginning *Green political theory* started with a normative critique of both capitalism and communism by engaging in questions of justice, rights, democracy, citizenship, the state, and the environment. The second generation of *Green political theorists* have turned to discuss "the core debates within normative IR theory, particularly those concerned with human rights, cosmopolitan democracy, transnational civil society, and transnational public spheres."[18] Currently, this green branch of *Normative IR theory* mostly focuses on global environmental justice. By doing this, *Green IR theory* has shifted the state-centric framework to analyze normative insights into global environmental problems and climate change by promoting international cooperation and the role of IGOs and international NGOs in global environmental politics.[19]

As Erskine claims, "for the normative IR theorist, the global is an ethical realm and the various actors that inhabit it are not immune to charges of moral responsibility."[20] Thus, the IR researchers should be concerned with how to criticize, change, and improve the world. In order to do that *Normative IR Theory* does not only focus on international norms and values, but also important policy questions of how institutions and practices in international relations can construct the actual choices and interactions of international actors in foreign policy. Ethical considerations and explanations are already embedded in our global international practices:[21] international interactions are taking place within certain ethical foundations that manifest themselves in the decision-making and justifications that states and other international actors provide particularly in foreign policy. As a matter of fact, "a striking feature of writings on International Relations (IR) over the last three decades is the burgeoning interest in applying insights grounded in normative theory to the practice of foreign policy."[22] So what are these key normative issues addressed by *Normative IR Theory* in a globalized world of politics?

NORMATIVE DILEMMAS AND TRAGEDY IN
CONTEMPORARY INTERNATIONAL RELATIONS

In fact, looking through the magnifying glass, IR involves some of the most fundamental normative issues that decision makers as well as all human beings as citizens of the nation-states encounter in their lives such as war and peace; justice and injustice; human rights and international/domestic order; humanitarian intervention; nuclear proliferation; environmental protection; and many other ethical questions.[23] In his well-known book entitled *Ethics in International Relations: A Constitutive Theory*, Frost identifies at least thirteen pressing normative issues in contemporary world politics including the causes and conduct of war; nuclear weapons and their proliferation; individuals' agreement or refusal to participate in the use of force; how to combat international terrorism; humanitarian intervention; just/unjust wars and the involvement of other parties to them; refugee problems; secession; involvement of other parties in secessionist conflicts; economic and social distribution of world resources; preservation of the global ecology; role of international organizations; and finally, human rights problems.[24]

In order to provide answers to these hard cases of international politics, Frost attempts to construct a *Constitutive Theory,* and offers a list of the *settled norms* in IR.[25] As individuals, citizens, states, or other international actors "it is something we all engage with in some measure when we attempt to understand who we are and how we fit into the social arrangements within which we are constructed."[26] Thus, actors in IR interact with each other within specified social practices based on certain ethical values and international norms. Furthermore, they are all challenged with one vital ethical question: *"What would it be ethically right for us to do in these circumstances?"*[27] Answering this crucial question "requires that one understands the ethical dimensions of what has gone before, the ethical dimensions of the present state of affairs, the ethical aspects of various policy options and the ethical dimensions of the means whose use is under consideration."[28] Accordingly, the viable answers to be given depend on the past and the prevailing state of international order and international society: in the post–Cold War era, the security foundations; the character of global governance and institutionalization; the character of power politics; the normative structure of international society with evolving/emerging international norms have all been changing.

This indeed has reshaped the sorts of questions currently being asked by normative theorists. On one hand, these changes have complicated the decision-making and implementation processes in foreign policy; on the other hand, the *new ethical issues* or *old issues with newly-acknowledged ethical dimensions* emerged in the last three decades have compelled IR theorists to analyze a wide range of issues within these new circumstances in world politics. Initially engaged in problems surrounding both war and global inequality, *Normative IR Theory* currently tackles a myriad of ethical problems. These include issues such as individual human rights, global civil society, private military companies, migrants, refugees, humanitarian intervention, globalized forces, global/international terrorism, counter-terrorism, proliferation of WMDs, global health issues (i.e., contagious diseases, pandemics, COVID-19 vaccines, etc.), climate change, global warming, and other pressing environmental issues, animal rights, global poverty, the new digital age and social media, internet privacy, disinformation, disability issues, gender issues, euthanasia, bioethics, genetic selection, embryo research, AI and robot ethics, and so on.

The list of new ethical issues or newly-acknowledged ethical dimensions of old issues could be expanded.[29] However, this not the only area needs attention from normative theorists: "the so-called *War on Terror* reinvigorated interest in the ethics of war, and brought with it new topics for study, including the ethics of torture, the status of nonstate actors in armed conflict, the justice of pre-emptive force, and our duties to others after wars end."[30] Thus, IR scholars have been increasingly researching on issues related ethical foreign policy as a problem of international relations, especially regarding the debate about the ethics of humanitarian intervention and the criteria of *Just War theory*.[31]

Another issue area that IR scholars have been focusing on from an ethical perspective is environmental problems: "Recent technological developments and new scientific tools regarding socioecological systems have created new global settings, which bring to the core new environmental problems, approaches, challenges, and conflicts."[32] IR scholars like Luca Valera and Juan Carlos Castilla assert that the current crisis in a globalized world today is not merely an environmental crisis, "but also socio-environmental: as humans, we are part of this crisis and responsible actors for finding possible solutions."[33] Hence, technological and even political solutions are not suffice to solve the current environmental crisis as they rather need ethical responses. What we need is "a clear picture of the empirical situation, but we also need a clear picture of the normative sphere of the web of interconnected and interdependent moral demands linked to climate change."[34] Therefore, climate change is a complex global problem posing humanitarian catastrophes for the current as well as the future generations; it also poses ethical questions such as reasonability, fairness, uncertainty, intergenerational and global distributive justice.[35]

Global health issues and governance has been another concern for IR scholars in the last two decades—particularly evaluating the inherent connection between ethics, human rights, and health issues.[36] In fact, it dates back to 1990s as the struggle for HIV/AIDS treatment for fair equal access to necessary health care and medication has been a turning point in the global governance of health. The development and global distribution of an effective Coronavirus vaccine is one of the latest illustrations of ethical concerns in global politics discussed not only by politicians, international community and the media, but also by IR researchers.[37] Mainly there are two major approaches to the politics of global health: the *statist perspective* versus the *globalist perspective*. Whereas the *statist perspective* is mostly state-based approach to health issues prioritising the state's economic and political stability threatened by infectious diseases, and using the concept of *health security*, the *globalist perspective* focuses on the individual's vulnerability and well-being by using the concept of *human security*. Therefore, in this globalized world, people's access to life-sustaining medicines are not only affected and controlled by their national governments, but also by a network of global health actors like intergovernmental organizations, international NGOs, multinational laboratories and factories.[38] In this respect, *bioethics* comes to the fore as it concerns the "clinical and research ethics in humans and other living organisms, from the 'everyday' ethical decisions made in common medical practice to the 'frontier' ethical dilemmas around the development and impact of new technologies."[39] Bioethical issues include the allocation of health care and systemic inequalities—particularly in poor societies in the Global South; the clinical trials of pharmaceutical companies; the collection of biological samples and genetic data. Thus, these relatively new ethical problems have started to inform the discussions within IR theories.[40]

A more recent example of an ethical research agenda on a global issue is referred to our central communicative practice of internet: Matthias C. Kettemann asserts that "a normative order of the internet has emerged, which is made up of norms of varied regulatory genesis and legitimacy."[41] Kettemann argues that the international norms apply to the internet are required to be systematized since they are "materially and normatively connected to the use and development of the internet nationally, regionally, and internationally."[42] As a novel ethical dilemma, *internet research ethics* involve many different questions of ethical obligations of researchers such as protection of the privacy of their subjects while using internet and social media; national and international ethical standards applied to research on global networks, communities and information flows; online anonymity and confidentiality; protection of minors as subjects; personal harm in digital platforms; inequalities in data access; and data quality.[43]

In the last decade or so *Normative IR* theorists have been engaging in a debate on the role of *tragedy* in world politics, and how to theorize tragedy and the tragic. The debate on *tragedy* has been mostly done through articles published in *International Relations* by IR theorists such as Mervyn Frost,

James Mayall, Nicholas Rengger, Richard Ned Lebow, Chris Brown, and Peter Euben.[44] The main question all these IR scholars have asked and tried to answer is "whether tragedy brings specific insight to our understanding of the relationship between international politics and ethics. . . . Does tragedy have something to say to international relations, its future conceptualization, and practice?"[45] Thus, they focus on whether and how the concept of tragedy provides useful insights to international ethics.

In fact, *tragedy* provides useful insights to both contemporary IR theory and practice for avoiding tragic outcomes in international politics. The history of international relations is most often based on different tragedies as explained by classical *Realists* and other theorists. Whereas *Realist* approaches argue that tragic perspectives help us to gain a deeper understanding of *realpolitik* and the selfish nature of human-beings, *Normative IR Theory* asserts that the concept of tragedy enables us to see ethical dilemmas clearly—this gives us an opportunity to transform the practice of international relations for better. As defined by Frost, *tragedy* "is a term used to refer to a special relationship between an act undertaken for ethical reasons and its negative or painful consequences. . . . It invites an ethical evaluation of a series of events consisting of an act and its consequences."[46] Different examples of these tragic outcomes occurred as a result of the ethical actions of international actors revealing the complexity of our own ethical practices. As there are "multiple sets of values encounter and potentially conflict with one another, and it can thereby help in disentangling ethical differences and dilemmas."[47]

Brown asserts that "tragedy involves a situation where duties are in radical conflict, such that whatever is done will involve wrongdoing . . . the only way to preserve integrity and honour is to accept the tragic nature of one's choice: that is, to acknowledge that to act is to do wrong."[48] As the practitioners of international relations often face ethical dilemmas, the ethical choices they make result in tragedies in international politics. For example, decision makers are faced with difficult policy options of humanitarian intervention, migrant and refugee issues or distributive justice in international affairs. The consequences of many tragedies were reflected on the creation of new international orders based on international norms, rules, law, and power relationships. Actually, the modern international order has been designed to prevent the recurrence of such tragedies of world wars, genocide, mass destruction, environmental catastrophes, and so on. Hence, tragedies may facilitate a transformation of social practices and institutions in the contemporary world order; "tragedy's potential utility lies in the contribution it can make to processes of resolution and reconciliation"[49] in international affairs.

CONCLUSION

The *normative turn* in IR theory dating back to 1980s has greatly contributed to the theoretical development of the discipline notably through the emergence of the post-Positivist IR theories with the end of the Cold War. When IR theorists set their sights on examining newly uncovered ethical issues that posed normative dilemmas to both decision makers and global community, *Normative IR theory* has assisted them through the ethically complex and contradictory world politics: new concepts, new interpretations, and new policy options were introduced and developed further. Thus, "the issues addressed by this body of scholarship [*Normative IR theory*] are situated resolutely at the very heart of international politics. Indeed, *Normative IR theory* embraces theoretical perspectives and priorities that the discipline cannot ignore if it is to be both meaningful to those who study it and relevant to practice."[50]

Thus, *normative turn* in IR theory has also contributed to the methodological debates within the discipline as they have pointed to the *positivist bias* of the dominant IR theories. After all, as Frost puts it "international interactions are always ethically informed, but that this aspect is often hidden and not made apparent"[51] in international relations—especially by *Rationalist IR theories*. However, *Normative IR theory* has paved the way for IR theorists to understand and to theorize the normative dilemmas in world politics as they have started to dominate the international agenda in the post–Cold War era.

Normative IR theory is usually portrayed as a newly conceived subfield within the discipline of IR, hence, it "is a young, and perhaps still somewhat immature, sibling in a growing family of IR theories."[52] Nevertheless, this did not prevent it to contribute to the research agendas of many IR scholars since the 1990s. In fact, *Normative IR theory* encompasses a variety theories and approaches examining moral standings of international actors, decisions, and ethical dilemmas in global politics.

So, what do the *normative dilemmas* and *tragedy* imply for contemporary IR theory? As Erskine puts it succinctly, "none of the issues, insights, or questions listed here would appear on our radar screens as IR scholars if we did not acknowledge the importance of the ethical dimension of international politics."[53] In a rapidly changing and challenging world, *Normative IR theory* aims at extending international norms and ethical commitments in order to further human rights, global justice and equality for all peoples through better practices and institutions: "to the extent that normative theory presents an evaluation of international politics as ethical life which can be recognized by others, it can be said to be an integral part of the ways in which the world has changed or is changing."[54]

In the post–Cold War era, both sovereign states and international organizations have felt the urge to justify their foreign policy decisions/actions in ethical terms. So normative issues have become more policy relevant as IR actors provided ethical arguments for their policies over humanitarian intervention, climate change, refuge problems, or global health issues, etc. in order to be accountable to their citizens and to the international community. The renewed interest in *Normative IR theory* is yet to continue since any evaluation of global politics today would be incomplete without an appraisal of international norms, normative dilemmas, and the moral responsibility of international actors.

REFERENCES

Amstutz, Mark R. *International Ethics: Concepts, Theories, and Cases in Global Politics.* Oxford: Rowman & Littlefield Publishers, 2013.

Bakan, Zerrin Ayşe. "Soğuk Savaş Sonrasında Devlet Egemenliğinin Sınırlarına Normatif Bir Bakış," *Avrasya Dosyası* 8, No. 3 (2002): 140–153.

Bakan, Zerrin Ayşe. "Uluslararası İlişkiler Teorileri Arasında Normatif Teorinin Yeri ve Kapsamı," *Avrasya Dosyası* 8, No. 2 (2002): 427–444.

Bakan, Zerrin Ayşe. "Normative Theory in IR: A Constitutive Approach," *Ankara University Sbf Journal* 63, No. 1 (2008): 3–16.

Banks, Michael. "The Inter-Paradigm Debate." In *International Relations: A Handbook of Current Theory,* edited by Margot Light and A.J.R. Groom, 7–26. London: Pinter, 1985.

Beardsworth, Richard. "Tragedy, World Politics and Ethical Community," *International Relations* 2, No. 1 (2008): 127–137.

Benney, Tabitha M. "Climate Change, Sustainable Development, and Vulnerability." In R*outledge Handbook of Ethics and International Relations,* edited by Brent J. Steele and Eric A. Heinze, 392–404. London: Routledge, 2018.

Brown, Chris. "International Ethics: Fad, Fantasy or Field?," *Paradigms* 8, No. 1 (1994): 1–12.

Brown, Chris. *International Relations Theory: New Normative Approaches.* London: Harvester-Wheatsheaf, 1992.

Brown, Chris. *Sovereignty, Rights and Justice: International Political Theory Today.* Cambridge: Polity, 2002.

Brown, Chris. "Tragedy, 'Tragic Choices' and Contemporary International Political Theory," *International Relations* 21, No. 1 (2007): 5–13.

Bulley, Dan. "The Politics of Ethical Foreign Policy: A Responsibility to Protect Whom?" *European Journal of International Relations* 16, No. 3 (2010): 441–461.

Burchill, Scott and Linklater, Andrew, et al, eds. *Theories of International Relations.* Hampshire: Palgrave Macmillan, 2005.

Cochran, Molly. *Normative Theory in International Relations: A Pragmatic Approach.* Cambridge: Cambridge University Press, 1999.

Daği, İhsan D. "Normatif Yaklaşımlar: Adalet, Eşitlik ve İnsan Hakları." In *Devlet, Sistem ve Kimlik: Uluslararası İlişkilerde Temel Yaklaşımlar*, edited by Atila Eralp, 185–226. İstanbul: İletişim Yayınları, 2001.

Demirbaş, Çağrı Emin and Alper, Gamze. "Uluslararası İlişkilerde Kozmopolitanizm-Komüniteryanizm Ayrışmasının Ana Hatları," *Uluslararası İlişkiler Çalışmaları Dergisi* 2, No. 1 (2022): 1–18.

Douglas, Thomas. "Genetic Selection." In *Ethics and the Contemporary World*, edited by David Edmonds, 303–317. London: Routledge, 2019.

Dunne, Tim. "The English School." In *International Relations Theories: Discipline and Diversity*, edited by Tim Dunne, Milja Kurki, and Steve Smith, 132–152. Oxford: Oxford University Press, 2012.

Dunne, Tim. "Ethical Foreign Policy in a Multipolar World." In *The Oxford Handbook of International Political Theory*, edited by Chris Brown and Robyn Eckersley, 495–507. Oxford: Oxford University Press, 2018.

Duryea, Scott N. "In Search of Monsters to Destroy: NATO's Prosecution of the Kosovo Intervention in the Just War Tradition," *Global Security and Intelligence Studies* 6, No. 2 (2021): 45–71.

Eckersley, Robyn. "Green Theory." In *International Relations Theories: Discipline and Diversity*, edited by Tim Dunne, Milja Kurki, and Steve Smith, 266–286. Oxford: Oxford University Press, 2012.

Edmonds, David, ed. *Ethics and the Contemporary World.* London: Routledge, 2019.

Erskine, Toni. "Normative International Relations Theory." In *International Relations Theories: Discipline and Diversity*, edited by Tim Dunne, Milja Kurki, and Steve Smith, 36–58. Oxford: Oxford University Press, 2010.

Fay, Timothy. "Applying Classical Realism, Institutional Liberalism and Normative Theory to the Development and Distribution of a COVID-19 Vaccine," *Gettysburg Social Sciences Review* 5, No. 1, Article 9 (2021): https://Cupola.Gettysburg.Edu/Gssr/Vol5/Iss1/9, Accessed 01/09/2022.

Frost, Mervyn. *Towards a Normative Theory of International Relations.* Cambridge: Cambridge University Press, 1986.

Frost, Mervyn. "The Role of Normative Theory in IR," *Millennium* 23, No. 1 (1994):109–118.

Frost, Mervyn. *Ethics in International Relations.* Cambridge: Cambridge University Press, 1996.

Frost, Mervyn. "A Turn Not Taken: Ethics in IR at the Millennium," *Review of International Studies,* 24/Special Issue: The Eighty Years' Crisis 1919–1999: 119–132.

Frost, Mervyn. "Tragedy, Ethics and International Relations," *International Relations* 17, No. 4 (2003): 477–495.

Frost, Mervyn. *Global Ethics: Anarchy, Freedom and International Relations.* London: Routledge, 2009.

Gray, Tim. "Normative Theory of International Relations and the 'Mackerel War' in the North East Atlantic," *Marine Policy* No. 131 (2021): 1–10.

Hoffman, Mark. "Critical Theory and the Inter-Paradigm Debate," *Millennium: Journal of International Studies* 16, No. 2 (1987): 231–249.

Hollis, Martin and Smith, Steve. *Explaining and Understanding International Relations.* Oxford: Clarendon Press, 1990.

Holzgrefe, J.L. and Keohane, Robert O., eds. *Humanitarian Intervention: Ethical, Legal and Political Dilemmas.* Cambridge: Cambridge University Press, 2003.

Hurrell, Andrew and Macdonald, Terry. "Ethics and Norms in International Relations." In *Handbook of International Relations,* edited by Walter Carlsnaes, Thomas Risse, and Beth A. Simmons, 57–84. London: Sage, 2013.

Hutchings, Kimberly. *International Political Theory: Rethinking Ethics in a Global Era.* London: Sage Publications, 1999.

Karacasulu, Nilüfer and Karakir, İrem Aşkar Karakır. "Cosmopolitan-Communitarian Dichotomy: Towards a Third Way?" *İşletme Fakültesi Dergisi* 16, No. 2 (2015): 21–48.

Kettemann, Matthias C. *The Normative Order of the Internet: A Theory of Rule and Regulation Online.* Oxford: Oxford University Press, 2020.

Küçük, Mustafa. "Uluslararası İlişkiler Kuramında 'Konstrüktivist Dönüşü' Anlamak," *Ege Academic Review* 9, No. 2 (2009): 771–795.

Langlois, Adèle. "Global Bioethics." In *Routledge Handbook of Ethics and International Relations,* edited by Brent J. Steele and Eric A. Heinze, 253–267. London: Routledge, 2018.

London, Leslie. "What Is a Human-Rights Based Approach to Health and Does It Matter?" *Health and Human Rights* 10, No. 1 (2008): 65–80.

Mann, Jonathan M. "Medicine and Public Health, Ethics and Human Rights," *Hastings Center Report* 27, No. 3 (1997): 6–13.

Mills, Elizabeth. "At a Crossroads: Health and Vulnerability in the Era of HIV." In *Routledge Handbook of Ethics and International Relations,* edited by Brent J. Steele and Eric A. Heinze, 378–391. London: Routledge, 2018.

Mitchell, Ronald B. "International Environmental Politics." In *Handbook of International Relations,* edited by Walter Carlsnaes, Thomas Risse, and Beth A. Simmons, 801–826. London: Sage, 2013.

Parlar Dal, Emel. "A Normative Approach to Contemporary Turkish Foreign Policy: The Cosmopolitanism–Communitarianism Divide," *International Journal: Canada's Journal of Global Policy Analysis* 70, No. 3 (2015): 1–13.

Reus-Smit, Christian. "Constructivism." In *Theories of International Relations,* edited by Scott Burchill, Andrew Linklater, et al., 188–212. Hampshire: Palgrave Macmillan, 2005.

Singer, Peter. *Ethics in the Real World: 86 Brief Essays on Things That Matter.* Princeton: Princeton University Press, 2016.

Sjoberg, Laura and J. Ann Tickner. "Feminist Perspectives on International Relations." In *Handbook of International Relations,* edited by Walter Carlsnaes, Thomas Risse, and Beth A. Simmons, 170–194. London: Sage, 2013.

Smith, Steve. "Reflectivist and Constructivist Approaches to International Theory." In *The Globalization of World Politics,* edited by John Baylis and Steve Smith, 224–249. Oxford: Oxford University Press, 2001.

True, Jacqui. "Feminism." In *Theories of International Relations,* edited by Scott Burchill, Andrew Linklater, et al., 213–234. Hampshire: Palgrave Macmillan, 2005.

Valera, Luca Valera and Castilla, Juan Carlos, eds. *Global Changes: Ethics, Politics and Environment in the Contemporary Technological World*, Ethics of Science and Technology Assessment 46, Springer Nature Switzerland, 2020.

Wedderburn, Alister. "Tragedy, Genealogy and Theories of International Relations," *European Journal of International Relations* 24, No.1 (2018): 177–197.

Wendt, Alexander. *Social Theory of International Politics.* Cambridge: Cambridge University Press, 1999.

Zellentin, Alexa. "Climate Change and International Ethics." In *The Routledge Handbook to Rethinking Ethics in International Relations*, edited by Birgit Schippers, 195–207. London: Routledge, 2020.

Zimmer, Michael and Kinder-Kurland, Katharina, eds. *Internet Research Ethics for the Social Age: New Challenges, Cases, and Contexts.* New York: Peter Lang Publishing, 2017.

NOTES

1. Mervyn Frost, *Global Ethics: Anarchy, Freedom and International Relations* (London: Routledge, 2009), 1.

2. For discussions, see: Robert W. Cox, "Social Forces, States and World Orders," *Millennium: Journal of International Studies* 10, no. 2 (1981): 126–155; Mark Hoffman, "Critical Theory and the Inter-Paradigm Debate," *Millennium: Journal of International Studies* 16, no. 2 (1987): 231–249; Martin Hollis and Steve Smith, *Explaining and Understanding International Relations* (Oxford: Clarendon Press, 1990).

3. Cox, "Social Forces, States," 128.

4. Scott Burchill and Andrew Linklater, "Introduction," in *Theories of International Relations*, eds. Scott Burchill, Andrew Linklater, et al. (Hampshire: Palgrave Macmillan, 2005), 9.

5. Molly Cochran, *Normative Theory in International Relations: A Pragmatic Approach* (Cambridge: Cambridge University Press, 2004), 1.

6. For discussions, see: Mervyn Frost, *Towards a Normative Theory of International Relations* (Cambridge: Cambridge University Press, 1986); Chris Brown, *International Relations Theory: New Normative Approaches* (London: Harvester-Wheatsheaf, 1992); Mervyn Frost, "The Role of Normative Theory in IR," *Millennium* 23, no.1 (1994): 109–118; Kimberly Hutchings, *International Political Theory: Rethinking Ethics in a Global Era,* (London: Sage Publications, 1999); İhsan D. Dağı, "Normatif Yaklaşımlar: Adalet, Eşitlik ve İnsan Hakları," in *Devlet, Sistem ve Kimlik: Uluslararası İlişkilerde Temel Yaklaşımlar,* ed. Atila Eralp (İstanbul: İletişim Yayınları, 2001), 185–226; Zerrin Ayşe Bakan, "Uluslararası İlişkiler Teorileri Arasında Normatif Teorinin Yeri ve Kapsamı," *Avrasya Dosyası* 8, no. 2 (2002): 427–444; Andrew Hurrell and Terry Macdonald, "Ethics and Norms in International Relations," in *Handbook of International Relations,* eds. Walter Carlsnaes, Thomas Risse, and Beth A. Simmons (London: Sage, 2013), 57–84.

7. Brown, *International Relations Theory,* 3.

8. Cochran, *Normative Theory in International Relations,* 52.

9. For discussions, see: Toni Erskine, "Normative International Relations Theory," in *International Relations Theories: Discipline and Diversity,* eds. Tim Dunne, Milja Kurki, and Steve Smith (Oxford: Oxford University Press, 2010), 36–58; Nilüfer Karacasulu and İrem Aşkar Karakır, "Cosmopolitan-Communitarian Dichotomy: Towards A Third Way?" *İşletme Fakültesi Dergisi* 16, no. 2 (2015): 21–48; Çağrı Emin Demirbaş and Gamze Alper, "Uluslararası İlişkilerde Kozmopolitanizm-Komüniteryanizm Ayrışmasının Ana Hatları," *Uluslararası İlişkiler Çalışmaları Dergisi* 2, no. 1 (2022): 1–18.

10. Tim Dunne, "The English School," in *International Relations Theories: Discipline and Diversity,* eds. Tim Dunne, Milja Kurki, and Steve Smith (Oxford: Oxford University Press, 2012), 136.

11. Andrew Linklater, "The English School," in *Theories of International Relations,* eds. Scott Burchill, Andrew Linklater, et al. (Hampshire: Palgrave Macmillan, 2005), 88.

12. See: Alexander Wendt, *Social Theory of International Politics* (Cambridge: Cambridge University Press, 1999).

13. Christian Reus-Smit, "Constructivism," in *Theories of International Relations,* eds. Scott Burchill, Andrew Linklater, et al. (Hampshire: Palgrave Macmillan, 2005), 196.

14. Christian Reus-Smit, "Constructivism," 207.

15. For example, see: Mustafa Küçük, "Uluslararası İlişkiler Kuramında 'Konstrüktivist Dönüşü' Anlamak," *Ege Academic Review* 9, no. 2 (2009): 771–795.

16. Jacqui True, "Feminism," in *Theories of International Relations,* eds. Scott Burchill, Andrew Linklater, et al. (Hampshire: Palgrave Macmillan, 2005), 213.

17. See: Jacqui True, "Feminism," 213–234; Laura Sjoberg and J. Ann Tickner, "Feminist Perspectives on International Relations," in *Handbook of International Relations,* eds. Walter Carlsnaes, Thomas Risse, and Beth A. Simmons (London: Sage, 2013), 170–194.

18. Robyn Eckersley, "Green Theory," in *International Relations Theories: Discipline and Diversity,* eds. Tim Dunne, Milja Kurki, and Steve Smith (Oxford: Oxford University Press, 2012), 269.

19. See: Ronald B. Mitchell, "International Environmental Politics," in *Handbook of International Relations,* eds. Walter Carlsnaes, Thomas Risse, and Beth A. Simmons (London: Sage, 2013), 801–826.

20. Erskine, "Normative International Relations Theory," 48.

21. See: Frost, *Global Ethics,* 1–53.

22. Tim Dunne, "Ethical Foreign Policy in a Multipolar World," in *The Oxford Handbook of International Political Theory,* eds. Chris Brown and Robyn Eckersley (Oxford: Oxford University Press, 2018), 497.

23. For some different aspects, see: Zerrin Ayşe Bakan, "Soğuk Savaş Sonrasında Devlet Egemenliğinin Sınırlarına Normatif Bir Bakış," *Avrasya Dosyası* 8, no. 3 (2002): 140–153; Emel Parlar Dal, "A Normative Approach to Contemporary Turkish Foreign Policy: The Cosmopolitanism–Communitarianism Divide," *International Journal: Canada's Journal of Global Policy Analysis* 70, no. 3 (2015): 1–13; Tim

Gray, "Normative Theory of International Relations and the 'Mackerel War' in the North East Atlantic," *Marine Policy* no. 131 (2021): 1–10.

24. Mervyn Frost, *Ethics in International Relations: A Constitutive Theory* (Cambridge: Cambridge University Press, 1996), 76–77.

25. For a discussion of Mervyn Frost's Constitutive Theory, see: Zerrin Ayşe Bakan, "Normative Theory in IR: A Constitutive Approach," *Ankara University SBF Journal* 63, no. 1 (2008): 3–16.

26. Mervyn Frost, *Constituting Human Rights: Global Civil Society and the Society of Democratic States* (London: Routledge, 2002), 137.

27. Frost, *Constituting Human Rights*, 137.

28. Frost, *Global Ethics*, 7.

29. For detailed discussions of different ethical issues in global politics, see: Mark R. Amstutz, *International Ethics: Concepts, Theories, and Cases in Global Politics* (Oxford: Rowman & Littlefield Publishers, 2013); Peter Singer, *Ethics in the Real World: 86 Brief Essays on Things That Matter* (Princeton: Princeton University Press, 2016); David Edmonds, ed., *Ethics and the Contemporary World* (London: Routledge, 2019).

30. Erskine, "Normative International Relations Theory," 54–55.

31. See: J.L. Holzgrefe and Robert O. Keohane, eds., *Humanitarian Intervention: Ethical, Legal and Political Dilemmas* (Cambridge: Cambridge University Press, 2003); Dan Bulley, "The Politics of Ethical Foreign Policy: A Responsibility to Protect Whom?" *European Journal of International Relations* 16, no. 3 (2010): 441–461; Scott N. Duryea, "In Search of Monsters to Destroy: NATO's Prosecution of the Kosovo Intervention in the Just War Tradition," *Global Security and Intelligence Studies* 6, no. 2 (2021): 45–71.

32. Luca Valera and Juan Carlos Castilla, "Introduction," in *Global Changes: Ethics, Politics and Environment in the Contemporary Technological World*, eds. Luca Valera and Juan Carlos Castilla (Ethics of Science and Technology Assessment 46, Springer Nature Switzerland, 2020), 1.

33. Valera and Castilla, *Global Changes*, 191.

34. Alexa Zellentin, "Climate Change and International Ethics," in *The Routledge Handbook to Rethinking Ethics in International Relations*, ed. Birgit Schippers (London: Routledge, 2020), 204.

35. See: Tabitha M. Benney, "Climate Change, Sustainable Development, and Vulnerability," in *Routledge Handbook of Ethics and International Relations*, eds. Brent J. Steele and Eric A. Heinze (London: Routledge, 2018), 392–404.

36. See: Jonathan M. Mann, "Medicine and Public Health, Ethics and Human Rights," *Hastings Center Report* 27, no. 3 (1997): 6–13; Leslie London, "What Is a Human-Rights Based Approach to Health and Does It Matter?" *Health and Human Rights* 10, no. 1 (2008): 65–80.

37. For example, see: Timothy Fay, "Applying Classical Realism, Institutional Liberalism and Normative Theory to the Development and Distribution of a COVID-19 Vaccine," *Gettysburg Social Sciences Review* 5, no. 1, Article 9 (2021), available at: https://cupola.gettysburg.edu/gssr/vol5/iss1/9, Accessed 01/09/2022.

38. See: Elizabeth Mills, "At a Crossroads: Health and Vulnerability in the Era of HIV," in *Routledge Handbook of Ethics and International Relations,* eds. Brent J. Steele and Eric A. Heinze (London: Routledge, 2018), 378–391.

39. Adèle Langlois, "Global Bioethics," in *Routledge Handbook of Ethics and International Relations,* eds. Brent J. Steele and Eric A. Heinze (London: Routledge, 2018), 253.

40. See: Langlois, "Global Bioethics," 253–267; Thomas Douglas, "Genetic Selection," in *Ethics and the Contemporary World,* ed. David Edmonds (London: Routledge, 2019), 303–317.

41. Matthias C. Kettemann, *The Normative Order of the Internet: A Theory of Rule and Regulation Online* (Oxford: Oxford University Press, 2020), vii.

42. Kettemann, *The Normative Order of the Internet,* 1.

43. See: Michael Zimmer and Katharina Kinder-Kurland (Eds.), *Internet Research Ethics for the Social Age: New Challenges, Cases, and Contexts* (New York: Peter Lang Publishing, 2017).

44. For a good account of the debate, see: Richard Beardsworth, "Tragedy, World Politics and Ethical Community," *International Relations* 2, no. 1 (2008): 127–137.

45. Beardsworth, "Tragedy, World Politics and Ethical Community," 1.

46. Mervyn Frost, "Tragedy, Ethics and International Relations," *International Relations* 17, no. 4 (2003): 482.

47. Alister Wedderburn, "Tragedy, Genealogy and Theories of International Relations," *European Journal of International Relations* 24, no. 1 (2018): 191.

48. Chris Brown, "Tragedy, 'Tragic Choices' and Contemporary International Political Theory," *International Relations* 21, no. 1 (2007): 9.

49. Wedderburn, "Tragedy, Genealogy and Theories of International Relations," 191.

50. Erskine, "Normative International Relations Theory," 55.

51. Frost, *Global Ethics,* 1–53.

52. Erskine, "Normative International Relations Theory," 40.

53. Erskine, "Normative International Relations Theory," 55.

54. Hutchings, *International Political Theory,* 184.

Chapter 4

Constructivism in International Relations

Yücel Bozdağlıoğlu

INTRODUCTION

The end of the Cold War became a milestone in international relations and dramatically altered the international system. Its consequences both changed the way international politics had been studied and brought new challenges to the dominant theories of international relations. Along with the end of the Cold War, other factors such as a noticeable erosion in state sovereignty as was evident in humanitarian interventions and "globalization—the intensification of economic, political, social, and cultural relations across borders—also tended to raise doubts about the explanatory power of existing theories and approaches."[1] As a result, new theories and approaches critical of mainstream theories began to surface. Their criticisms mainly dwelled on rationalist theories—mainly Neorealism and Neoliberalism—and their failure to predict the peaceful end of the Cold War.

Among those theories, Constructivism has risen pretty quickly and presented fairly solid arguments against the validity of rationalist theories. Constructivists criticized Neorealism's "static materialist" view while emphasizing the *social dimension* of international politics and highlighting the *possibility of change* in the international system. Alexander Wendt, who is one of the first and the most influential scholars in the Constructivist school, stated that his aim was to develop "a theory of the international system as a *social construction*."[2] Along with historical cases like the end of the Cold War, developments in other disciplines including sociology, philosophy, and psychology also inspired Constructivists to build alternative explanations to rationalist theories.

Writings of Nicholas Onuf and Alexander Wendt first introduced Constructivism to the discipline of International Relations. Among all constructivist IR theorists, however, Alexander Wendt stands out as one of the most important figures in Constructivist IR theory. As one scholar put it, "He is now regarded as one of the discipline's most important theorists, having developed a model of international politics anchored in a theory of science twenty years after Waltz's *Theory of International Politics.*"[3] His book *Social Theory of International Politics* (1999) has been regarded as the most comprehensive work on Constructivist IR theory.

Since its first appearance in International Relations in the late 1980s, Constructivism has evolved significantly and different versions of Constructivism have emerged. Many IR scholars agree that Constructivism is a theory that can be best placed between rationalist and reflectivist theories of international relations.

Despite variations in Constructivist theory, all of them share the basic assumptions on the mutually constitutive relationship between agents and structures, the importance of normative structures as well as material structures and the formation of state identities, interests, and preferences. To better elaborate Constructivist view on international relations, the chapter will start with Neorealist arguments about structure and state identities/interests and proceed with the Constructivist critique of Neorealism.

REALISM

Realism dominated the Cold War period. Hans Morgenthau's seminal book *Politics among Nations: The Struggle for Power and Peace*[4] became a handbook for almost every scholar studying international relations. It not only affected the study of international relations but also shaped the foreign policies of almost every country in the world. Power and national interest became buzzwords in the implementation of states' foreign policies.

Drawing on the writings of Thucydides, Niccolo Machiavelli, Thomas Hobbes, and E. H. Carr, Morgenthau developed a realist theory of international politics in which he argued that "international politics, like all politics, is a struggle for power. Whatever the ultimate aims of international politics, power is always the immediate aim."[5] Morgenthau went on to argue that the international system is anarchy. The most important effect of anarchy is the lack of trust among states, which forces states to rely on their own resources. Therefore, the system is a self-help system, and states as rational actors look out for their selfish interests and constantly seek to maximize their power to guarantee their survival.

Morgenthau's version of Realism, which was later labeled as *Classical Realism*, argues that the desire for more power is rooted in human nature. Echoing Machiavelli and Hobbes, Morgenthau believes in the flawed nature of humanity, which he claims, is the primary cause for states to continuously engage in a struggle to increase their power. When he summarized the six principles of Realism, he suggested that "political realism believes that politics, like society in general, is governed by objective laws that have their roots in human nature."[6] As Elman states,

> *The absence of the international equivalent of a state's government is a permissive condition that gives human appetites free reign. In short, classical realism explains conflictual behavior by human failings. . . . For classical realists international politics can be characterized as evil: bad things happen because the people making foreign policy are sometimes bad.*[7]

Classical Realism was attacked by other theoretical approaches like Neoliberalism, Feminism, and Critical Theory. However, the most influential critique came from other realists. Kenneth Waltz became the leading proponent of a radically revised version of Classical Realism labeled Neorealism (also called Structural or Systemic Realism). His book *Theory of International Politics* quickly replaced Morgenthau's *Politics among Nations*. According to Waltz, a scientific IR theory must focus on the international system, not on the internal characteristics or leaders of states. Waltz developed a systemic theory in which he diverged from Classical Realism on the causes of state behavior in the system.

According to Waltz, flawed human nature does not have anything to do with why states constantly seek power in the international system. Instead, he focused on the structure of the international system to explain why states want more power. Waltz argued that the international system is anarchic and under anarchy, states are primarily concerned about survival. Since the system is a self-help system, states must rely on their own capabilities, i.e., power to ensure their own survival.[8]

Unlike Classical Realism, which focuses on state leaders and their decisions, Neorealism pays more attention to the structure of the international system. "Leaders are relatively unimportant because structures compel them to act in certain ways. Structures more or less determine actions."[9] Waltz defines the structure of the international system in terms of three factors: ordering principles, characteristics of units, and material capabilities.[10] Since there is no higher authority above states, the system is anarchic where each state is responsible for its own security. Therefore, anarchy is the ordering principle of the system. Additionally, under anarchy, states perform similar tasks which make them functionally similar. The functional similarity is the natural result of anarchy because "anarchy entails coordination among a system's units, and that implies their sameness."[11] Under anarchy, states' most important concern is to survive and all their efforts and actions are directed to that end. States as rational actors will behave to guarantee survival which will entail their functional similarity. "For Waltz, the assumption of anarchy means that states will be unwilling to risk functional differentiation, in other words, an international division of labor. Anarchy compels each state to focus on its core preference—maintaining its sovereignty, i.e., its own survival—without relying on external help."[12]

According to Neorealism, anarchy and the functional similarity of units are constant. The only element that can change is the distribution of capabilities. States face similar tasks in the system, but they differ in their abilities to perform them. States are "distinguished primarily by their greater or lesser capabilities for performing similar tasks . . . the structure of a system changes with changes in the distribution of capabilities across the system's units."[13] Therefore, the distribution of capabilities becomes the only determining factor of the structure. International change occurs when the distribution of capabilities changes and when the balance of power shifts dramatically. Changes in the system, or systemic change, then, depend on the distribution of material capabilities that move the system from anarchy to hierarchy or vice versa. Since material capabilities are an essential part of the structure, the structure is considered a *material* concept.

Neorealism suggests that states possess considerable differences at the unit level such as culture or regime types. But these differences matter "relatively little for how they act toward other states"[14] because the structure of the international system is the main force that determines state behavior. The structure of the international system, once formed, becomes a force that the units cannot control or change. It constrains and puts limits on the behavior of the units. "Structures encourage certain behaviors and penalize those who do not respond to the encouragement."[15] States, in this account, must therefore act in accordance with the requirements of the system, or they will cease to exist.

Neorealism treats states as rational and egoistic actors that pursue their self-interest in the system. They are also *"pre-social* in the sense that their identities and interests are autogenous."[16] They socialize with others in the system with already-defined identities and interests. Their identities and interests are formed before interaction, therefore they are exogenous to social interaction. Under the conditions of anarchy, it is logical to assume that states must acquire egoistic identities and take care of themselves or they will risk their survival. The above argument implies that since states have egoistic identities and consequently egoistic interests imposed upon them by the anarchic structure they all will be concerned about cheating and relative gains in their relations with others. This situation in turn will curb their willingness to cooperate because they are unable to change the structure and their selfish identities under anarchy.[17]

In sum, Neorealism argues that material structure shapes state behavior and state identities and interests are given and exogenous to social interaction. That means, states, theoretically, come to the system with already-defined identities and interests.

Constructivists target exactly these two points: structure and identity/interest formation, which we will turn to in the next section.

CONSTRUCTIVISM

Constructivism covers a wide range of theoretical perspectives whose common denominators include "an emphasis on the importance of normative as well as material structures, on the role of identity in shaping political action and on the mutually constitutive relationship between agents and structures."[18] While all Constructivist approaches agree on the definition of structure and the role of identity in international politics, they mainly diverge on epistemology and methodology on the one hand and the levels of analysis on the other.

Despite differences, all variants of Constructivism agree on the following points: (1) social structures are as important as material structures, (2) social structures have not only a regulative effect but also a constitutive effect on actor identities and interests, and (3) agents and structures are mutually constitutive. This part of the chapter will focus on Constructivist arguments on structure and identity/interest formation by using Alexander Wendt's ideas.

ALEXANDER WENDT AND SYSTEMIC CONSTRUCTIVISM

Alexander Wendt is one of the most important and influential scholars in the constructivist school. He agrees with other Constructivists that the structure of the international system is social and that identity is the basis of interests. He adopted a systemic approach to show that state identities and interests are formed at the system level and they are endogenous to state interaction. His analysis mainly criticizes Neorealist understandings of structure and identity and interest formation and develops an alternative Constructivist approach.

Constructivism and Social Structure

Neorealism focuses on the material aspects of the international system. According to Neorealism, the structure of the international system consists of material factors—i.e., military capabilities. Constructivists, on the other hand, emphasize the social dimension of international politics and argue that the world we live in is, indeed, *socially constructed*. According to Constructivism, ideas, norms, knowledge, and culture have structural characteristics and play important roles in international relations. Constructivists underline the importance of "collectively held or intersubjective ideas and understandings on social life."[19] Constructivism does not deny the existence of material factors in international relations but argues that ideational factors do also have a strong influence on political action. Thus, ideas have a causal effect on behavior.

According to Wendt constructivism has two basic tenets: "(1) the structures of human association are determined primarily by shared ideas rather than material forces, and (2) the identities and interests of purposive actors are constructed by these shared ideas rather than given by nature."[20] Wendt holds that Waltz's definition of structure does not say much about state behavior. For him, the Neorealist definition of structure "does not predict whether two states will be friends or foes, will recognize each other's sovereignty, will have dynastic ties, will be revisionist or status quo powers"[21] because these factors are essentially *intersubjective* and affect states' interaction with each other under anarchy. Alternatively, he develops the concept of a "structure of identity and interest" and contends that "without assumptions about the structure of identities and interests in the system, Waltz's definition of structure cannot predict the content or dynamics of anarchy."[22] Thus, Wendt's ontology of international relations is social.

Wendt's definition of social structure has important implications that set his theory apart from rationalist theories. As explained before, Neorealism argues that political structure once formed becomes a force above states that affects their behaviors. States do not have much to change the structure but to succumb to its requirements. There is a one-way relationship between agents and structures, structures affecting the behaviors of states, not the other way around. Wendt suggests that for Neorealism "only the behavior of states is affected by system structure, not their identities and interests."[23] Constructivism, on the other hand, argues that agents and structures are *mutually constitutive* and emphasizes the process of interaction between them. "The ontology is one of mutual constitution, where neither unit of analysis—agents or structures—is reduced to the other and made 'ontologically primitive.'"[24] In other words, Constructivism argues that agents and structures are mutually constructed and continuously shape each other. States, through behavioral or discursive processes, constitute norms, rules, and principles. Social structures also can affect state identities and interests and consequently behaviors. Once these norms are generally accepted, they constitute the culture of the international system.

Wendt goes on to argue that anarchy has different cultures and therefore different logics. Anarchy presented by Neorealism in which states are self-interested egoists represents only one culture or logic. In Neorealism, it is anarchy that leads to self-help because under the condition in which there is no supreme authority, states do not have any choice but to be selfish. Constructivists argue that this statement reflects only one logic or culture of anarchy. Anarchy can have different cultures depending on the nature of prevalent norms, rules, principles, shared knowledge, and expectations. "In other words, instead of a single anarchy and a singular logic, there are different understandings of anarchy."[25] Whether the system will be conflictual or cooperative then will depend on the type of culture that is prevalent in the system.

Wendt argues that "self-help and power politics do not follow either logically or causally from anarchy and that if we find ourselves in a self-help world, this is due to process, not structure."[26] In other words, the Neorealist premise that anarchy necessarily entails self-help cannot be verified because "whether it does or not cannot be decided a priori; it depends on the interaction between states."[27] Different processes or practices create different logics of anarchy. This is because, through these processes and practices, states create their identities and consequently their interests. This structure of identities and interests informs states what course of action they will adopt toward other states in the system. States in the process of interaction may develop different cultures under anarchy and self-help is just one of them, "not an essential feature of anarchy. *Anarchy is what states make of it.*"[28] In Wendt's view self-help is just an institution that is created and sustained through the process.[29]

Wendt distinguishes three separate cultures in which states' behaviors, identities, and interests vary considerably: *Hobbesian culture, Lockean culture, and Kantian culture.* There are different ideas, norms, and rules prevalent in each culture in which states acquire different identities and interests. The *Hobbesian culture* is characterized by a constant enmity between states that see each other as enemies. It is a world of *all-against-all* in which states prioritize power and interests. Norms and rules that dominate the system reflect the ideas of Thomas Hobbes who argued that a society without a supreme ruler resembles a state of nature.[30]

In the *Lockean culture*, a perspective drawn from the writings of philosopher John Locke, on the other hand, although states view each other as rivals, they nevertheless "recognize each other's sovereignty, and therefore submit to a minimum standard of common norms."[31] There is, of course, competition between states, but this competition does not come to the point that they constantly try to destroy each other.

In a *Kantian system*, states no longer see each other as enemies or rivals, but as friends, and "the scope of shared norms is much more extensive."[32] Drawing from Immanuel Kant's ideas, Wendt argues that this culture is the closest one to a collective security system where states identify with each other and define their interests collectively. In other words, in a Kantian culture states form a community. These Constructivist arguments suggest that the system does not have to be a self-help system under anarchy. Depending on the nature of states' interaction, the system may have different cultures and define their identities and interests accordingly. These identities and interests in turn will shape their behaviors toward each other.

There are two important implications from the above arguments. First, Constructivism implies that material capabilities acquire different meanings for states under different cultures. Neorealism proposes that states must try to preserve their relative power position in the system and take necessary measures against rising states (balancing is the most important of them) because power is the most important threat to a state's existence. In this sense, threat has an objective quality.

Constructivism, however, indicates that material capabilities owned by a state do not necessarily constitute a threat to other states because threat is an intersubjective construction. Constructivists include material power and interests in their analysis but suggest that they are part of social structures "but their meaning and effects depend upon the social structure of the system, and specifically on which of the three 'cultures' of anarchy is dominant"[33]— Hobbesian, Lockean, or Kantian. This is because, according to Wendt, "material sources only acquire meaning for human action through the structure of shared knowledge in which they are embedded."[34] As a result, states will act differently toward enemies than they do toward friends even if the former holds more material capabilities than the latter. Wendt illustrates the point with the following example: "500 British nuclear weapons are less threatening to the United States than 5 North Korean nuclear weapons because the British are friends and the North Koreans are not."[35] Here, material power is interpreted through and defined by ideas that actors hold about each other.

The second is related to systemic change. According to Neorealism systemic change occurs when the distribution of capabilities changes. Waltz argues that systemic change occurs through great wars since they can alter the distribution of power thus, he leaves little room for change. Constructivists, on the other hand, argue that systemic change is more possible than neorealism suggests. For Constructivists, systemic change occurs when the prevailing norms that make up the culture of the system change. Thus, in constructivism, systemic change means cultural change. What makes this change possible is

discursive social practices that reproduce or transform each actor's view of self and other. A Hobbesian system will be sustained only if actors continue to act toward each other in egoistic, militaristic ways. If actors gesture differently, showing that they are casting the other in a less self-centered manner, then over time, a Hobbesian culture can move to a Lockean and possibly a Kantian form.[36]

Constructivism and Identity Formation

The second core criticism that Constructivism directed against Neorealism is the formation and role of state identities and interests. Constructivism presented a very distinctive view of state identities and interests. Neorealism holds that state identities and interests are givens. In the anarchical international system, states must acquire egoistic identities and interests or they will risk their existence. Constructivism, on the other hand, argues that states acquire identities through social interaction, and as a result, state identity becomes endogenous to interaction among states. This is contrary to Neorealism which argues that states start interaction with already acquired egoistic identities.

According to Neorealism state interests are assumed to be also egoistic. Constructivism, on the other hand, assumes that state interests are not determined independently from state identities. In other words, identity comes before and is the basis of interests; states first acquire their identities through social interaction and then determine what their interests are. In Wendt's terms, states cannot know what their interests are before they know who they are.[37] If states' identities change, "then actors' perspective on certain situations may also change, which may prompt a redefinition of interests."[38]

How state identities are constructed and how they change occupy a central place in the constructivist research program. Constructivists attribute special importance to identity because it implies a state's "preferences and consequent actions."[39] Since identities define states' interests they have a powerful explanatory power in foreign policy analysis. Identity provides actors with "an understanding of self and their place in the social world, and its relationships with others."[40] It gives actors who they and others are in a specific structural context-i.e., intersubjective structure.

When explaining the formation and role of state identity, Wendt makes a distinction between states' corporate and social identities. Drawing from psychology and social psychology, Wendt argues that states, like individuals, hold two types of identities: corporate and social. Corporate identity (personal identity in psychology) "refers to the intrinsic, self-organizing qualities that constitute actor individuality."[41] This type of identity generates four basic interests: 1) physical security, 2) predictability in relationships to the world, 3) recognition as an actor by others, and 4) economic development. How a state satisfies these corporate interests "depends on how it defines the self in relation to the other, which is a function of social identities at both domestic and systemic levels of analysis."[42]

Since Wendt's constructivist approach adopts a system-level (systemic) analysis, he excludes the corporate identities of states from his analysis and tries to show how states form their social identities, and consequently interests, through systemic interaction. Wendt argues that the roots of corporate identities lie in domestic politics and therefore they are of no interest to his Systemic Constructivism. This way, Wendt aims to show how state identities and interests are endogenous, not exogenous as Neorealism suggests, to interaction.

Social identity, on the other hand, is defined as "a set of meanings that an actor attributes to itself as a social object while taking the perspective of others, that is, as a social object."[43] While actors have one corporate identity, they usually have multiple social identities. Identities are relational and actors acquire identities by participating in collective meanings. States may have multiple social identities and which identity will be more salient depends on the specific social context. It should be kept in mind that while identity gives actors a sense of who they are in a social situation, however, what they mean to others will depend on the intersubjective structure.[44]

In addition to a specific institutional environment, social identities require an "other" for their construction as well. For example, having an identity of a student requires an institutional environment, which, in this case, is a school. This institutional environment also defines related identities which, in this case again, are teachers. These identities are mutually constituted. Thus, social identities need an "other" and an appropriate interaction context.

According to Wendt's Systemic Constructivism, systemic interaction through which states socialize with each other has a decisive impact on identity and interest construction. "Wendt's conception of how collective state identities develop is that this occurs through an interactional process between states on the level of the international system. What matters to the unfolding of this process and the 'culture' of the international system is how states encounter one another for the first time."[45] For Wendt, states do not have any social identity, and consequently, any interest before interaction. In other words, since social identity formation is an intersubjective process of meaning creation, states before interaction have no conception of the self and the other. Only through interaction do they come to define themselves and others and only after do they know "who they are" they define their interests. This view contrasts with the Neorealist and Neoliberal assumption that states only have one preexisting egoist identity.

For Wendt, "interests and identities of actors emerge only in an interactive process."[46] As a result, Systemic Constructivism assumes that the history of interaction between actors will determine the nature of the system. In other words, whether or not states acquire "selfish" or "collective" identities and interests depends on the nature and "manner in which social identities involve an identification with the fate of the other. Identification is a continuum from negative to positive—from conceiving the other as anathema to the self to conceiving it as an extension of the self."[47]

For Wendt, since states have no sense of self and other before interaction, they also do not have any social identity and interests—egoistic or collective. When they get into interaction, depending on mutual gestures, states will develop identities and consequently interests. If states identify negatively with each other, then, as realists suggest, the system will be a competitive security system and a Hobbesian culture will dominate. States may identify with each other positively and develop collective identities which will lead to a Kantian culture. Finally, state identities may evolve into one of rivalry where a Lockean culture takes precedence over other cultures. This explains the title of Wendt's famous article: "Anarchy is what states make of it."[48] Identities that states construct during the interaction are not static. They can change over time and across contexts leading to the creation of new definitions of self and other.

Alexander Wendt's Systemic Constructivism was criticized by other theories and other constructivists on many grounds and paved the way for the emergence of different variants of Constructivism. Wendt adopts a third-image perspective and focuses solely on systemic interaction between state actors at the international system level. He ignores domestic sources of identity formation and excludes domestic sources of identity from his analysis. His approach, in turn, limits the explanatory power of constructivist theory. Since Wendt is committed to system-level analysis in his theory he leaves out corporate sources of state identity. Instead, he is more interested in how different types of state identity are produced and reproduced by structural contexts, systemic processes, and strategic practices. There is, however, a major problem with this approach: "it confines the processes that shape international societies within an unnecessarily and unproductively narrow realm."[49] In other words, Wendt's approach looks at identity formation from the perspective of the system and leaves out other possible factors such as the individual state or representatives of a state.[50]

Jutta Weldes criticizes Wendt's treatment of the state as "a black box, internal workings of which are irrelevant to the construction of state identities."[51] In Wendt's analysis, the meanings that objects have for states and the identities and interests of states are created only through and restricted to systemic interaction. Systemic interaction, then, becomes the starting point in Wendt's analysis. Before states socialize with each other, Wendt assumes, they do not have any conception of self and other. This brings us to the conclusion that states do not have any history and consequently any conceptions of friend and enemy before systemic interaction. These conceptions will be produced after the interaction starts. Whether they will be friends or enemies will depend on how they interpret their gestures.

Many constructivists disagree with this point. Inayatullah and Blaney, for example, criticize Wendt for ignoring actors in the pre-social world. They argue that actors construct a sense of self and an understanding of others long before interaction and they bring ideas, purposes, intentions, and images to interaction.[52]

Furthermore, "the meanings which objects, events, and actions have for 'states' are necessarily the meanings they have for those individuals who act in the name of the state."[53] These state officials have some ideas about the world, the international system, and the place of their state within that system. These ideas, in turn, are "necessarily rooted in meanings already produced, at least in part, in domestic political and cultural contexts."[54] In other words, actors usually construct themselves and others long before the actual contact most often through discursive practices; that is through *representations*.[55] Depending on the nature of these representations (negative or positive), actors produce and reproduce meanings and identities that make a certain course of action possible or impossible.[56]

VARIANTS OF CONSTRUCTIVISM

These critics' emphasis on domestic roots of identity led to the emergence of two alternative constructivist research programs: Unit-Level and Holistic Constructivism. This section will examine these constructivist programs and the main differences between them.

Unit-Level Constructivism

Unit-Level Constructivism starts with the critique of the systemic approach and contends that systemic constructivism's focus on the role of the international environment and norms in constructing state identities and interests leaves out the important role that domestic factors play in the formation of state identities and interests. "Instead of focusing on the external, international domain, unit-level constructivists concentrate on the relationship between domestic social and legal norms and the identities and interests of states, the very factors bracketed by Wendt."[57]

Arguing that international norms did not have similar effects in different states, unit-level constructivists turned their attention to domestic factors responsible for such variation. Their argument is that systemic theorizing is inadequate because it ignores the internal makeup of states and domestic norms in guiding state behavior in the international system. Many analysts focused on the roles of strategic and organizational cultures, ideology, domestic institutions, and state-society relations in guiding state behavior in the international system. Jepperson, Wendt, and Katzenstein, for example, argue that "investigating the domestic sources of foreign policy focuses attention on the degree to which the identities of actors are constructed by state-society relations."[58] They suggest that shared conceptions of identity in the domestic context can have important effects on state policies.[59]

Peter Katzenstein and Nobuo Okawara maintain that Japan's security policy is mainly shaped by both the domestic normative context—social and legal—and the structure of the state.[60] They suggest that the incoherency in Japan's security policy in the 1920s and 1930s and the dramatic shift in the post–World War II era cannot be explained by structural factors. They, instead, turn their attention to "the effects of Japan's domestic structures and norms."[61] Their argument rests on the assumption that Japan's security policy is deeply influenced by—along with the structure of the state—"the social and legal norms that help shape the interests which inform Japanese security policy."[62] They explain the change in Japan's militaristic foreign policy into a pacifist one after World War II with Japan's domestic norms and argue that Japan was able to change domestic norms that constituted its (militaristic) national identity without systemic interaction. This change in the domestic environment accordingly influenced Japan's behavior in the international system.

In her analysis of France's military doctrine, Elizabeth Kier claims that structural analyses are insufficient in explaining changes in military doctrine. Instead, she offers a cultural perspective and suggests that beliefs about the military's role in society held by dominant political actors and the domestic distribution of power are responsible for the formation of French military doctrine.[63]

In a similar manner, Alastair Iain Johnston problematized China's realpolitik behavior. He argues that "China has historically exhibited a relatively consistent hard realpolitik or *parabellum* strategic culture that has persisted across different structural contexts into the Maoist period (and beyond)."[64] He convincingly demonstrates that this strategic culture, not the logic of anarchy, which has been internalized by Chinese decision-makers is responsible for China's strategic behavior in the system throughout centuries. He concludes that the root causes of states' strategic behaviors in the system lie in domestic ideational structures; a point that is missing in Wendt's analysis.[65]

Holistic Constructivism

Holistic Constructivism aims at removing the traditional dichotomy between system and unit levels of analysis and tries to bridge the two domains. Holistic Constructivists criticized Systemic Constructivism for not adequately explaining the change. This critique led some constructivists who want to explain forms of international change to adopt a more encompassing, holistic perspective. In the words of Reus-Smit,

> to accommodate the full spectrum of conditioning factors, they forgo the parsimonious elegance of systemic theorizing, and bring the "corporate" and "social" together into a unified analytical perspective, treating "domestic" and "international" structures and processes as two faces of a single social and political order.[66]

Holistic Constructivism argues that states' corporate and social identities continuously interact with each other and states' foreign policies are the product of this interaction. Interactions between corporate (domestic level) and social identities (international level) will result in the production and reproduction of self and other. "According to this approach, any transformation in the corporate identity of a state—as a result of domestic conditions—will eventually affect the identity formation at the international level where states will try to reset their priorities in accordance with the new identity."[67] International developments, on the other hand, may force states to reevaluate their corporate identities and make adjustments to both identity and behavior. From this perspective, domestic (national) identity as well as shared norms of international society have causal effects on states' interests and behaviors.

Holistic Constructivism rests on the idea that states start systemic interaction with an already defined corporate identity. The corporate identity of the state, depending on its definition, informs states with whom to interact and with what intention. In other words, defining the states' constitutive elements (or basically the internal character of the state) will determine the foreign policy of the state.[68]

"Identity is reinforced (or not) by contacts with others."[69] Systemic interaction, depending on its nature, can confirm or transform already-held identities, which is also a function of domestic politics because systemic interaction can be interpreted and internalized differently by different individuals and organizations with different cultural backgrounds and identities. This is an interactive process in which systemic interaction can shape the identity by adding more elements (such as norms and values) that may exacerbate the debate over the national identity at the domestic level.[70]

CONCLUSION

Constructivism is a social theory of international relations. It has been inspired by sociological theories and emphasizes the social aspects of international life. It highlights the importance of culture, identity, and norms in international relations which were ignored by rationalist theories. Two contributions that Constructivism has made to the discipline are worth mentioning here: 1) structures are social and agents and structures are mutually constitutive, and 2) identities and interests of states are not pre-given; instead, they are formed during the process of interaction.

For Constructivists, structures are not only made up of material capabilities but also shared understandings, norms, and ideas. These ideas in turn form the culture of the system and shape not only behavior but also the identity and interests of actors. In this sense, the Neorealist claim that anarchy entails only self-help becomes invalid since self-help is one of the logics (or cultures) of anarchy. Under anarchy, states can develop different identities and interests ranging from cooperative (collective) to conflictual. Depending on what type of culture dominates the anarchical system, state identities, interests, and behaviors can vary considerably. While social structures shape states' identities and behaviors, states through practices can also change structures.

Secondly, Constructivism offers a different understanding of identity and interest formation. For Neorealism and other rationalist theories, state identity and interests are given. States form those identities and interests in the pre-social world. Constructivism, on the other hand, argues that states do not have any conceptions of self and other before interaction with other states in the system, therefore, they cannot have identity and interests. States' social identities are formed only through interaction with others and these identities determine state interests. Identity, in Constructivism, is the basis of interests.

Despite criticisms arguing that Constructivism is not a substantive theory, but an approach, of international relations, it has been managed to occupy the center stage in the discipline. Despite its relatively short history, it has dominated the study of international relations and opened up new lines of inquiry.

REFERENCES

Bozdağlıoğlu, Yücel. *Turkish Foreign Policy and Turkish Identity: A Constructivist Approach* (New York and London: Routledge, 2003).

Checkel, Jeffrey T. "The Constructivist Turn in International Relations Theory,"
    World Politics, 50 (1998): 324–348.
Copeland, Dale C. "The constructivist challenge to structural realism," in Stefano
    Guzzini and Anna Leander, ed., Constructivism and International Relations:
    Alexander Wendt and His critics (London and New York: Routledge, 2006): 1–20.
Doty, Roxanne Lynn. "Foreign Policy as Social Construction: A Post-Positivist
    Analysis of U.S. Counterinsurgency Policy in the Philippines," International
    Studies Quarterly, 37 (1993): 297–320.
Elman, Colin. "Realism," in Martin Griffiths, ed., International Relations Theory for
    the Twenty-First Century (London and New York: Routledge, 2007): 11–20.
Finnemore, Martha and Kathryn Sikkink. "TAKING STOCK: The Constructivist
    Research Program in International Relations and Comparative Politics," Annu. Rev.
    Polit. Sci., 4 (2001): 391–416.
Flockhart, Trine. "Constructivism and Foreign Policy," in Steve Smith, Amelia
    Hadfield, Tim Dunne, ed., Foreign Policy: Theories, Actors, Cases, Third Edition
    (2016): 79–94.
Hopf, Ted. "The Promise of Constructivism in International Relations Theory,"
    International Security, 23, No. 1 (Summer 1998): 171–200.
Inayatullah, Naeem and David L. Blaney. "Knowing Encounters: Beyond Parochialism
    in International Relations Theory," in Yosef Lapid and Friedrich Kratochwil, ed.,
    The Return of Culture and Identity in IR Theory (Boulder, London: Lynne Rienner
    Publishers, 1996): 65–84.
Jackson, Robert and Georg Sørensen. Introduction to International Relations
    Theories and Approach (Oxford: Oxford University Press, 2013).
Jepperson, Ronald L., Alexander Wendt, and Peter J. Katzenstein. "Norms, Identity,
    and Culture in National Security," in Peter Katzenstein, ed., The Culture of
    National Security: Norms and Identity in World Politics (New York: Columbia
    University Press, 1996): 33–75.
Johnston, Alastair Iain. "Cultural Realism and Strategy in Maoist China," in Peter
    Katzenstein, ed., The Culture of National Security: Norms and Identity in World
    Politics (New York: Columbia University Press, 1996): 216–268.
Katzenstein, Peter J. and Nobuo Okawara. "Japan's National Security: Structures,
    Norms, and Policies," International Security, 17, No. 4 (Spring 1993): 84–118.
Kier, Elizabeth. "Culture and French Military Doctrine before World War II," in Peter
    Katzenstein, ed., The Culture of National Security: Norms and Identity in World
    Politics (New York: Columbia University Press, 1996): 186–215.
Mearsheimer, John J. "Structural Realism," in Tim Dunne, Milja Kurki, and Steve
    Smith, ed., International Relations Theories: Discipline and Diversity (Oxford:
    Oxford University Press, 2013): 77–93.
Morgenthau, Hans J. Politics among Nations: The Struggle for Power and Peace
    (New York: Alfred A. Knopf, Inc., 1948).
Nia, Mahdi Mohammad. "A Holistic Constructivist Approach to Iran's Foreign
    Policy," International Journal of Business and Social Science, 2, No. 4 (2011):
    279–294.

Reus-Smit, Christian. *The Moral Purpose of the State: Culture, Social Identity, and Institutional Rationality in International Relations* (Princeton: Princeton University Press, 1999).

Reus-Smit, Christian. "Constructivism," in Scott Burchill et al., ed., *Theories of International Relations,* Third Edition (New York: Palgrave, 2005), 188–212.

Schörnig, Niklas. "Neorealism," in Siegfried Schieder and Manuela Spindler, ed., *Theories of International Relations* (New York and London: Routledge, 2014): 37–55.

Steans, Jill et al. *An Introduction to International Relations Theory: Perspectives and Themes,* Third Edition (London and New York: Pearson, 2010).

Ulbert, Cornelia. "Social Constructivism," in Siegfried Schieder and Manuela Spindler, ed., *Theories of International Relations* (New York: Routledge, 2014): 248–268.

Viotti, Paul R. and Mark V. Kauppi. *International Relations Theory* (New York: Longman, 2012).

Waltz, Kenneth N. *Theory of International Politics* (Reading: Addison-Wesley Publishing Company, 1979).

Waltz, Kenneth N. "Anarchic Orders and Balances of Power," in Robert O. Keohane, ed., *Neorealism and Its Critics* (New York: Columbia University Press, 1986): 98–130.

Weldes, Jutta. "Constructing National Interests," *European Journal of International Relations,* 2 (1996): 275–318.

Wendt, Alexander. "The agent-structure problem in International Relations," *International Organization,* 41, No. 3 (1987): 335–370.

Wendt, Alexander. "Anarchy is what states make of it: The social construction of power politics," *International Organization,* 46, No. 2 (1992): 391–425.

Wendt, Alexander. "Collective identity formation and the international state," *American Political Science Review,* 88 (1994): 384–396.

Wendt, Alexander. "Constructing International Politics," *International Security,* 20 (1995): 71–83.

Wendt, Alexander. *Social Theory of International Politics* (Cambridge: Cambridge University Press, 1999).

Zehfuss, Maja. *Constructivism in International Relations: The politics of reality* (Cambridge: Cambridge University Press, 2004).

NOTES

1. Paul R. Viotti and Mark V. Kauppi, *International Relations Theory* (New York: Longman, 2012), 277.

2. Alexander Wendt, *Social Theory of International Politics* (Cambridge: Cambridge University Press, 1999), xiii. Emphasis added.

3. Cornelia Ulbert, "Social Constructivism," in Siegfried Schieder and Manuela Spindler, ed., *Theories of International Relations* (New York: Routledge, 2014), 250.

4. Hans J. Morgenthau, *Politics among Nations: The Struggle for Power and Peace* (New York: Alfred A. Knopf, Inc., 1948).

5. Morgenthau, *Politics among Nations,* 13.

6. Morgenthau, *Politics among Nations,* 19.

7. Colin Elman, "Realism," in Martin Griffiths, ed., *International Relations Theory for the Twenty-First Century* (London and New York: Routledge, 2007), 12.

8. Christian Reus-Smit, "Constructivism," in Scott Burchill et al., ed., *Theories of International Relations,* Third Edition (New York: Palgrave, 2005), 190.

9. Robert Jackson and Georg Sørensen, *Introduction to International Relations Theories and Approach* (Oxford: Oxford University Press, 2013), 79.

10. Kenneth N. Waltz, *Theory of International Politics* (Reading: Addison-Wesley Publishing Company, 1979), 79.

11. Waltz, *Theory of International Politics,* 93.

12. Niklas Schörnig, "Neorealism," in Siegfried Schieder and Manuela Spindler, ed., *Theories of International Relations* (New York and London: Routledge, 2014), 42.

13. Waltz, *Theory of International Politics,* 97.

14. John J. Mearsheimer, "Structural Realism," in Tim Dunne, Milja Kurki, and Steve Smith, ed., *International Relations Theories: Discipline and Diversity* (Oxford: Oxford University Press, 2013), 78.

15. Kenneth N. Waltz, "Anarchic Orders and Balances of Power," in Robert O. Keohane, ed., *Neorealism and Its Critics* (New York: Columbia University Press, 1986), 103.

16. Reus-Smit, "Constructivism," 192.

17. Yücel Bozdağlıoğlu, *Turkish Foreign Policy and Turkish Identity: A Constructivist Approach* (New York and London: Routledge, 2003), 14.

18. Reus-Smit, "Constructivism," 188.

19. Martha Finnemore and Kathryn Sikkink, "TAKING STOCK: The Constructivist Research Program in International Relations and Comparative Politics," *Annu. Rev. Polit. Sci.,* 4 (2001), 392.

20. Wendt, *Social Theory,* 1.

21. Alexander Wendt, "Anarchy is what states make of it: The social construction of power politics," *International Organization,* 46, No. 2 (1992), 396.

22. Wendt, "Anarchy," 396.

23. Wendt, *Social Theory,* 248.

24. Jeffrey T. Checkel, "The Constructivist Turn in International Relations Theory," *World Politics,* 50 (1998), 326. Also refer to Alexander Wendt, "The agent-structure problem in International Relations," *International Organization,* 41, No. 3 (1987).

25. Viotti and Kauppi, *International Relations,* 294.

26. Wendt, "Anarchy," 394.

27. Jackson and Sørensen, *Introduction to International,* 216.

28. Ibid., 395.

29. Maja Zehfuss, *Constructivism in International Relations: The politics of reality* (Cambridge: Cambridge University Press, 2004), 14.

30. Wendt, *Social Theory,* 250.

31. Jill Steans, et al., *An Introduction to International Relations Theory: Perspectives and Themes*, Third Edition (London and New York: Pearson, 2010), 195.

32. Steans, et al., *An Introduction to International Relations Theory*, 195.

33. Viotti and Kauppi, *International Relations*, 294.

34. Alexander Wendt, "Constructing International Politics," *International Security*, 20 (1995), 73.

35. Wendt, "Constructing International Politics," 73.

36. Dale C. Copeland, "The constructivist challenge to structural realism," in Stefano Guzzini and Anna Leander, ed., *Constructivism and International Relations: Alexander Wendt and His Critics* (London and New York: Routledge, 2006), 7.

37. Wendt, "Anarchy."

38. Ulbert, "Social Constructivism," 255.

39. Ted Hopf, "The Promise of Constructivism in International Relations Theory," *International Security*, 23, No. 1 (Summer 1998), 175.

40. Trine Flockhart, "Constructivism and Foreign Policy," in Steve Smith, Amelia Hadfield, and Tim Dunne, ed., *Foreign Policy: Theories, Actors, Cases*, Third Edition (2016), 87.

41. Alexander Wendt, "Collective identity formation and the international state," *American Political Science Review*, 88 (1994), 385.

42. Wendt, "Collective identity," 385.

43. Wendt, "Collective identity," 385.

44. Hopf, "The Promise of Constructivism," 175.

45. Ulbert, "Social Constructivism," 258.

46. Naeem Inayatullah and David L. Blaney, "Knowing Encounters: Beyond Parochialism in International Relations Theory," in Yosef Lapid and Friedrich Kratochwil, ed., *The Return of Culture and Identity in IR Theory* (Boulder, London: Lynne Rienner Publishers, 1996), 71.

47. Wendt, "Collective identity," 386.

48. Wendt, "Anarchy."

49. Reus-Smit, "Constructivism," 199.

50. Ulbert, "Social Constructivism," 259.

51. Jutta Weldes, "Constructing National Interests," *European Journal of International Relations*, 2 (1996), 280.

52. Inayatullah and Blaney, "Knowing Encounters," 73.

53. Weldes, "Constructing National Interests," 280.

54. Weldes, "Constructing National Interests," 280.

55. Roxanne Lynn Doty, "Foreign Policy as Social Construction: A Post- Positivist Analysis of U.S. Counterinsurgency Policy in the Philippines," *International Studies Quarterly*, 37 (1993).

56. Bozdağlıoğlu, *Turkish Foreign Policy*, 25.

57. Reus-Smit, "Constructivism," 200.

58. Ronald L. Jepperson, Alexander Wendt, and Peter J. Katzenstein, "Norms, Identity, and Culture in National Security," in Peter Katzenstein, ed., *The Culture of National Security: Norms and Identity in World Politics* (New York: Columbia University Press, 1996), 51.

59. Jepperson, Wendt, and Katzenstein, "Norms, Identity, and Culture," 51.

60. Peter J. Katzenstein and Nobuo Okawara, "Japan's National Security: Structures, Norms, and Policies," *International Security*, 17, No. 4 (Spring, 1993), 86.

61. Katzenstein and Okawara, "Japan's National Security," 88.

62. Katzenstein and Okawara, "Japan's National Security," 97.

63. Elizabeth Kier, "Culture and French Military Doctrine before World War II," in Peter Katzenstein, ed., *The Culture of National Security*, 186–187.

64. Alastair İain Johnston, "Cultural Realism and Strategy in Maoist China," in Peter Katzenstein, ed., *The Culture of National Security*, 217.

65. Johnston, "Cultural Realism," 268.

66. Christian Reus-Smit, *The Moral Purpose of the State: Culture, Social Identity, and Institutional Rationality in International Relations* (Princeton: Princeton University Press, 1999), 167.

67. Mahdi Mohammad Nia, "A Holistic Constructivist Approach to Iran's Foreign Policy," *International Journal of Business and Social Science*, 2, No. 4 (2011), 282.

68. Bozdağlıoğlu, *Turkish Foreign Policy*, 28.

69. Jepperson, Wendt, and Katzenstein, "Norms, Identity, and Culture," 61.

70. Bozdağlıoğlu, *Turkish Foreign Policy*, 28.

PART III

Critical Approach to Security

Chapter 5

Aberystwyth School of Security Studies

Bülent Sarper Ağır

INTRODUCTION

Academic debates on the definition, meaning, and nature of security concepts have vastly intensified among scholars of the International Relations (IR) discipline since the end of the Cold War.[1] As a part of these debates, new security conceptions and theories have emerged. In this respect, when a student of Security Studies examines the literature, most probably s/he will find references to both concepts of "Critical Security Studies" and "critical security studies." While the former one with uppercase particularly implies the security conception and assumptions of Aberystwyth School, the latter one with lowercase represents approximately all new and critical security perspectives that challenge the traditional security conception. There are similarities and differences among these critical perspectives in the context of the meaning of security, the referent object of security, and its methodology. Therefore, critical security studies cannot be identified as a homogenous field.[2]

The scholars with critical perspectives on security refuse the assumption of priority of the sovereign state as the referent object of security and argue for the necessity of deepening and widening of the security conception. In this respect, the first significant analytical attempt of the Aberystwyth School is to deepen the security conception. This attempt of the School leads scholars of Security Studies to question the state actor and consider the other referent objects of security. Another attempt of the School is to widen the security conception in order to regard all insecurities that threaten the referent objects of security.[3] However, Ken Booth and Richard Wyn Jones, regarded as the two important representatives of the School, not only criticize the traditional security conception in terms of deepening and widening security concepts but also argue for a reconceptualization of security studies by focusing on the emancipation of human beings. According to Booth and Wyn Jones, the realist security conception in the sense of "power" and "order" does not lead to "real" security.[4] Therefore, Aberystwyth School aims to provide a social transformation through revealing and, if possible, eliminating all obstacles to the emancipation of human beings. Aberystwyth School's main assumptions on security concepts will be examined in this section of the book.

INSPIRATION SOURCES AND DEVELOPMENT PROCESS OF ABERYSTWYTH SCHOOL

Aberystwyth School was first developed within the Critical Security Studies Master's Program of the International Politics Department of the University of Wales. Ken Booth, Richard Wyn Jones, Keith Krause, and Michael C. Williams have made crucial contributions to the development process of Aberystwyth School. Although the first usage of the term "Aberystwyth School" is not obvious in the Security Studies literature, Steve Smith's influential article titled "The Increasing Insecurity of Security Studies: Conceptualising Security in the last Twenty Years" is considered the first user of "Aberystwyth School" term.[5] Aberystwyth School gives a start to its critics by arguing that state-centric security conception does not generate satisfactory explanations for the post–Cold War security environment. In this context, Aberystwyth School questions the narrow, militarized, positivist, and theoretically realist security conception.

Comprehending security as a derivative concept, emphasizing the necessity of widening of security agenda beyond the narrow conception of traditional security agenda, privileging the individual as the referent object of security instead of the state, regarding security problems in the context of the emancipation concept, considering the threats as socially constructed matter, and examining the relationship between self and other are the main characteristics of Aberystwyth School's security conception.[6] However, the most important feature of the Aberystwyth School is to comprehend security as emancipation that requires the abolishment of all constraints such as poverty, violence, and political pressure for the realization of human potential. In order to examine the origin of such a security perspective, it is important to make some explanations about critical theory and its implications on security concepts and practice.

Aberystwyth School attempts to reevaluate and revisit the traditional security conception through a critical manner. Pursuing such a critical attitude about the concept of security benefits from important intellectual sources such as Marxism, Frankfurt School, Gramscian hegemony conception, Peace Studies, and critical theory of IR discipline. For instance, Peace Studies makes a crucial contribution to the development process of Aberystwyth School through its positive peace conceptualization and broadening of violence concept by including structural violence and cultural violence in addition to physical violence.[7] Thus, Aberystwyth School could find a proper conceptual base for its efforts to broaden the agenda of security. Moreover, in terms of the contributions of the Frankfurt School and Gramscian thought, Aberystwyth School reevaluates the dominant position of traditional security conception by using the hegemony concept.

Traditional theories with a positivist approach do not effectively critique society since they consider the social world as given and "out there." Because such a critique requires scientifically "unverified" value judgments. According to Max Horkheimer, the traditional theory is about the reproduction of the status quo.[8] Nevertheless, critical theory calls into question the legitimacy of existing social and political institutions and attempts to examine their transformation process. While classical Marxism argues that life determines the mind, not vice versa, Frankfurt School claims a mutual relationship exists between the mind, thoughts and ideals, and economic infrastructure. Hence, thinkers of the Frankfurt School were intensively inspired by Antonio Gramsci's views and his concept of hegemony, for which class domination in the society has not resulted from economy and power relations but from ideas of the bourgeoisie that create hierarchy and authority in the society.[9] Frankfurt School criticizes the unequal and hierarchic structures that limit the free development of individuals. Therefore, the most significant contribution of the Frankfurt School to critical security studies is the concept of "emancipation." In this respect, the Aberystwyth School, under the effect of the Frankfurt School, has chosen to analyze the post–Cold War security issues by examining the sources of insecurities and possible ways of achieving emancipatory goals.

In a general sense, critical security studies emerged as a reaction to the problem-solving theories in the Security Studies sub-field.[10] Since a problem-solving theory considers the nature of international politics as given, practical and academic attention is attested to specific actors and issues. In Security Studies, this actor is the state, and the main problem that should be solved is the inter-state war.[11] Such a status quo–oriented perspective regards the determinant power of an anarchic international system over state behaviors as a given condition. Although neorealist theory attempts to display the existing conditions of international politics as natural and constant, Robert Cox, an influential representative of the critical theory of IR, focuses on how social and political relations and institutions emerge and in what ways they are subject to transformation.[12] For Cox, who introduced his critics to dominant theories of international relations with a Gramscian perspective, "theory is always for someone and for some purposes."[13] If values and ideas reflect specific social relationships, knowledge cannot be timeless and objective in contrast to realist argument. In this context, all objective and value-free theories, thoughts, and analyses should be reviewed critically. Hence, it is significant to appreciate critical theory's attempts to question the dominant order by analyzing and revealing social forces that could lead to an emancipatory change.[14]

Furthermore, Aberystwyth School seeks to display the roles and effects of security representations, normative choices, and security practices on social and political circumstances. Because thinking about security is not an intellectually neutral effort. Theories that reflect specific interests and values lead to a choice about who or what should be privileged.[15] Under the effect of values, norms, and ideas, the analyst cannot abstract himself/herself from the analyzed objects. Therefore, for Aberystwyth School, there is a need to change the ways of comprehending security. In this context, the purpose of critical security should be to reveal the "neutral knowledge allegation" behind politics. Revealing the political content of knowledge can facilitate social change and progress. The structures of world politics are also not constant since they are socially constructed.[16] One of the most important contributions of the Aberystwyth School is to bring together the security concept and critical theory.

SECURITY AS A POLITICAL PHENOMENON

Definitional ambiguity in the security concept[17] has led to the emergence of critical security approaches, since they reject the idea that security has a constant meaning. For Ken Booth, the conceptualizaton of security is required to reveal the real insecurities of individuals and human collectivities.[18] That is why, security can be achieved through the elimination of threats, and the contexts that produce them.[19] For Aberystwyth School, the priority should not be about how security will be ensured, but the sources of security issues. Hence, positive security that comprises social, economic, and cultural structures should have a priority. Thus, as long as the concept of security is about the improvement of human welfare, it will have a positive meaning for Aberystwyth School.[20]

Survival is important and necessary due to its vitality for the continuation of the existence of a state. However, the survival of the state does not necessarily mean the security of individuals. Consequently, the concept of "survival plus" which means the security beyond the survival of the state aims to create the appropriate environment for the perfection of human beings themselves.[21] In this framework, Booth argues that "survival is being alive; security is living."[22] In other words, security refers to positive life conditions beyond the survival needs of the state. According to Aberystwyth School, security is worthwhile for human collectivities and should be understood as a positive value. Therefore, security is conceptualized as a condition of emancipation of individuals from insecurities.[23]

For Aberystwyth School, security is a derivative concept based on *a priori* political understanding. Therefore, different ideological perspectives and discourses about politics deliver different opinions and discourses about security. While traditional security conception defines Security Studies in terms of the study of the threat, use, and control of military force,[24] critical approaches to security focus on normative choices and their political implications. Therefore, Aberystwyth School addresses the question of what security does politically.[25] In that case, it can be argued that the most important challenge of Aberystwyth School to traditional security conception is to deal with security as a political phenomenon.[26]

Security as a derivative concept implies that security outcomes result from different political aims and facts. In other words, for the Aberystwyth School, which questions the objective world conception of traditional security thinking, security would get different meanings depending on different worldviews and different rhetorics.[27] Thus, the security conception of one actor will derive from his/her political opinions, ideas, beliefs, and thoughts. For example, referent object of security, security threats, and instruments for providing security will be understood differently for a Marxist, racist, feminist, or other political ideologies. As another example, the dominant security conception of the Cold War period was derived from a focus on the political, ideological, and geopolitical conflict between the United States of America and the Union of Soviet Socialist Republics.[28] For Aberystwyth School, this way of security conception was derived from neorealist thinking and the nature of the anarchic international system. Therefore, different worldviews lead to different security conceptions. In that case, knowledge of security has a constitutive effect on the political realm.[29] As a result, Aberystwyth School addresses security theory as a political activity and brings politics back to security studies by seeking to display the connection between security theory and political order.

BROADENING THE SECURITY
AGENDA FOR NEW TOPICS

Aberystwyth School claims that dominant security rhetoric does not deal with the essence of security, since the narrow security agenda of traditional conception does not analyze the real security problems of individuals, social groups, and humanity. Therefore, it points to the necessity of broadening of security agenda and questions the state-centric and military-based conception of the traditional perspective. Aberystwyth School seeks a reconceptualization of the security concept in a holistic sense. In this respect, considering security with a widening agenda represents the search for extending beyond the artificial limitations of realist security conception. Aberystwyth School emphasizes the need for analyzing of different dimensions of security by bringing up the matter of why some issues such as human rights and socio-economic problems are excluded from the security agenda.[30]

Critique of traditional security conception leads to questioning of "true security." Ken Booth emphasizes the consideration of real lives in the real world by stating the concept of "true security."[31] In this context, the concept of security should be employed in the sense of threatening issues for individuals instead of "real" threats to the state. Because real threats to the welfare of individuals should constitute the main subject matter of the security studies. If the security agenda is enlarged in this direction, the general issues of human welfare will be inevitably addressed. Therefore, Aberystwyth School defines peace and security in terms of the absence of all forms of violence, namely physical, structural, and cultural ones.[32]

Individuals will be emancipated in a real sense when they are not threatened by military and non-military security issues. This circumstance would inevitably lead to a wider security conception. Although survival is only described in the context of security needs of the state by traditional security conception, security necessitates more than the survival of the state. According to Ken Booth, security is "an instrumental value in that it allows individuals and groups (to a relative degree) to establish the conditions of existence with some expectations of constructing a human life beyond the merely animal."[33] Security denotes a genuine absence of threats and the consequent maximization not only of an individual's life-*chances* but also of their life-*choices*.[34] That is why, thinking about and studying security concept would also require considering the basic issues about the nature of political life.

In addition to classical security issues such as power competitions among state actors, there are many issues such as violations of human rights, minority issues, repressive regimes, environmental degradation, migration, diseases, and poverty that have a significant place in contemporary security thinking.[35] Indeed, Ken Booth states that revealing underlying realities of security and insecurity necessitates addressing such issues as human rights problems and violations, repressive and assimilative minority policies, and violence against women at all levels, respectively physical, structural, and cultural.[36] Although this perspective would inevitably lead to a broadening of security agenda, it does not imply ignoring the security problems pointed out by traditional security conception. Because military threats to the territorial integrity of the state would also continue to be a threat to the security of individuals and nations. However, there are also other sorts of crucial security threats such as environmental degradation, socio-economic problems, ethnic conflict, disease, poverty, political repression, human rights violations, organized crime, and terrorism to the life of individuals.[37]

For scholars of Aberystwyth School, states should not be given a central position in security analysis since they have different characteristics, and they can be a part of security problems rather than their solutions. Therefore, security can be in the best way ensured through human emancipation that is described as the elimination of social, physical, economic, political, and other sorts of limitations for the realization of the potential of individuals and social groups. In the following sections, critiques introduced by the Aberystwyth School about the state as a referent object of security, its emphasis on the security of individual, and the emancipation concept will be examined respectively.

INDIVIDUAL AS THE REFERENT OBJECT OF SECURITY

While one of the two main debates in Security Studies during the 1990s is about the broadening of the security agenda by including non-military threats, another one is about determining the proper referent object of security.[38] In this respect, it is stated that individuals, identity-based social groups, nations, and a whole global community are defined as potential referent objects of security apart from the state. The security concept has been defined in a broadened way in terms of both referent objects of security and its context since the last three decades. Therefore, although the state maintains its central position in security studies, its previous privileged position as a referent object of security is extensively contested. Because, broadening of security agenda is necessarily required to analyze various referent objects of security apart from the state actor. At this point, scholars of critical security studies have intensified their discussions on the appropriateness of the state as a referent object of security and its security-providing role.

In the framework of this discussion, Ken Booth claims that the state cannot be a proper referent object of security due to three reasons. First, while some states are in search of security, others are not, and therefore, states are not credible actors as privileged referent objects. While some states try to provide their own security needs, they can constitute crucial insecurities for some important part of their own societies and fail to respond to the security needs of their own citizens. That is why, it is important to state that it is not possible to think about the state as the main security provider in all cases. In other words, the security of the state does not automatically mean the security of individuals who live within it. Second, the state as a security provider does not represent the ends, but means. It is not logical to make privilege the security of means in contrast to the security of ends. Third, differences among states both in terms of quality and capacity make it impossible for states to develop a comprehensive approach to security. Therefore, state-centric security approaches do not provide theoretical and conceptual tools in order to analyze the insecurities of human collectivities and individuals.[39] Hence, Aberystwyth School seeks to give a central position to human emancipation instead of the security of the state. Such an effort requires to regard individuals as the privileged referent object of security. Such a conceptualization that gives priority to human emancipation is a radical break from the dominant security conception based on the national security notion.[40]

Even though Barry Buzan advocates the broadening of the security agenda by including non-military security issues, his broader vision for the security agenda does not provide a complete critique of traditional security conception. Although Buzan states that an individual can be a referent object of security, he has continued to follow the state-centric security conception. Moreover, Buzan claims that the state should be the focus of security conceptualization due to its historical and existential role as an actor addressing all security issues.[41] In contrast to security conceptions that prioritize the individual as the referent object of security, according to Buzan, the state should remain the referent object of analysis of international security due to three reasons. First of all, it is the state actor which would address the security issues at the levels of sub-state, state, and the international system. Secondly, the state is the primary actor in reducing insecurity. Thirdly, the state is the dominant actor of the international political system.[42] However, as it is mentioned in the literature of critical security studies, the idea that advocates the sole referent object position of the state in security studies is largely questioned.

There are some reasons that lead to the consideration of the state as the dominant actor of security studies. Firstly, the state is the only actor which has the legitimacy on the use of violence in international society. Secondly, the state is regarded as the best-endowed actor for responding to security threats. Thirdly, since established security thinking is based on a state-centric and military-based conception, analytical perspectives in security analysis are conditioned to focus on the state.[43] In addition to these evaluations, the state has a high level of capacity and flexibility to adapt itself to new conditions.

Although the state is perceived as the provider of security for its citizens, it has become the dominant referent object of security within the competitive and conflictual structure of the sovereign state system. Therefore, state-centric traditional security conception has tended to ignore the cruciality of non-state actors in its theoretical and conceptual frameworks for a long time. As a result of this attitude, the effects of sub-state actors on state behaviors and choices have to remain highly limited within national and international arenas. However, in contemporary world politics, the main assumptions in the direction of the centrality of the state and military security issues are less important for the discipline of IR. The state is no longer the only and main actor, and consequently, it has a less privileged position when it is compared with previous eras.[44] Broadened security agenda is required to take into consideration activities of non-state actors such as social and transnational movements and non-governmental actors. Therefore, the analytical perspective of the Aberystwyth School is necessary because of both the incapability of state actor for providing security of its citizens, and the efforts of non-state actors for responding to various needs of individuals.[45]

Richard Wyn Jones claims that a cautious perspective should be maintained for the assumption of the state's protector position for its own citizens. For him, when a narrow perspective of security is applied, the efforts of governments for increasing power capacities and armament attempts in the name of national security will constitute potential threats to the physical security and freedoms of their own citizens. Critical security studies state that a sovereign state is one of the main reasons of insecurity, and it is a part of the problem rather than the solution.[46] This circumstance is not only valid for the disadvantegeous countries of Global South, but also for the countries of Global North. Consequently, while states give attention to threats against their survival, they tend to neglect the threats to individuals. However, in parallel with focusing on the security of individuals, Aberystwyth School claims that a theory should be for the "voiceless, the unrepresented and the powerless."[47] In this context, Aberystwyth School states that it should be focused on the needs and interests of the most "vulnerable" ones instead of concerns of state security.

The choice in respect to state actor as the appropriate referent object of security will only complicate the security thinking given the current realities and facts of global security. Because there are many potential referent objects of security. Even though it seems to be logical to focus on state security and inter-state security threats (most notably military threats) due to the dominant position of the state in the international system, security studies should give sincere attention to other referent objects given the increasing varieties of actors in global politics. Although there is a disagreement about the referent object matter within the Security Studies, there is no scarcity in terms of options. As a result, Aberystwyth School does not ignore the importance of state actor for contemporary security issues. Although the state is still important for the understanding of contemporary global politics, the Aberystwyth School questions and criticizes the ethical and practical position of the state as a privileged actor in international relations.[48] Because making the individual a referent object of security necessitates to critically analyze the state actor. For the Aberystwyth School, in the final analysis, the state is a means of realizing the potential of individuals and human collectivities for their own aims.[49] Therefore, the ends of security should not be replaced by the means of it.

As a representation of the growing importance of individual security in Security Studies, it is worth examining the human security concept. The debates on human security have not emerged as a new theoretical attempt but as an emphasis on humanitarian values and needs within the process of determining a new political agenda about security in the post–Cold War era. The human security conception's emphasis on the need of broadening of security agenda, the connection between freedom and security, and prioritizing of the individual instead of the state can be considered as the main common points with critical security studies. Indeed, critical security conception has a high level of sensitivity to the security needs of individuals and humanity. According to this perspective, military, political, environmental, societal, and economic threats primarily threaten people in the first instance.

United Nations Development Programme's (UNDP) 1994 Human Development Report represents a turning point for the inclusion of the human security concept into the Security Studies sub-field.[50] In this Report, it is stated that the most important concerns for human security are grounded in socio-economic problems and human rights violations. Accordingly, the concepts of personal security, community security, economic security, food security, environmental security, political security, and health security are described as categories of human security. Although military security problems among states continue to harm human beings, some issues such as environmental disasters, infectious diseases, and poverty have much more crucial consequences.[51] Therefore, focusing on the security of individuals is required to consider global threats to the security and welfare of human beings.

EMANCIPATION AS SECURITY

The philosophical origin of the emancipation concept can be traced back to the Enlightenment era and classical Marxism. In terms of Enlightenment, emancipation implies the opposing views about superstition, ignorance, inequality, custom, and traditional authority structures such as the Church and monarchic dynasties. In terms of classical Marxism, emancipation means the abolishment of exploitative relationships conducted by the capitalist class. In this context, critical theory can be viewed as the rediscovery of modernization theory's emancipatory attempt. However, Aberystwyth School introduces an emancipatory goal for security of individuals as opposed to the modernist way of security thinking that is based on state-centric and military-based security conception.[52] As the most significant distinguishing feature of the Aberystwyth School from other critical perspectives on security, the comprehension of security in the context of the emancipation concept introduces a critique of the modernist conceptualization of security.[53]

In order to emphasize the centrality of the emancipation concept for Aberystwyth School, it is considered as the heart of a critical theory of world security.[54] Ken Booth explains the importance of the emancipation concept for security studies in the following ways: "Security and emancipation are two sides of the same coin. Emancipation, not power or order, produces true security. Emancipation, theoretically, is security."[55] In respect to the question of how "true" security will be provided, Aberystwyth School claims that there can be an alternative reality, and that is why, security should be understood as emancipation.[56]

According to Aberystwyth School, emancipation should be comprehended as not a final end, but as a process. In other words, emancipation is not a constant idea or destination, but a direction for a better world order. That is why, emancipation means to resist oppression and struggle for a society based on fundamental freedoms, equality, justice, human development, and progress.[57] Because, it is not easy to pursue a life under the domination of political, economic, social, and cultural repressive power structures. Ken Booth explains the connection between security and emancipation in his seminal article titled "Security and Emancipation" in the following way: "Security means the absence of threats. Emancipation is the freeing of people (individuals and groups) from those physical and human constraints which stop them carrying out what they would freely choose to do. War and the threat of war is one of those constraints, together with poverty, poor education, political oppression and so on."[58] Threats to individuals and societies can include physical violence such as war, conflict, and terrorist activities, structural violence such as socio-economic problems, unemployment, poverty, lack or absence of health-care service, and/or cultural violence such as discriminatory or assimilative policies to identity-based social groups. Accordingly, the concept of emancipation has contributed to the development of positive peace conception. The natural result of such a conception that takes into consideration the existential conditions of individuals is to regard the individual as the main referent object of security. Indeed, "true" security conditions determine the quality of an individual's life. Therefore, even though it is difficult to clearly describe emancipation in a theoretical sense, it can be easier to identify it in practical conditions in the framework of physical, structural, and cultural violence.[59]

According to Ken Booth, "true" security will emerge if individuals and social groups are not abused by others.[60] Emancipation needs to be understood in a way that security should be ensured by considering the needs of others, not at the expense of them. Therefore, emancipation represents an inclusive conception.[61] However traditional security conception has an exclusive logic and seeks to construct a national community that serves the interests of the state machinery.[62] Therefore, Aberystwyth School rejects the egoist, exclusive and statist security conception. For instance, accepting war as a reality of world politics is a part of the problem. However, Aberystwyth School claims that there is a need to be skeptical about the actual benefits of an exclusive focus on war and conflict.[63] Therefore, the critical theory approach seeks to extend the idea of moral and political community beyond the frontiers of the state, and at the same time to "deepen" it within national frontiers.

Rejecting the state as the subject of security studies represents an attempt to express an alternative security ontology. While such an alternative attempt targets to emancipate masses who are the victims of state-centric security conception, it cannot identify any clear idea on how power will be transformed in the direction of human emancipation.[64] If there is a practical importance of Aberystwyth School's security conception, it should display the significance of emancipation for the real life institutions and relations. In this sense, there is a need for emancipatory practices in order to strongly emphasize its revelance for world security. However, Aberystwyth School expresses general principles rather than an action plan. Because insecurities and restrictions of individuals differentiate according to time and space. Therefore, it is not possible to determine a concrete criterion for emancipatory action. For progressive social change, it is recommended to support social movements that aim to generate emancipation. Critical security studies can play an important role in supporting social movements by introducing a critique of the current order and legitimizing alternative thoughts.[65] However, it is not obvious in what ways social movements will be supported.

There is no universal definition on the meaning of emancipation, and emancipation can be abused for the legitimization of illiberal practices. For instance, according to Mohammed Ayoob, the concept of emancipation is not proper for non-Western societies. In these societies, ethnic groups' searches for emancipation in the framework of self-determination right can be a cause of disorder and anarchy.[66] However, for Aberystwyth School, emancipation is not synonymous with Westernization. In other words, emancipation does not mean the same thing for all individuals and cultures. Therefore, emancipation as a target should know no national, racial, sexual, or other frontiers.[67] Accordingly, emancipatory practices must be contingent upon the identification of the particular insecurities experienced by groups and individuals.[68] Although emancipation includes some Western values, it cannot be claimed that Western values are the bases of a "new" society. According to Aberystwyth School, the concept of emancipation does not have any conception to construct its monopoly over absolute truth.[69] In other words, Aberystwyth School's emancipation approach is not based on a constant vision of an ideal society, since such a vision would necessitate imposition of an "ideal social order" on the rest of general society.

As a result, while the emancipatory security conception privileges the societal conception of security, it is in contradiction with the traditional security conception's search for order. Because Ken Booth claims that emancipation should prevail against the concerns about power and order.[70] The aim of critical theory with its normative nature is to direct attention to social and political oppressions and provide intellectual tools to people in order to promote an emancipatory change in the society. Relatedly, emancipation aims to overcome the false consciousness of the masses that tend to comprehend security in the context of narratives of traditional security conception. Therefore, Aberystwyth School links the study of security to the expansive goal of human emancipation. Thus, the School advocates a normative perspective to the study of security through questioning the ethical and political position of the state-centric security conception. Emphasizing the emancipated society as a purpose of security studies requires to tackle with real security issues of individuals in many parts of the world. Consequently, security should be normatively revisited in the context of emancipation that requires giving attention to positive peace conditions in which all types of violence are eliminated.

IDENTITY AND OTHERING

Aberystwyth School regards the identity-related security issues as an important topic of world security in contrast to the traditional security conception for which states react to anarchic international system's conditions, and they are considered as given. Since the end of the Cold War, identity has become one of the most important concepts with its implications on security through integration and fragmentation processes in contemporary world politics. Therefore, Aberystwyth School attempts to examine the identity issues and othering processes that cause marginalization of identity-based social groups.[71] While Aberystwyth School examines the issue of othering, it gives attention to the distinction of subject and object. Accordingly, by determining a framework of observation in accordance with her/his own conditions, the observer limits the observed object and thus avoids objectivity. Therefore, theories developed as a result of unilateral observation are for specific cases and actors. When the current international security issues are analyzed or sought solutions for them, the Western world gives itself a central position and makes the non-Western world "others."[72] In this respect, it is claimed that the efforts for solving current international security issues are primarily formulated in order to provide the security of the West.[73] While the threatened values are Western values, threats against them emanate from non-Western societies. Therefore, dominant relations, thoughts, and actions of contemporary global politics create a hegemony, and finding solutions to the security problems of this hegemony reflects a unilateral choice without regarding the security needs of all societies of the world.

Aberystwyth School analyzes the concept of hegemony by giving attention to the unequal and hierarchic structure of the international system as the source of insecurity. According to Antonio Gramsci, the hegemony that is created by not only power, but also consent leads to become prevalent of dominant group's ethical, political, and cultural values within the society and acceptance by other groups or classes.[74] Thus, the ideology of the dominant social class becomes a "common conception" of society. Some institutions such as media, culture, education system, and civil society play an important role in the production process of this common conception.[75] Thereby, socio-economical, political, and cultural relations and practices become a base of historical bloc of existing order.

The contemporary hegemonic structure is mostly based on the discourses and concepts of human rights and freedoms, democracy, and a capitalist economy. In a sense, these discourses and concepts constitute the strategic culture of the West. The actors and societies who do not embrace these discourses and concepts ideationally and practically are subject to an othering process. These "others" are mostly non-Western societies and actors. This process has gained a new dimension and momentum with the discourse of "Islamic terrorism" after the September 11, 2001 terrorist attacks. For example, some parts of non-Western societies are labelled as "usual suspects" of insecurities such as terrorism, organized crime, irregular migration, or street violence.[76] Thus, they are regarded as security threats to Western values and their hegemony. Such an attitude has resulted in the othering process based on identity and exclusionary political implications. In this respect, while xenophobia in Western societies has significantly increased, military interventions conducted in the direction of the strategy of "global war on terrorism" have caused massive violations of human rights and freedoms. In that case, it can be argued that the efforts of the West to overcome security problems have contributed to bringing about a global insecurity atmosphere.

As a result, Aberystwyth School states that dramatic differences in terms of power capacities between countries of Global North and Global South contribute to global insecurity, and the reasons and motivations of the September 11 terrorist attacks should be analyzed in this context. In contrast to the othering process based on an identity that has gained a global characteristic after September 11, Aberystwyth School draws attention to the existence of identity-based oppressive structures that lead to the construction of dominative relationships. Therefore, it advocates emancipatory communities based on inclusionary and egalitarian notions of identity. In this context, it is stated that human emancipation—both that of individuals and humanity in general—provides the guide for relations both within communities and between them.[77] Therefore, it is important to recede from a security conception based on practices of violence and exclusion.

CONCLUSION

The state-centric and military-based security conception aims to provide security needs of the state without questioning the constitution processes of dominant thoughts, practices, and social conditions. On the other hand, Aberystwyth School rejects the objective knowledge of security, and calls into question the legitimacy of existing social and political institutions and conceptions. In this respect, Aberystwyth School has opened up the study of security by posing questions that were not raised in any meaningful sense by the traditional approach to security. Gramscian thought, critical social theory of the Frankfurt School, and critical theory of the IR discipline have affected the development of the Aberystwyth School's security conception. Therefore, the clear and original contribution of the Aberystwyth School is to provide important connections between Critical Theory and the concept of security. By inspiration from the critical theory, Aberystwyth School analyzes the traditional security conception and seeks to examine the involvement of structural components and practices in the continuation of repression, inequality, and injustice in world politics.

According to the Aberystwyth School, which makes an effort to reveal the limitations of traditional security conception, security is a derivative concept based on a priori political understanding. While traditional security conception defines Security Studies in terms of the study of the threat, use, and control of military force,[78] critical approaches to the security focus on the normative choices and their political implications. Therefore, Aberystwyth School addresses the question of what security does politically.[79] In that case, it can be argued that the most important challenge of Aberystwyth School to traditional security conception is to deal with security as a political phenomenon.[80]

For Aberystwyth School, the security agenda should be broadened due to the limitations of the narrow approach of traditional security conception. Because the narrow security agenda of traditional conception does not analyze the security problems of social groups and individuals. Relatedly, Aberystwyth School questions the state actor in terms of discussions of appropriate referent object of security. In this respect, it is stated that individuals, identity-based social groups, nations, and a whole global community are defined as potential referent objects of security apart from the state. Therefore, security should be revisited in the context of emancipation and normative basis. Rethinking security as emancipation entails giving attention to positive peace conditions through examining the reasons of structural and cultural violence. As a result, the most significant distingiushing feature of Aberystwyth School is the comprehension of security in the context of the emancipation concept.

REFERENCES

Ağır, Bülent Sarper. "Critical Security Studies." In *Theories of International Relations II*, edited by Tayyar Arı, 110–135. Eskişehir: Anadolu University Publications, 2019.

Ağır, Bülent Sarper. "Migration and Immigrants as the 'Usual Suspects' of European Insecurity." *Security Dialogues* 10, no. 1 (2019): 7–18.

Ayoob, Mohammed. "Defining Security: A Subaltern Realist Perspective." In *Critical Security Studies: Concepts and Cases*, edited by Keith Krause and Michael C. Williams, 121–146. London: UCL Press, 1997.

Baldwin, David A. "The Concept of Security." *Review of International Studies* 23, no. 1 (1997): 5–26.

Bilgin, Pınar. "Individual Security and Societal Dimensions of Security." *International Studies Review* 5, no. 2 (2003): 203–222.

Bilgin, Pınar. "Critical Theory." In *Security Studies: An Introduction*, edited by Paul Williams, 89–102. London: Routledge, 2008.

Birdişli, Fikret. *Teori ve Pratikte Uluslararası Güvenlik*. Ankara: Seçkin Yayıncılık, 2014.

Birdişli, Fikret. "Eleştirel Güvenlik Çalışmaları Kapsamında Frankfurt Okulu ve Soğuk Savaş Sonrası Güvenlik Sorunlarına Eleştirel Bir Yaklaşım: Galler Ekolü." *Güvenlik Stratejileri Dergisi* 10, no. 20 (2014): 229–256.

Booth, Ken. "Security and Emancipation." *Review of International Studies* 17, no. 4 (1991): 313–326.

Booth, Ken. "Human Wrongs and International Relations." *International Affairs* 71, no. 1 (1995): 103–126.

Booth, Ken. "Security and Self: Reflections of a Fallen Realist." In *Critical Security Studies: Concepts and Cases*, edited by Keith Krause and Michael C. Williams, 83–119. London: UCL Press, 1997.

Booth, Ken. "Three Tyrannies." In *Human Rights in Global Politics*, edited by Tim Dunne and Nicholas J. Wheeler, 31–70. Cambridge: Cambridge University Press, 1999.

Booth, Ken. "Realities of Security: Editor"s Introduction." *International Relations* 18, no. 1 (2004): 5–8.

Booth, Ken, ed. *Critical Security Studies and World Politics*. Boulder: Lynne Rienner, 2005.

Booth, Ken. *Theory of World Security*. Cambridge: Cambridge University Press, 2007.

Booth, Ken. "The Human Faces of Terror: Reflections in a Cracked Looking-Glass." *Critical Studies on Terrorism* 1, no. 1 (2008): 65–79.

Browning, Christopher S. and McDonald, Matt. "The Future of Critical Security Studies: Ethics and the Politics of Security." *European Journal of International Relations* 19, no. 2 (2013): 235–255.

Buzan, Barry. *People, States, and Fear: An Agenda for International Security Studies in the Post-Cold War Era*. Second Edition, London: Wheatsheaf, 1991.

CASE Collective. "Critical Approaches to Security in Europe: A Networked Manifesto." *Security Dialogue* 37, no. 4 (2006): 443–487.

Cox, Robert. "Social Forces, States, and World Orders: Beyond International Relations Theory." *Millennium Journal of International Studies* 10, no. 2 (1981): 126–155.

Floyd, Rita. "Human Security and the Copenhagen School's Securitization Approach: Conceptualizing Human Security as a Securitizing Move." *Human Security Journal* 5 (2007): 38–49.

Galtung, Johan. "Violence, Peace and Peace Research." *Journal of Peace Research* 6, no. 3 (1969): 167–191.

Heywood, Andrew. *Global Politics*. London: Palgrave Macmillan, 2011.

Hobden, Stephan and Jones, Richard Wyn. "Marxist Theories of International Relations." In *The Globalization of World Politics: An Introduction to International Relations*, edited by John Baylis and Steve Smith, 200–223. New York: Oxford University Press, 2001.

Hynek, Nick and Chandler, David. "No Emancipatory Alternative, No Critical Security Studies." *Critical Studies on Security* 1, no. 1 (2013): 46–63.

Jones, Richard Wyn. "'Message in a Bottle'? Theory and Praxis in Critical Security Studies." *Contemporary Security Policy* 16, no. 3 (1995): 299–319.

Jones, Richard Wyn. *Security, Strategy, and Critical Theory*. Boulder: Lynne Rienner, 1999.

Krause, Keith and Williams, Michael C. "Broadening the Agenda of Security: Politics and Methods." *Mershon International Studies Review* 40, no. 2 (1996): 229–254.

Krause, Keith and Williams, Michael C. "From Strategy to Security: Foundations of Critical Security Studies." In *Critical Security Studies: Concepts and Cases*, edited by Keith Krause and Michael C. Williams, 33–59. London: UCL Press, 1997.

Mutimer, David. "Critical Security Studies: A Schismatic History." In *Contemporary Security Studies*, edited by Alan Collins, 93–105. Oxford: Oxford University Press, 2010.

Nunes, João. "Reclaiming the Political: Emancipation and Critique in Security Studies." *Security Dialogue* 43, no. 4 (2012): 345–361.

Columba, Peoples , Columba   and Vaughan-Williams, Nick. *Critical Security Studies: An Introduction*. London: Routledge, 2015.

Sheenan, Michael. "Community, Anarchy and Critical Security." Paper for the ECPR Joint Sessions Workshop Redefining Security, Mannheim, March 26–31, 1999.

Sheenan, Michael. *International Security: An Analytical Survey*. Boulder: Lynne Rienner Publishers, 2005.

Smith, Steve. "The Increasing Insecurity of Security Studies: Conceptualizing Security in the Last Twenty Years." *Contemporary Security Policy* 20, no. 3 (1999): 72–101.

United Nations Development Programme. *Human Development Report.* Oxford: Oxford University Press, 1994.

Wæver, Ole. "Aberystwyth, Paris, Copenhagen: New Schools in Security Theory and Their Origins between Core and Periphery," 2004. Accessed March 10, 2022. http: //www.scribd.com/doc/40010349/Ole-Waever-Aberystwyth-Paris-enNew-Schools -in-Security-Theory-and-Their-Origins-Between-Core-andPeriphery.

Walt, Stephen M. "The Renaissance of Security Studies." *International Studies Quarterly* 35, no. 2 (1991): 211–239.

Williams, Michael C. "Words, Images, Enemies: Securitization and International Politics." *International Studies Quarterly* 47, no. 4 (2003): 511–531.

Wolfers, Arnold. "National Security as an Ambiguous Symbol." *Political Science Quarterly* 67, no. 4 (1952): 481–502.

NOTES

1. Keith Krause and Michael C. Williams, "Broadening the Agenda of Security: Politics and Methods," *Mershon International Studies Review* 40, no. 2 (1996): 229.

2. Columba Peoples and Nick Vaughan-Williams, *Critical Security Studies: An Introduction* (London: Routledge, 2015), 1.

3. Pınar Bilgin, "Critical Theory," in *Security Studies: An Introduction,* ed. Paul Williams (London: Routledge, 2008), 98.

4. David Mutimer, "Critical Security Studies: A Schismatic History," in *Contemporary Security Studies,* ed. Alan Collins (Oxford: Oxford University Press, 2010), 91.

5. Steve Smith, "The Increasing Insecurity of Security Studies: Conceptualizing Security in the Last Twenty Years," *Contemporary Security Policy* 20, no. 3 (1999): 89.

6. Michael Sheenan, *International Security: An Analytical Survey* (Boulder: Lynne Rienner Publishers, 2005), 157; Krause and Williams, "Broadening the Agenda," 48; Ole Wæver, "Aberystwyth, Paris, Copenhagen: New Schools in Security Theory and Their Origins between Core and Periphery," 2004, accessed on March 10, 2022, http: //www.scribd.com/doc/40010349/Ole-Waever-Aberystwyth-Paris-enNew-Schools-in -Security-Theory-and-Their-Origins-Between-Core-andPeriphery.

7. Johan Galtung, "Violence, Peace and Peace Research," *Journal of Peace Research* 6, no. 3 (1969): 167–191.

8. Sheenan, *International Security,* 154.

9. Andrew Heywood, *Global Politics* (London: Palgrave Macmillan, 2011), 69.

10. Bülent Sarper Ağır, "Critical Security Studies," in *Theory of International Relations II,* ed. Tayyar Arı (Eskişehir: Anadolu University Publications, 2019), 113–114.

11. Peoples and Vaughan-Williams, *Critical Security Studies,* 18–19.

12. Robert Cox, "Social Forces, States, and World Orders: Beyond International Relations Theory," *Millennium Journal of International Studies* 10, no. 2 (1981): 126–155.

13. Cox, "Social Forces, States," 128.

14. Hobden and Jones, "Marxist Theories," 212.

15. Sheenan, *International Security*, 157.

16. Mutimer, "Critical Security Studies," 93–96.

17. Arnold Wolfers, "National Security as an Ambiguous Symbol," *Political Science Quarterly* 67, no. 4 (1952): 481–502; David Baldwin, "The Concept of Security," *Review of International Studies* 23, no. 1 (1997): 5–26.

18. Ken Booth, *Critical Security Studies and World Politics* (Boulder: Lynne Rienner, 2005).

19. Ken Booth, "Security and Emancipation," *Review of International Studies* 17, no. 4 (1991): 313–326.

20. Peoples and Vaughan-Williams, *Critical Security Studies*, 18.

21. Ken Booth, *Theory of World Security* (Cambridge: Cambridge University Press, 2007), 39.

22. Booth, *Theory of World Security*, 106.

23. Ken Booth, "The Human Faces of Terror: Reflections in a Cracked Looking-Glass," *Critical Studies on Terrorism* 1, no. 1 (2008): 65–79.

24. Stephen Walt, "The Renaissance of Security Studies," *International Studies Quarterly* 35, no. 2 (1991): 211–239.

25. Christopher S. Browning and Matt McDonald, "The Future of Critical Security Studies: Ethics and the Politics of Security," *European Journal of International Relations* 19, no. 2 (2013): 235–255.

26. João Nunes, "Reclaiming the Political: Emancipation and Critique in Security Studies," *Security Dialogue* 43, no. 4 (2012): 345–361.

27. Ken Booth, "Security and Self: Reflections of a Fallen Realist," in *Critical Security Studies: Concepts and Cases*, ed. Keith Krause and Michael C. Williams (London: UCL Press, 1997), 97.

28. Peoples and Vaughan-Williams, *Critical Security Studies*, 22.

29. Booth, "Security and Self," 104–119.

30. Ağır, "Critical Security Studies," 118.

31. Ken Booth, "Human Wrongs and International Relations," *International Affairs* 71, no. 1 (1995): 123.

32. Ağır, "Critical Security Studies," 119.

33. Booth, *Theory of World Security*, 106–107.

34. Peoples and Vaughan-Williams, *Critical Security Studies*, 25.

35. Ağır, "Critical Security Studies," 119.

36. Ken Booth, "Realities of Security: Editor's Introduction," *International Relations* 18, no. 1 (2004): 5–8.

37. Booth, "Security and Emancipation," 318.

38. Michael C. Williams, "Words, Images, Enemies: Securitization and International Politics," *International Studies Quarterly* 47, no. 4 (2003): 513.

39. Booth, "Security and Emancipation."

40. Nick Hynek and David Chandler, "No Emancipatory Alternative, No Critical Security Studies," *Critical Studies on Security* 1, no. 1 (2013): 50.

41. Barry Buzan, *People, States, and Fear: An Agenda for International Security Studies in the Post-Cold War Era*, Second Edition (London: Wheatsheaf, 1991), 329.

42. Buzan, *People, States, and Fear.*

43. Pınar Bilgin, "Individual Security and Societal Dimensions of Security," *International Studies Review* 5, no. 2 (2003): 216.

44. Smith, "The Increasing Insecurity," 77.

45. Bilgin, "Individual Security," 216–217.

46. Richard Wyn Jones, "'Message in a Bottle'? Theory and Praxis in Critical Security Studies," *Contemporary Security Policy* 16, no. 3 (1995): 310.

47. Richard Wyn Jones, *Security, Strategy, and Critical Theory* (Boulder: Lynne Rienner, 1999), 159.

48. Sheenan, *International Security*, 162.

49. Booth, "Security and Emancipation," 319.

50. United Nations Development Programme, Human Development Report (Oxford: Oxford University Press, 1994).

51. Rita Floyd, "Human Security and the Copenhagen School's Securitization Approach: Conceptualizing Human Security as a Securitizing Move," *Human Security Journal* 5 (2007): 39.

52. CASE Collective, "Critical Approaches to Security in Europe: A Networked Manifesto," *Security Dialogue* 37, no. 4 (2006): 448.

53. Ağır, "Critical Security Studies," 124–125.

54. Booth, *Theory of World Security*, 110.

55. Booth, "Security and Emancipation," 319.

56. Sheenan, *International Security*, 158–159.

57. Booth, *Theory of World Security*, 111.

58. Booth, "Security and Emancipation," 319.

59. Bilgin, "Critical Theory," 100.

60. Booth, "Security and Emancipation," 319.

61. Booth, "Three Tyrannies," 65.

62. Browning and McDonald, "The Future of Critical."

63. Peoples and Vaughan-Williams, *Critical Security Studies*, 20.

64. Hynek and Chandler, "No Emancipatory Alternative," 50.

65. Peoples and Vaughan-Williams, *Critical Security Studies*, 25; Jones, *Security, Strategy*, 161.

66. Peoples and Vaughan-Williams, *Critical Security Studies*, 30; Mohammad Ayoob, "Defining Security: A Subaltern Realist Perspective," in *Critical Security Studies: Concepts and Cases*, ed. Keith Krause and Michael C. Williams (London: UCL Press, 1997), 127.

67. Sheenan, *International Security*.

68. Peoples and Vaughan-Williams, *Critical Security Studies*, 32.

69. Booth, "Three Tyrannies," 42.

70. Booth, "Security and Emancipation," 319.

71. Krause and Williams, "Broadening the Agenda," 48.

72. Fikret Birdişli, "Eleştirel Güvenlik Çalışmaları Kapsamında Frankfurt Okulu ve Soğuk Savaş Sonrası Güvenlik Sorunlarına Eleştirel Bir Yaklaşım: Galler Ekolü," *Güvenlik Stratejileri Dergisi* 10, no. 20 (2014): 245.

73. Fikret Birdişli, *Teori ve Pratikte Uluslararası Güvenlik* (Ankara: Seçkin Yayıncılık, 2014), 73.

74. Ağır, "Critical Security Studies," 127.

75. Hobden and Jones, "Marxist Theories," 210.

76. Bülent Sarper Ağır, "Migration and Immigrants as the 'Usual Suspects' of European Insecurity," *Security Dialogues* 10, no. 1 (2019): 7–18.

77. Peoples and Vaughan-Williams, *Critical Security Studies*, 26.

78. Walt, "The Rennaissance of Security."

79. Browning and McDonald, "The Future of Critical."

80. Nunes, "Reclaiming the Political," 346–347.

Chapter 6

Copenhagen School of Security Studies

Bülent Sarper Ağır

INTRODUCTION

Addressing war and peace phenomena has played a constructive role in the development process of the discipline of International Relations (IR). The emergence of the discipline is a clear response to the traumas of the First World War. Since the issues of war and peace are interrelated with the security needs at all levels—individual, societal, national, international—most of the recent debates in contemporary IR have been focusing on the concept of security. Due to the contested characteristics of security, the concept has been subjected to different theoretical assessments.

Traditional security conception persists in defining the field of security exclusively in terms of "the study of threat, use, and control of military force."[1] In this respect, the security concept has been traditionally employed in a rather narrow sense—i.e., as almost synonymous with military power. According to this simplistic logic, more military power will lead to more security for the state and consequently its citizens. Therefore, traditional security conception insists that non-military issues can only become a topic of Security Studies to the extent that they can lead to physical violence and conflict.[2] On the other hand, there is uncertainty in terms of the definition and content of security, the nature of threats, and the responsibility for providing security. Indeed, new/critical security approaches consider individuals and societal groups as the referent objects of security instead of state actor, and thus, they identify a broadened security agenda including political, economic, societal, and environmental issues in addition to military ones.[3] Hence in an epistemological sense, traditional security conception as a reaction to

125

objective conditions has been extensively questioned due to the dynamic conditions of global security.

The end of the Cold War directly influenced the agenda of security policies and led to a political and academic discussion in terms of the nature and meaning of security and the need for its reconceptualization. This discussion extends from the epistemological and ontological foundations of security to the content of the security agenda and appropriate referent objects of security. Indeed, the central position of state actor and the dominance of national security in security studies have been questioned due to the global economic interdependence, and the fragmentation of multicultural states in the respect of ethnic, religious, and sectarian differences.

There is a close connection between contextual change and conceptual innovation. As a middle ground between traditional security conception and new/critical security studies, the Copenhagen School's studies on security can be evaluated as a reaction to the changes in the security realm during the ending process of the Cold War and its aftermath. Although the Copenhagen School recognizes the importance of state actor in the security realm and its security concerns, it has sought to introduce a new security framework by considering the widening perspective of the security agenda in terms of both threats and actors. In this context, a common feature of the studies of the Copenhagen School is to focus on previously "neglected" issues and develop conceptual and theoretical perspectives to go beyond the traditional security studies.

CHANGING DYNAMICS OF SECURITY: FROM TRADITIONAL TO CRITICAL

There is a lively debate on the meaning, nature, content, and means of security and responsibility for providing security among the scholars of Security Studies. The basic and most probably sole consensus of such a debate is the contested nature of the security concept. For David Baldwin, security can be formulated as "a low probability of damage to acquired values."[4] According to Barry Buzan, security includes the efforts for survival against threats.[5] While some scholars argue that there is a paradigm shift that leads to change in security conception, some scholars believe that traditional security conception still maintains its importance and validity. The latter questions the conceptual simplicity of traditional security conception and seeks to develop alternative security conceptions and definitions.

With the end of the Cold War and the acceleration of the globalization process, security conception has been subjected to extensive academic debates on whether or not it should be broadened and/or deepened. For instance, the separation of non-physical security from territorial security; diversification of security threats and the emergence of new security threats; the emergence of identity as a crucial security issue; and questioning of state actor as a security provider are the reflections of interconnectedness between the concepts of globalization and security.[6] Although the globalization process does not shift the emphasis of states' primacy on traditional security issues, the emergence of new types of threats and actors has led to the erosion of the central position of the state as a security provider. Therefore, it is argued that state actor has become less capable of meeting the security requirements of its own people.[7] While the nature of war has mostly transformed from inter-state wars to civil wars and ethnic conflicts, transboundary issues such as environmental degradation, migration, terrorism, and supranational processes such as the formation of the European Union (EU) constitute new security concerns in a multiplicity manner. Consequently, since the end of the Cold War, discussions on the security concept have included two contrasting perspectives—narrow security conception versus widening security conception.

According to traditional security conception, security is related to competitive and mostly conflictual relationships between states; and military threats constitute the main issues of traditional security conception. In this respect, it is important to examine the relationship between the security concept and the notion of anarchic international system that influences the development of assumptions of traditional security conception.[8] The notion of international anarchy is described as the absence of an effective higher unit that reacts automatically, universally, and irrespectively to the emergency conditions of any state in the modern world system.[9] All in all, the existence of anarchy describes the structural condition of the international system and constitutes the ontological base of the traditional security conception.

According to traditional security conception, sovereignty, independence, and territorial integrity are the core values that may lead a state to going war to defend them.[10] The containment or deterrent capacity of a state for confronting any threats to its core values defines the general framework of national security policy. In this context, the dominant issues of the security agenda are military security and political security issues. If a state regards any development as a threat to its national security, it can try to operationalize the balance of power mechanism to ensure its survival. The importance of power politics and military capacity for national survival demonstrates the power acquisition by state actors as a systemic condition.[11] States seek to expand their armaments efforts or make an alliance to increase their military deterrence. However, it is important to state that security issues are not only conditioned by the structure of the international system and interactions of states within it, but also by their internal characteristics and issues.[12] In this respect, intra-state conflicts and security dynamics demonstrate the analytical and conceptual limitations of traditional security conception for addressing contemporary security issues. Indeed, the state is only analyzed politically and institutionally without considering its societal dimension by traditional security studies. Because ontological and epistemological bases of neorealism do not consider the socially constructed aspect of social reality.

In the context of a need for considering non-traditional security issues, new security approaches have advocated the widening and deepening of security conception. A significant part of newly published literature in Security Studies claims that state-centric security approaches could not explain all dimensions of security.[13] Indeed, the classical dividing line between high politics and low politics of the realpolitik worldview does not reflect the current characteristics and tendencies in the security domain. In terms of the origin of security threats, new security approaches claim that many threats to humanity do emanate from environmental problems, pandemics, global terrorism, poverty, and migration rather than aggressor states.[14] Thus, in addition to military security issues, non-military aspects of security such as political, economic, societal, and environmental issues are increasingly recognized as crucial parts of the security agenda. Thus, new security perspectives argue that non-military solutions such as democratization, state-building, development of civil society, economic growth, and sustainable development will be more helpful than military ones for resolution of security issues.[15] Indeed, the shift in the nature and origin of security threats has also led to a change in solution methods of security issues in the post–Cold War era.

A EUROPEAN SECURITY PERSPECTIVE: COPENHAGEN SCHOOL

The concept of security has an important place in the post-positivist debates on international relations. On the one hand, some favor the widening and deepening of security conception, on the other hand, some scholars argue that such an attempt will destroy the conceptual meaning of security. The Copenhagen School constitutes a middle/third way between these two contrasting views on security concept. While the Copenhagen School emphasizes the problems of widening of security conception indiscriminately, it also intends to go beyond the narrow security perspective of traditional security conception.[16] In other words, while the Copenhagen School recognizes the need for softening the connection between security and military issues, it also argues that there is a requirement for developing criteria to differentiate security issues from politics.

The Copenhagen Peace Research Institute (COPRI) was established as an independent research institute by the Danish Parliament in 1985 aimed at supporting and strengthening multidisciplinary research on peace and security.[17] "Non-military Aspects of European Security"—one of the research projects of COPR—was developed in 1988. The basic motivation of this research project was to address the consequences of the end of the Cold War on European security architecture. The participants of this project group have maintained continuity and coherence in their academic studies on security concept; and subsequently, they are called "School" in the Security Studies sub-field of IR.[18]

The primary studies of the Copenhagen School on security concept are closely concerned with European security dynamics. Addressing the effects of significant developments and processes of international politics on European security dynamics, the Copenhagen School focuses on collective security problems rather than national security. It is concerned with the possibility of the creation of peaceful relations among European peoples and states rather than focusing on the protection of a specific state.[19]

Innovative concepts and views about security conception primarily emerged from the efforts of understanding the uncertainties and risks of European security problematic. There is a close and endogenous relationship between empirical developments of European security and conceptual developments in the studies of the Copenhagen School.[20] For instance, in the book entitled *European Polyphony: Perspectives Beyond East-West Confrontation* (1989),[21] the Copenhagen School examined the national security conceptions of Eastern and Western European states. It emphasized that security dynamics in Europe not only depended on two superpowers, and that there was also a more endogenous and European character in national security conceptions in the continent. While previous studies of the Copenhagen School focused on conceptual innovations for explaining European security dynamics, the book *Security: A New Framework for Analysis* (1998) focused on the security dynamics of different regions of the world.[22] Thus, the Copenhagen School has acquired a universal character and become more inclusive in the geographic sense. In this respect, the book entitled *Regions and Powers: The Structure of International Security* (2003)[23] primarily analyzed the regional security dynamics of North America, South America, Europe, the post-Soviet region, the Middle East, South Africa, Central Africa, South Asia, and East Asia.

Two motivations promote the interest of the Copenhagen School in the widening of security agenda. Firstly, the European security agenda has tended to gradually broaden beyond the military security issues since the mid-1980s. Such an attitude caused a concern for the developing conceptual apparatuses to explain the politically widening security debates. Moreover, the studies of the Copenhagen School are not only motivated by the empirical concern towards European security; it had an academic concern to make the original contributions to theoretical and conceptual debates in Security Studies.[24]

The basic concepts that characterize the security approach of the Copenhagen School have not been primarily developed within the collective studies of the School. Although the social constructivist perspective on security conception, sectoral security concept, and regional security complex theory are developed by the members of the School, they are scholarly produced by individual studies of the School's members rather than a collective project. The security conceptualizations and theoretical frameworks of the Copenhagen School are theoretically and empirically used by scholars of Security Studies.

Methodologically, the Copenhagen School presents an approach that brings together the objective perspective of neorealism and intersubjective knowledge conception of social constructivism. In terms of securitization, there is also room for the subjective perspective of post-modernism. In this respect, the Copenhagen School constitutes a bridge between advocators of traditional security conception and widening security conception in the security debates of the post–Cold War era. Despite its middle ground position in Security Studies, it can be argued that while the Copenhagen School implements a social constructivist model, it still maintains some foundations of neorealist tradition.[25] For instance, although the Copenhagen School accepts the idea of securitization of non-military security issues and referent object position of non-state actors, it only recognizes the state as a securitizing actor. Thus, it is clear that the state-centric security approach has a place in the security conception of the Copenhagen School.

The questioning of the objective logic of security has resulted in a series of conceptual innovations of the Copenhagen School. While the Copenhagen School does not regard security as an objective phenomenon, it avoids the reduction of security to a subjective phenomenon. According to the Copenhagen School, security should be comprehended as an intersubjective phenomenon instead of neither objective nor subjective.

The security approach of the Copenhagen School makes a connection among the levels of individual, state, and the international system as it argues that the state can be threatened both internally and externally. Hence, the Copenhagen School has made a separation between five sectors of security (military, political, economic, societal, and environmental), and five levels of analysis (international, regional, state, societal, and individual).[26] Thus the Copenhagen School has introduced an inclusive perspective in terms of dynamics, agendas, referent objects, and actors of security. Such a variety in respect to analysis facilitates the implementation of the conceptual framework of the Copenhagen School to almost all empirical cases.

The basic difference between the security framework of the Copenhagen School and the traditional security conception is the choice of a multi-sectoral perspective for the security agenda instead of a narrow security agenda. The advocators of widening the security agenda should keep an open mind for any source of security threat, actor, and type of referent object of security when the interconnectedness among security sectors is considered. However, traditional security conception gives priority to only one security sector (military) and one actor (state), and makes a connection with other security sectors only if they cause a direct use of military force. Consequently, the studies of the Copenhagen School are the most systematic explanations for the widening of the security agenda in Security Studies. The Copenhagen School recognizes the need for defining a broadened security conception without enlarging its perspective on the issue of international order. In this respect, the security conception of the Copenhagen School is based on three main conceptualizations; securitization, sectoral security, and regional security complex theory.

SECTORAL SECURITY

By rejecting the limited perspective of the traditional conception of security concept, the Copenhagen School argues that security is a type of politics that can be applied to a wide range of issues. If survival of the collective units is considered the defining foundation of Security Studies, security analysis can be applied to different sectors without losing the basic characteristics of the security concept. It is a clear response to the limited perspective of traditional security conception with the issues of military security and political security.[27]

The concept of sectoral security reveals that security conditions of human collectivities can be threatened by the developments and the dynamics of five security sectors—military, political, societal, economic, and environmental. The concept of sectoral security has made its contribution for comprehending non-military aspects of security by providing analytical categories for examination of non-military security issues. The state actor is the basic referent object of security in the military security sector, and it is identified concerning threats to territorial integrity, independence, and sovereignty of the state. These externally defined threats are mostly military in their nature.[28] The most apparent aspect of state action within the security realm is the military security sector. Moreover, military tools and instruments have significant domination over the outputs of other security sectors.[29] These characteristics of military security explain the dominant position of military factors in the conceptions of national security and international security.

In the political security sector, legitimacy of governing authority, organizational stability of the state, and ideology of the state are the core values that need to be secured. Threats to political security can be related to ideological and sub-state reasons and conditions through which the state authority and sovereignty can be threatened by significant parts of its people, or the state itself can become a source of threat to its people.[30] Under such circumstances, its legitimacy and authority can be internally questioned.

When the scholars of Security Studies were engaged in studying the security needs of identity-based social groups, they lacked the conceptual and theoretical endowments. That's why the works of the Copenhagen School on societal security represent a valuable attempt to address some crucial weaknesses in existing theories of security. Societal security is about the perceptions of and security situation of identity-based social groups particularly in terms of their relations with other social groups and the state. More specifically, it is about the sustainability—within acceptable conditions for evolution—of traditional patterns of language, culture, association, and religious and national identity, and customs.[31] The concept of societal security addresses the circumstances in which the collective identity of a social group can be threatened by cultural changes, political integration projects like the EU's effort for a common and inclusionary European identity, and large-scale population movements.

In the economic security sector, the concept of security concerns the access ability and capacity of the state actor to necessary markets, finance, and sources to maintain the sustainability of state power and welfare.[32] When it comes to the environmental security sector, it concerns the protection of the ecosystem at both local and global levels since it is vital for all activities of humanity. The referent objects of environmental security are widely defined to include the survival needs of all species, the climate system of our planet, and the protection of biodiversity.

Even though sectors of security identify different sets of issues, they are an integral part of a complex whole. The aim of choosing among security sectors is to reduce the complexity to facilitate security analysis.[33] Given the analytical aim of the sectoral security approach is to differentiate the military, political, economic, societal, and environmental interaction types from each other, there will be disparities for each security sector in terms of particular units, values, nature of the threat, and survival.[34] Therefore, the sources of existential threat for each security sector cannot be addressed in respect to the same framework. Moreover, there is dynamic transitivity between different security sectors. Therefore, attempts that limit the security to only one sector will lead to serious problems in understanding the security more comprehensively.

In its first study on the sectors of security, the Copenhagen School formulated the role of security sectors to demonstrate the different vulnerabilities of the state in terms of its national security.[35] On the other hand, in the book entitled *Identity, Migration and the New Security Agenda in Europe* (1993), the Copenhagen School changed its previous attitude that regards the state as the main referent object of all security sectors, since other referent objects of security apart from the state should be considered to operationalize the sectoral security approach. Thus, the sectoral security approach has transformed from a categorization tool for the determination of important factors for the security of the state into a security concept to explain the transformation of the European security dynamic in the post–Cold War era.[36] Sectoral analysis of security has become more systematic with the publication of the *Security: A New Framework for Analysis* book of the Copenhagen School. This book addressed the referent objects of security, threats, and vulnerabilities, securitizing units that identify the security issue, and finally functional actors that influence the security dynamics in a security sector within the framework of the concept of security sectors.[37]

As a result, the sectoral security approach is vital for the security conception of the Copenhagen School for at least three reasons: First, sectoral security seeks to combine the traditional security conception and new security approaches through maintaining a strong connection with state-centric and military-based security studies. Second, sectoral security reflects the real conditions and issues of human beings by indicating different dimensions of security such as sovereignty, welfare, identity, and sustainability. Third, security sectors provide a way of comprehension for the different qualities of security that are features of the wider security agenda.[38] Although some features of security are common for all security sectors, each sector has its own actors, referent objects, security dynamics, and contradictions.

REGIONAL SECURITY COMPLEX THEORY

The neorealist approach to security studies deals with developing a more general security perspective by taking the systemic factors and conditions into consideration. However, most of the conflicts in international politics have regional origins, dimensions, and dynamics as could be observed with the end of the Cold War. In this respect, Barry Buzan developed the idea of a security complex to introduce the regional level to Security Studies. A Regional security complex can be conceptualized as a geographically well-defined regional security system in which security perceptions and practices are interdependent among regional actors rather than non-regional ones.

Classical regional security complex theory considers regional security complexes as the products of mutual interactions of security concerns of states in a specific region. In this respect, the first characteristic of a regional complex is the existence of at least two or more states. Secondly, component states of a regional security complex constitute a geographically coherent grouping. Thirdly, the relationship among these states is marked by security interdependence that has to be deep and durable, although not permanent.[39] In addition to these characteristics, there are three main components of an essential structure in a security complex. These are (1) the arrangement of the units and the differentiation among them, (2) the patterns of amity and enmity, and (3) the distribution of power among the principal units.[40] Any shift in these components would naturally and normally necessitate a redefinition of the complex. Therefore, a regional security complex can be analyzed in both static and dynamic terms.

In its first definition, a regional security complex theory is defined as a set of states whose major security perceptions and concerns are so interlinked that their national security problems cannot reasonably be analyzed or resolved apart from one another.[41] It is clear that classical formulation of regional security complex theory gives a privileged position to a state actor, and focuses on military and political security sectors and accepts sub-regional systems as an analytical object. Thus, it generates an analytical framework for the examination of regional security systems.

The debates on the need for widening of traditional security conception beyond its military-based perspective, rearrangement of sectoral security perspective to regard the referent objects of security apart from a state actor, and social constructivist perspective of the Copenhagen School in the post–Cold War era all led to the questioning and revisiting of the original meaning of regional security complex theory.[42] For instance, in the definition of societal security concept in the book *Identity, Migration and the New Security Agenda in Europe,* the Copenhagen School questions the security conception of the classical regional security complex theory that focuses on inter-state security relations and dynamics of the military and political security.[43] Moreover, the classical conception of regional security complex theory that is based on geographical proximity and subsequently emerged objective security interdependency had to be amended as a result of the inter-subjective perspective of the Copenhagen School. In this respect, the Copenhagen School has applied the sectoral security conception to the classical regional security complex theory. Thus, the analysis of the regional security complex has gained new dimensions and potential. The regional focus of classical security complex theory has been merged with broadened agenda of security studies.

There are two possible ways of opening the regional security complex theory to sectors other than the military-political and to actors/units other than states: homogeneous security complex and heterogeneous security complex. According to the homogeneous security complex approach, security complexes focus on specific security sectors; for instance, security conception can only be composed of the power struggle between states in the anarchic international system in which specific interactions occur among the like-units of the international system. As a sector-dependent approach, a homogeneous security complex requires a separate framework for each security sector. This logic leads to different types of complexes that occur in different sectors.[44] For instance, while military complexes are made up predominantly of states, a societal complex is composed of identity-based social groups.

The approach of heterogeneous security complexes questions the assumption that security complexes are locked into a specific security sector. According to the approach of a heterogeneous security complex, the regional logic can be integrated with different types of actors/units interacting across two or more security sectors. Such an approach has the advantage to combine the referent objects of security and security sectors. Thus, it enables the analyst to consider the whole picture within a framework.[45]

With the help of new perspectives on the concept of regional security complex, a security complex is redefined as a set of units whose major processes of securitization, desecuritization, or both are so interlinked that their security problems cannot be reasonably analyzed or resolved apart from one another.[46] The formative dynamics and structure of a security complex are normally generated by the units within it. In this process, their security perceptions and security interactions with each other are considered. Thus, the Copenhagen School introduced a revisited version of the classical security complex theory. Instead of material conditions and distribution of power as the main determinants of security relations in a specific region, intersubjective perceptions of units are strongly emphasized to outline the general security conditions of a region.

As a result, although a significant part of the studies of the Copenhagen School is related to the role and position of the state actor in security analysis, the regional level security analysis is also introduced as a different analysis level of security. In this respect, the concept of regional security complex is firstly used to explain the importance of the end of the Cold War for the transformation of regional security dynamics in Europe. Then, the Copenhagen School has applied the concept of regional security complex to the security interdependencies and dynamics of other regions in the world by considering the sectoral security conception and the epistemology of intersubjective security knowledge in its following studies. In this way, the Copenhagen School has sought to demonstrate the universal applicability of its conceptual frameworks.

SECURITIZATION

The Copenhagen School is opposed to the view of understanding of everything as a security issue, since such an attitude would lead to the loss of disciplinary boundaries of the Security Studies. Therefore, the securitization approach has been developed as a formula to make a separation between security issues and political issues. According to the securitization approach, if an issue is not constructed as a security threat through a speech act of a related actor such as a high-level decision-maker or political leader, it will not be characterized as a security threat. Thus, following Ole Wæver's securitization approach,[47] speech act analysis has stood out in the security conception of the Copenhagen School.

Issues in the public sphere can be categorized into three sub-categories; non-politicized, politicized, and securitized. Non-politicized issues mean that the state actor does not deal with them and that they are not a part of any public debate. Politicized issues are a part of public policy, and they require government decision and resource allocation. Securitized issues are considered as existential threats, and they require emergency measures and justify actions and decisions outside the normal political process.[48] Thus, an issue can be presented as a security issue and have an absolute priority due to the arguments in favor of its vitality in the political agenda.

According to the securitization approach, actors with authority for taking measures should present an issue as an existential threat to any referent object of security to be able to construct that issue as a security threat. Therefore, the actor claims a right to handle the issue through extraordinary means, to break the normal procedures and rules of the political realm.[49] The Copenhagen School describes the securitizing actors as "actors who securitize issues by declaring something—a referent object of security—existentially threatened."[50] Political leaders, bureaucrats, lobbies, and pressure groups can be considered as securitizing actors who perform security speech acts.

According to Ole Wæver, who emphasizes the role of political elites in the securitization of the issues, an issue can be transformed into a security issue when it is declared as a security threat by political elites.[51] Indeed securitization tends to be a process dominated by powerful actors who have some privileges in a society. Particularly political elites have a leading role in the securitization process since it is dependent on the capacity and influence of a securitizing actor. Security thinking in terms of a speech act is closely related to the power and knowledge duality that provides the authority to the state for the definition of security. However, structural factors in the process of definition of security constitute limitations for decision-makers. That is why the security speech act is not only made up of the speeches of decision-makers.

When a securitizing move is carried out for the state by statespeople, the separation line between securitizing actor and the referent object of security may not be so clear. For instance, state elites can claim that they have a right to speak in the name of state actor. Indeed, threat discourses are integral parts of state-building and elite legitimacy processes. When it is regarded that the primary security concern of a state is related to its sovereignty and territorial integrity, the focal point of state security and related instruments for achieving it would become obvious. However, it is not easy for other referent objects of the security. If a nationalist activist refers to security of a nation, his/her rhetoric is usually understood as the common perspective of the whole nation. On the other hand, it is well known that collective units like nations and ethnic groups may not have a common view or attitude about any issue.

When a securitizing actor identifies an issue outside of conditions of "normal politics"[52] by using the discourse of existential threat to a referent object, it means that it is faced with a securitization process. Since uttering of security concept is reminiscent of danger, existential threat, and urgency, declaring an issue as a security issue at the same time demands a primary status in the political realm. An actor with existential threat discourse claims a right to handle an issue through emergency ways and means. As a result of the successful securitization process, the related issue is handled in respect to the security realm, instead of a political one.

The real success of a securitization attempt is determined by the audience of the security speech act rather than a securitizing actor. Because the discourse itself that introduces the existential security threat to a referent object of security is just a securitizing move.[53] The securitization of an issue is totally achieved through accepting of such a securitization by a relevant audience. Unless there is such an acceptance by an audience, it is just possible to mention the existence of a securitizing move. One of the aims of security policy is to guide public opinion and provide its support for decisions and actions about security.

Since the approval of the audience for securitization is considered as a *sine qua non* condition, the Copenhagen School suggests an intersubjective process, instead of a subjective one. There is a "negotiation" process between the performing of a securitizing move by a securitizing actor through a security speech act and approval or rejection of it by a relevant audience.[54] Objective approaches in Security Studies view security and security threats as given realities and facts. Although the issues may have objectivity, they can be only transformed into a security issue through the speech act of a securitizing actor, and then they can be securitized as a result of the approval of the audience. Consequently, securitization is required for the construction of an existential threat through security speech acts based on intersubjectivity of security knowledge.

Security measures can consist of some practices such as suspension of some political and civil rights and freedoms. Therefore, Ole Wæver offers the concept of "desecuritization" as much as possible due to the so-called untouchable nature of security issues.[55] Desecuritization of an issue requires providing the necessary conditions for normal attitudes and behaviors through locating the issue outside the security realm. Thus, it will be facilitated to solve an issue in the normal political process through cooperation, negotiation, and dialogue. Wæver, who identifies the desecuritization as an ideal option, claims that the act of securitization has the potential to pave the way for overrated securitization and therefore, it can create "societies of fear."[56] That is why Michael C. Williams claims that securitization should be avoided.[57] However, practical conditions for desecuritization of an issue are not clearly defined by the Copenhagen School.

Thierry Balzacq argues that the securitization approach does not provide a ground for examination of security practices in real conditions. For instance, the wizardly authority of the security concept overlooks the objective context of the security units.[58] The classical securitization approach of the Copenhagen School has not adequately considered the importance of political and social contextual factors in which the security speech act takes shape.[59] Conversely, the nature of the audience and its cultural, social, and psychological conditions have to be analyzed for the success of the securitizing move. However, using "security" concept during the securitization process changes the existing context and creates a new one.[60] The form of understanding and practicing of security concept directly influences the political and social life. Because security concept determines the political priorities.

As a result, the majority of the security analyses of the Copenhagen School concern the role of the state in the security field. Contrary to the book *Security: A New Framework for Analysis*, the Copenhagen School has given a central role to the state actor in security analysis in the book *Regions and Powers*.[61] The growing centrality of the state in security analysis is closely related to the primary position of the state in terms of securitizing actors and threatened referent objects of security. In this framework, it is argued that the Copenhagen School continues to maintain a state-centric security conception and therefore, it does not represent a significant detachment from traditional security conception.

CONCLUSION

Several theories or research programs—often called "schools"—have emerged within Security Studies particularly since the end of the Cold War.[62] In this respect, as one of the critical schools of security studies that developed in Europe, the Copenhagen School has made significant contributions to Security Studies by introducing a substantial body of innovative concepts to rethink the security concept such as security sectors, securitization, and regional security complex theory.[63] Thus, the School has directed its major research to the widening scope of security, the discursive construction of a security threat, and the importance of regional level analysis for international security.

While the Copenhagen School recognizes the necessity of softening the linkage between security and military issues, it emphasizes the efforts that aim at organizing criteria for providing a distinction between security issues and normal politics. In addition, the Copenhagen School does not recognize the mono-sectoral (military and political) attitude of traditional security conception. On the contrary, it argues that security is a kind of politics that can be applied to a wide range of security issues. If we regard the survival needs of collective units and/or principles as the defining core of Security Studies, then we would have a basis for applying security analysis to a variety of sectors (military, political, economic, societal, and environmental) without losing the essential quality of the security concept.

Even though a consensus seems to be emerging on the need for a widening of security concept, disagreement persists about where to draw the line. To expand the notion of security too far would not be practical, since it would merely create the need for an additional term for "traditional security." In this respect, the concept of securitization replaces the focus on physical violence and military issues with a focus on the inter-subjective construction of security threats in a broader agenda.[64] In the context of the epistemological dimension of the securitization concept, the works of the Copenhagen School constitute the most concerted attempt to develop a framework for the study of security in the constructivist tradition. The securitization process can have different "referent objects," depending on whether they belong to an economic, environmental, political, military, or societal sector. Indeed, existential threats may be directed toward various referent objects of security other than the state. Consequently, as a middle ground between traditional security conception and new/critical perspectives on security, the strength of the Copenhagen School—to a significant extent—relies on the implementation of its theoretical and conceptual innovations in empirical studies.

REFERENCES

Ağır, Bülent S. "Reconsidering Security Predicament of Weak States in the Context of Human Security and Societal Security." *European Journal of Human Security* 2, (2018): 31–53.

Baldwin, David A. "The Concept of Security." *Review of International Studies* 23, no. 1 (1997): 5–26.

Balzacq, Thierry. "Three Faces of Securitization: Political Agency, Audience and Context." *European Journal of International Relations* 11, no. 2 (2005): 171–201.

Burchill, Scott. "Realism and Neorealism." In *Theories of International Relations*, edited by Scott Burchill and Andrew Linklater, 67–92. London: Macmillan Press, 1996.

Buzan, Barry. *People, States and Fear: National Security Problem in International Relations.* Sussex: Wheatsheaf, 1983.

Buzan, Barry. *People, States and Fear: An Agenda for International Security Studies in the Post-Cold War Era.* London: Lynne Rienner, 1991.

Buzan, Barry. "Rethinking Security after the Cold War." *Cooperation and Conflict* 32, no. 1 (1997): 5–28.

Buzan, Barry and Lene Hansen. *The Evolution of International Security Studies.* Cambridge: Cambridge University Press, 2009.

Buzan, Barry, Morten Kelstrup, Pierre Lemaitre, Elzbieta Tromer and Ole Wæver. *The European Security Order Recast: Scenarios for the Post-Cold War Era.* London: Pinter, 1990.

Buzan, Barry and Ole Wæver. "Slippery, Contradictory? Sociologically Untenable?: The Copenhagen School Replies." *Review of International Studies* 23, no. 2 (1997): 241–250.

Buzan, Barry and Ole Wæver. *Regions and Powers: The Structure of International Security.* Cambridge: Cambridge University Press, 2003.

Buzan, Barry, Ole Wæver, and Jaap de Wilde. *Security: A New Framework for Analysis.* Boulder: Lynne Rienner, 1998.

C.A.S.E. Collective. "Critical Approaches to Security in Europe: A Networked Manifesto." *Security Dialogue* 37, no. 4 (2006): 443–487.

Clark, Ian. *Globalization and International Relations Theory.* New York: Oxford University Press, 1999.

Emmers, Ralf. "Securitization." In *Contemporary Security Studies*, edited by Alan Collins, 131–144. Oxford: Oxford University Press, 2010.

Huysmans, Jef. "Revisiting Copenhagen: Or, On the Creative Development of a Security Studies Agenda in Europe." *European Journal of International Relations* 4, no. 4 (1998): 479–505.

Knudsen, Olav F. "Post-Copenhagen Security Studies: Desecuritizing Securitization." *Security Dialogue* 32, no. 3 (2001): 355–368.

Krause, Keith and Michael C. Williams, *Critical Security Studies, Concepts and Cases.* London: UCL Press, 1997.

McDonald, Matt. "Securitization and the Construction of Security." *European Journal of International Relations* 14, no. 4, (2008): 563–587.

McSweeney, Bill. "Identity and Security: Buzan and the Copenhagen School." *Review of International Studies* 22, no. 1 (1996): 81–93.

McSweeney, Bill. *Security, Identity and Interests: A Sociology of International Relations.* Cambridge: Cambridge University Press, 1999.

Miller, Benjamin. "The Concept of Security: Should It Be Redefined?" *The Journal of Strategic Studies* 24, no. 2 (2001): 13–42.

Mutimer, David. "Critical Security Studies: Schismatic History." In *Contemporary Security Studies*, edited by Alan Collins, 53–74. Oxford: Oxford University Press, 2007.

Ripsman, Norrin M. and T. V. Paul. "Globalization and the National Security State: A Framework for Analysis." *International Studies Review* 7, no. 2 (2005): 202–222.

Stritzel, Holger. "Towards a Theory of Securitization: Copenhagen and Beyond." *European Journal of International Relations* 13, no. 3 (2007): 357–383.

Ullman, Richard. "Redefining Security." *International Security* 8, no. 1 (1983): 162–177.

Wæver, Ole. "Securitization and Desecuritization." In *On Security*, edited by Ronnie D. Lipschutz, 46–86. New York: Columbia University Press, 1995.

Wæver, Ole. "Aberystwyth, Paris, Copenhagen: New Schools in Security Theory and Their Origins between Core and Periphery," 2004. Accessed March 10, 2022. http://www.scribd.com/doc/40010349/Ole-Waever-Aberystwyth-Paris-enNew-Schools-in-Security-Theory-and-Their-Origins-Between-Core-andPeriphery.

Wæver, Ole, Pierre Lemaitre, and Elzbieta Tromer. *European Polyphony: Perspectives Beyond East-West Confrontation*. London: Macmillan, 1989.

Wæver, Ole, Barry Buzan, Morten Kelstrup and Pierre Lemaitre. *Identity, Migration and the New Security Agenda in Europe*. London: Pinter, 1993.

Walt, Stephen. "The Renaissance of Security Studies." *International Studies Quarterly* 35, no. 2 (1991): 211–239.

Waltz, Kenneth. *Theory of International Politics*. New York: McGraw-Hill Inc., 1979.

Williams, Michael C. "Words, Images, Enemies: Securitization and International Politics." *International Studies Quarterly* 47, no. 4 (2003): 511–532.

NOTES

1. For the traditional view of security conception, see Stephen Walt, "The Renaissance of Security Studies," *International Studies Quarterly* 35, no. 2 (1991): 211–239.

2. Bill McSweeney, *Security, Identity and Interests: A Sociology of International Relations* (Cambridge: Cambridge University Press, 1999), 35.

3. For critical security studies, see Keith Krause and Michael C. Williams, *Critical Security Studies, Concepts and Cases* (London: UCL Press, 1997).

4. David A. Baldwin, "The Concept of Security," *Review of International Studies* 23, no. 1 (1997): 13.

5. See Barry Buzan, *People, States and Fear: National Security Problem in International Relations* (Sussex: Wheatsheaf, 1983), 3–9; Barry Buzan, *People, States and Fear: An Agenda for International Security Studies in the Post-Cold Era* (London: Lynne Rienner, 1991), 3–12.

6. Ian Clark, *Globalization and International Relations Theory* (New York: Oxford University Press, 1999), 114.

7. Norrin M. Ripsman and T. V. Paul, "Globalization and the National Security State: A Framework for Analysis," *International Studies Review* 7, no. 2 (2005): 202–222.

8. Kenneth Waltz, *Theory of International Politics* (New York: McGraw-Hill Inc., 1979), 88–99.

9. Benjamin Miller, "The Concept of Security: Should It Be Redefined?," *The Journal of Strategic Studies* 24, no. 1 (2001): 15.

10. Miller, "The Concept of Security," 16–17.

11. Scott Burchill, "Realism and Neorealism," in *Theories of International Relations*, ed. Scott Burchill and Andrew Linklater (London: Macmillan Press, 1996), 86.

12. Bülent Sarper Ağır, "Reconsidering Security Predicament of Weak States in the Context of Human Security and Societal Security," *European Journal of Human Security* 2, (2018): 31–53.

13. For advocators of widening security conception, see Richard H. Ullman, "Redefining Security," *International Security* 8, no. 1 (1983): 129–153; Barry Buzan, "Rethinking Security after the Cold War," *Cooperation and Conflict* 32, no. 1 (1997): 5–28.

14. Miller, "The Concept of Security," 19.

15. Miller, "The Concept of Security," 20.

16. David Mutimer considers the Copenhagen School as a part of critical security studies. David Mutimer, "Critical Security Studies: Schismatic History," in *Contemporary Security Studies*, ed. Alan Collins (Oxford: Oxford University Press, 2007), 53–74. See about the middle or third way position of the Copenhagen School, Barry Buzan and Lene Hansen, *The Evolution of International Security Studies* (Cambridge: Cambridge University Press, 2009), 260.

17. The other main research projects of COPRI were European Security, Military Restructuring, Security in the Nordic and Baltic Sea Region, Intra-State Conflicts: Causes and Peace Strategies, and Global Governance and Peace. In January 2005, it was merged with Danish Institute for International Affairs. CASE Collective, "Critical Approaches to Security in Europe: A Networked Manifesto," *Security Dialogue* 37, no. 4 (2006): 447.

18. The term "Copenhagen School" is first used by Bill McSweeney in order to depict the views and studies of Barry Buzan, Ole Wæver, and other scholars on security concept in the framework of the Copenhagen Peace Research Institute. Bill McSweeney, "Identity and Security: Buzan and the Copenhagen School," *Review of International Studies* 22 (1996): 81–93.

19. Jef Huysmans, "Revisiting Copenhagen: Or, On the Creative Development of a Security Studies Agenda in Europe," *European Journal of International Relations* 4, no. 4 (1998): 484.

20. Huysmans, "Revisiting Copenhagen," 480.

21. Ole Wæver, Pierre Lemaitre, and Elzbieta Tromer, *European Polyphony: Perspectives Beyond East-West Confrontation* (London: Macmillan, 1989).

22. Huysmans, "Revisiting Copenhagen," 490.

23. Barry Buzan and Ole Wæver, *Regions and Powers: The Structure of International Security* (Cambridge: Cambridge University Press, 2003).

24. Huysmans, "Revisiting Copenhagen," 482.

25. Although all members of the School do not advocate the assumptions of neorealism, they agree that it has an important place in the analysis of international relations. Barry Buzan, Morten Kelstrup, Pierre Lemaitre, Elzbieta Tromer, and Ole Wæver, *The European Security Order Recast: Scenarios for the Post-Cold War Era* (London: Pinter, 1990).

26. Barry Buzan, Ole Wæver, and Jaap de Wilde, *Security: A New Framework for Analysis* (Boulder: Lynne Rienner, 1998).

27. Buzan, *People, States*, 15.

28. Buzan, Wæver, and de Wilde, *Security: A New*, 49–70.

29. Buzan, Kelstrup, Lemaitre, Tromer, and Wæver, *The European Security Order*, 4.

30. Buzan, Wæver and de Wilde, *Security: A New*, 141–162.

31. Ole Wæver, Barry Buzan, Morten Kelstrup, and Pierre Lemaitre, *Identity, Migration and the New Security Agenda in Europe* (London: Pinter, 1993), 17–40.

32. Buzan, Wæver, and de Wilde, *Security: A New*, 95–117.

33. Buzan, Wæver, and de Wilde, *Security: A New*, 8.

34. Buzan, Wæver, and de Wilde, *Security: A New*, 27.

35. Buzan, *People, States*, 116–134.

36. Wæver, Buzan, Kelstrup, and Lemaitre, *Identity, Migration*, 21–27.

37. Buzan, Wæver, and de Wilde, *Security: A New*.

38. Buzan, Wæver, and de Wilde, *Security: A New*, 195–196.

39. Buzan, Wæver, and de Wilde, *Security: A New*, 15.

40. Buzan, Wæver, and de Wilde, *Security: A New*, 13.

41. Buzan, Wæver, and de Wilde, *Security: A New*, 12.

42. Huysmans, "Revisiting Copenhagen," 497.

43. Wæver, Buzan, Kelstrup, and Lemaitre, *Identity, Migration*.

44. Buzan, Wæver, and de Wilde, *Security: A New*, 16–17.

45. Buzan, Wæver, and de Wilde, *Security: A New*, 16–17.

46. Buzan, Wæver, and de Wilde, *Security: A New*, 201.

47. Ole Wæver, "Securitization and Desecuritization," in *On Security*, ed. Ronnie Lipschutz (New York: Columbia University Press, 1995), 46–66.

48. Buzan, Wæver. and de Wilde, *Security: A New*, 23.

49. Buzan, Wæver, and de Wilde, *Security: A New*, 23–24.

50. Buzan, Wæver, and de Wilde, *Security: A New*, 36.

51. Wæver, "Securitization and Desecuritization," 54.

52. The Copenhagen School does not define the concept of "normal politics" in respect to the securitization concept.

53. Buzan, Wæver, and de Wilde, *Security: A New*, 24–25.

54. Holger Stritzel, "Towards a Theory of Securitization: Copenhagen and Beyond," *European Journal of International Relations* 13, no. 3 (2007): 362–363.

55. Wæver, "Securitization and Desecuritization," 56–57.

56. Wæver, "Securitization and Desecuritization," 64.

57. Michael C. Williams, "Words, Images, Enemies: Securitization and International Politics," *International Studies Quarterly* 47, no. 4 (2003): 523.

58. See for the discussion Thierry Balzacq, "The Three Faces of Securitization: Political Agency, Audience and Context," *European Journal of International Relations* 11, no. 2 (2005): 171–201.

59. Matt McDonald, "Securitization and the Construction of Security," *European Journal of International Relations* 14, no. 4 (2008): 571.

60. Stritzel, "Towards a Theory," 361.

61. Buzan and Wæver, *Regions and Powers.*

62. Ole Wæver, "Aberystwyth, Paris, Copenhagen: New Schools in Security Theory and Their Origins between Core and Periphery," 2004, accessed on March 10, 2022, http://www.scribd.com/doc/40010349/Ole-Waever-Aberystwyth-Paris-enNew -Schools-in-Security-Theory-and-Their-Origins-Between-Core-andPeriphery.

63. Ralf Emmers, "Securitization," in *Contemporary Security Studies*, ed. Alan Collins (Oxford: Oxford University Press, 2010), 137.

64. Olav F. Knudsen, "Post-Copenhagen Security Studies: Desecuritizing Securitization," *Security Dialogue* 32, no. 3 (2001): 358.

Chapter 7

Paris School and the Theory of Insecurity

Tayyar Arı

INTRODUCTION

The unexpected end of the Cold War and the failure of traditional mainstream theories to predict this process and analyze it adequately and satisfactorily led to the emergence of social critical theories and their popularity in international relations. Moreover, social and political developments, the increase in the role of transnational and supranational structures, and the fact that security reasons and security providers are not limited to the state have facilitated and encouraged the emergence and acceptance of new theories.

North America is especially known as the center of traditional and mainstream theories, while Europe has come to the fore with more critical theories. In this context, the influence of Europe in the post–Cold War era, in which the debates on enlargement and deepening of security studies have intensified, has significantly strengthened its place in security studies. It has been observed that environmental, social, political, and economic security has also been studied intensively, although the mainstream theories are based only on military security and national security. The critical theory led to a revolutionary transformation centered on human and social security rather than national security and answered the question of whose security. In the context of deepening, in contrast to the traditional mainstream theories that only take the state as the main actor and the only unit of analysis, the individual, society, and human have become the unit of analysis. As the level of analysis, the individual, group, state, regional, and global level replaces the state and system level. In this context, it is seen that the Securitization Theory, Emancipatory Theory, and Insecurity Theory, in other words, the Copenhagen

School, the Aberystwyth (Wales) School, and the Paris School, have begun to dominate security studies.[1]

This chapter explains the Paris School or theory of insecurity and, in this context, its similarities to and differences from other critical security approaches; and that is why for the Paris school, (in)securitization is not just a speech act that legitimizes the extraordinary and the exception, and why many different instruments are being used. The chapter also discusses important concepts such as speech act, surveillance, ban-opticon, governmentality, dispositive, Mobius strip, and internal-external security. And the relation between the migration problem and (in)security in Europe is also analyzed because according to Didier Bigo, the issue of migration is generally perceived as a security problem.

CRITICAL APPROACHES TO SECURITY

Along with the constructivist theory, known for the works of Alexander Wendt,[2] one of the first theories in the field of critical studies, it was revealed that national interest was not a static and fixed phenomenon but was constructed depending on intersubjective interactions and changed depending on identity. On the other hand, the international structure was seen as a socially constructed structure with an ever-changing and dynamic nature rather than as an anarchic structure consisting of power configurations. Wendt introduces that anarchy is not a common situation that does not change for everyone but rather an imaginative thing that differs depending on the states' perceptions and identities. The international social structure, identity, and interest constantly affect each other and change in a reconstructed interaction process. Therefore, the social structure came to the fore instead of material structures and subjectivity instead of objectivity. [3]

On the other hand, the Copenhagen School,[4] one of the first initiatives in the context of critical security theories, reveals that security is not an objective phenomenon. While traditional security approaches focused only on military security, political, economic, social, and environmental security issues were also included in the topics within the framework of the concept of security sectors. In addition, it was revealed that the reference object of security was not only the state but also individual and social groups. In other words, there was expansion in the context of the subject of security and deepening in the context of the reference object of security.[5]

The Copenhagen school contributed three concepts to the field: 1) Securitization, 2) Security Sectors, and 3) Regional Security Complex. The first of these is more widely known, and the concept of Securitization Theory is mainly used instead of the concept of the Copenhagen School. Security

Sectors include economic, social, and environmental security, besides military and political security. The Regional Security Complex, on the other hand, is a concept put forward concerning the importance of the regional level in security analysis and focused on how security could be provided at the regional level.

Securitization theory criticizes the traditional meaning of security which was seen as an objective phenomenon. According to the securitization theory, the process starts when the securitizing actor encodes a subject or a group as an existential threat to the reference object. Convincing the audience means that securitization is successful, and it is possible to go beyond ordinary rules and legal principles and use extraordinary methods. The point to be noted here is the extraordinary nature of the threat and the need for exceptional methods to deal with it.[6] Before securitization, the issue was seen as an ordinary political issue and could be dealt with by normal legal and political means. However, after securitization is accomplished, the way for non-democratic methods is open to be seen as legitimate in the struggle against it. The coding of the threat and attribution of the extraordinary is a subjective situation entirely related to the perception and preference of the securitizing actor.[7] According to the Copenhagen school, securitization can be reversed by the securitizing actor, the problem is returned to the political arena again, or it may cease as a security issue. This process is known as desecuritization. [8]

On the other hand, the emancipatory theory is considered to be the pioneer of critical security theories because it is the first theory that comes to mind when critical security studies are mentioned. The school's views, also known as the Welsh School and whose contemporary representatives are Ken Booth and John Wyns, are mainly based on the Frankfurt School, and in a sense, it represents the Frankfurt School's approach to security. In the Welsh school,[9] as in the Frankfurt school, the concept of emancipation[10] is at the center of the theory. The concept of "emancipation" here, unlike "freedom" in liberal theory, means getting rid of the political, economic, and social conditions that condition people and force certain behaviors. It means getting rid of the conditions that prevent people from being aware of their own selves and living humanely. In this context, the concept of security becomes a normative concept, and it is aimed at getting rid of the false consciousness that surrounds people. People are reminded that they are not without choice and that they do not have to accept the conditions they are in. For Ken Booth, too, security can be achieved by rescuing people from the conditions surrounding them that make them insecure. The normative agenda is also prominent for the Frankfurt school, on which the Welsh School is based, and in this sense, the epistemological perspectives are anti-positivist. The theory is political and is not independent of people's tendencies and personal preferences. Robert Cox summed it up with the phrase "theory is always for someone and for some purposes." Therefore, in the 1920s, the Frankfurt School, which brought together names from different fields such as Theodore Adorno, Herbert Marcuse, Max Horkheimer, and Erich Fromm, did not emerge as an international relations theory or a security theory.[11]

According to the Aberystwyth School, like the Copenhagen School, security is a socially constructed phenomenon and is political. However, according to the Welsh School, not only is the security but also the security object constructed.[12] In addition, the issue of enlargement and deepening[13] is more prominent and includes social and humanitarian issues in the scope of security.

On the other hand, the Paris school shows that national and international, and security and insecurity are like the intertwined Mobius strip. In this process, the diversification and proliferation of threats and actors played an important role and led to the discussion of the traditional paradigm. This situation has made it necessary to associate internal security with external security and external security with internal security. In particular, the International School of Political Sociology or the Paris School, which focused its studies on EU examples, was skeptical of the sectoral distinction of security and insisted that security be essentially social. Although it differs from the Copenhagen school in many respects in general, it draws attention to the fact that securitization is a speech act process, but other tools are also used. However, as in other critical theories, it breaks with traditional realist/positivist theories in that it has a constructivist character and accepts that security is subjective and political rather than objective.[14]

THE PARIS SCHOOL AND THEORY OF INSECURITY

The Paris school and insecurity approach are mainly based on the philosophy of Foucault and Bourdieu. However, the name the PARIS school is not only due to the fact that the philosophers and scientists who developed the theory were of French origin and did their studies in Paris. According to Didier Bigo, one of the leading writers of the Paris school, the name of the school consists of the initials of Political Anthropological Research for International Sociology. The Paris school is an interdisciplinary approach to security that demonstrates how different disciplines explain security.[15]

The Paris school began in 2007 with the studies published in the journal *International Political Sociology*, edited by Didier Bigo. The journal started its publication in 2006 as one of the main publications of the ISA. In this context, Didier Bigo, R.B.J (Rob) Walker, and Jef Huysmans can be seen as the first names to contribute to this field. They have a mission aiming to highlight the sociological perspective that traditional IR theories have neglected, as well as focus on the "global" rather than the concept of "international," on which traditional theories focus. In other words, scholars of IPS preferred to focus on areas that traditional approaches neglect. They intended to eliminate the dominance of political science in the field by including transdisciplinary fields such as geography, anthropology, and history rather than merely making a sociological analysis. In a sense, they wanted to bridge the gap between IR, sociology, and social theory. In this context, the increase in sociological analyses in IR began to be discussed, and they pioneered the gradual spread of pluralism in IR. Considering the fields of study, areas such as feminism and post-colonialism came first. In addition, their critical and reflective nature and emphasis on post-modern and post-structuralist analyses were among their most distinctive features.[16]

> Certainly we want to continue fostering the productive transdisciplinary conversations that our predecessors established between IR, Political Theory, and Sociology. However, we are keen to enliven our interstitial starting place between the international-political-sociological by encouraging further transdisciplinary conversations across disciplines such as Anthropology, Geography, Criminology, History, Political Economy, Literature, and Creative Arts.[17]

CONCEPT OF SECURITY AND THE (IN)SECURITIZATION

The Paris school and Didier Bigo draw attention to the fact that the traditional approach of international relations associates security with state security and, in this context, looks at the problem as a problem of survival. According to conventional theories, issues such as internal security and crime are not considered issues that concern IR. However, the approach of European-centered critical security studies has changed this traditional perspective. In fact, although terrorism and organized crime were seen as the subject of IR to the extent that they are global, with 9/11, the real development on this issue started with Barry Buzan's work in 1983, which expanded security and added economic, social, and environmental security to the concepts of military and political security. In addition, the traditional approach to seeing the reference object of security as a state and a matter of survival has also changed to some extent. Although it was possible for the state to be the reference object, especially in these two and even the first three, it was possible to see certain groups and communities as the reference objects in the fourth and fifth. However, it can be said that the reference object itself is a subject of discussion because while any state or political party is trying to present a social problem, such as immigration, as a threat to a certain social segment, it may be trying to hide its interests behind the scenes. Or, a certain social group or political party may argue that the state is endangering national identity by not allowing immigration or making necessary border checks. Or they may argue that they are defending the security of society by opposing immigration. Therefore, both the extension of security and the object of reference are concepts that are controversial and open to criticism in the last instance. Bigo argues that international political sociology's view of security is needed in this sense. However, the Paris school thinks that the meaning of "international" is not very clear and should be discussed.[18]

Bigo also includes the analysis of sociology and criminology, which the traditional approaches of IRs leave out. However, the sociological approach was used by social constructivists and the Copenhagen school before Bigo, but for Bigo, sociology is central to analyzing security, not secondary or supplementary. According to Bigo, the security concept comprises a winner and a loser. In other words, when making one secure, you make another insecure. The ones who legitimize security can sometimes be local actors, sometimes states and national actors. The definition of what security is also requires defining what insecurity is. While one speaks of security and legitimizes the tools it uses, it means insecurity for the other.[19]

According to Başaran and Dido, security cannot be handled by being abstracted from practical realities. Instead, it is a special method developed against the group or actor that a dominant actor or group needs to be protected. "Security" operates as a distinctive method that legitimizes and imposes a political program for a dominant group to evaluate who should be protected, who can be sacrificed, and who can be designated as an object of fear and subject to coercion and control. In this process, the attempt to achieve maximum security leads to maximum insecurity, contrary to the claim of traditional security approaches. At the same time, declaring a reference object as an object of security or insecurity is purely political. Securitization, or rather (in)securitization, is central to understanding discursive and non-discursive practices of what is threat and what is fear, what is danger, or what should be protected.[20]

THE CONCEPT OF "INTERNATIONAL," MOBIUS STRIP, INDIFFERENCE, AND INTERNAL-EXTERNAL SECURITY

The Paris School scholars discuss the scope and meaning of the concept of "international," as it is mentioned above. The convergence and interlinking of the concepts of "international" and "sociology" must be put forward due to the great need for cooperation between these two fields. The journal members aimed to carry out an interdisciplinary study within this framework to show how intertwined sociology and international relations are. As a result of the efforts of international political sociology, the academic culture of international relations has begun to change to a certain extent.[21]

The Paris school claims, especially after the end of the Cold War, that the distinction between inside and outside in terms of security became blurred. In this context, while internal security officers, such as the police, gendarmerie, and other internal security elements, are looking for the enemy, that is, the source of security outside, external security units (soldiers and intelligence units) are also looking inside. In this context, the focus is on foreign nationals, immigrants, and people living in slums. While the internal security units (police, gendarmes, customs guards and border guards, and national police forces) are looking for the enemy beyond the borders, they concentrate on organized crime networks, immigrants, and asylum seekers.[22]

On the other hand, political sociology discusses the meaning of borders while opening up the concept of international for discussion. They draw attention to the fact that borders separating the inside from the outside and separating the inside from the international serve to define the other. In this context, it serves to express religious, cultural, and similar identities. Consequently, borders cause wars, conflicts, and exclusion, i.e., they become the cause of all exclusion and marginalization. Although the borders are the lines separating two nations, two states, or two identities under normal conditions, which is seen as indispensable in the classical understanding, school members draw attention to the fact that the borders do not correspond to such a strict separation anymore. Boundaries can no longer clearly distinguish between inside and outside because they are similar to the Mobius strip, intertwined, and cannot clearly define the areas of sovereignty.[23]

The Paris school also sees the concepts of security and insecurity as intertwined and difficult to separate from each other, like in the Mobius strip. The Paris school reveals that securitization/insecurity is a situation we constantly experience in our daily life. The intertwining of internal and external security and its appearance as a Mobius strip brought about the de-differentiation of internal and external security. Traditional theories reject the idea that internal security is under the control of the police (internal security elements) and external security is under the authority of soldiers and other army members. In addition, although there is an intersubjective process in the process of (in)securitization, they defend the existence of an objective situation and, like post-structuralists, completely oppose relativity. Reference is made to Bourdieu by arguing that the habitus/fields of the actors involved in the (in)securitization/securitization process and their capitals play an important role. In a later work, Didier Bigo prefers the concept of "patrimony of

Tayyar Arı

dispositions" used by Bruno Lahire instead of the capital and habitus he borrowed from Bourdieu.

> This terminology of the "patrimony of dispositions insisting on the generative capacity to act via the actors" "aptitudes and competences" has the advantage of adjusting the concept of the heritage of habitus by highlighting the concepts of legacy and inheritance (patrimony), without presupposing that the system of dispositions remains durable, transposable or generally permanent within an individual. On the contrary, the patrimony of dispositions insists on the strength and time of the actors' socialization by distinguishing between weak and strong systems of dispositions and competences and by discussing their transposability in each case and context.[24]

Attention should be drawn to the subjectivity of insecurity in the sense that it is also a process defined through the other. It is also pointed out that there is no security problem but that it actually stems from not accepting the existence of the other. According to the Paris school, security refers to a different understanding of securitization, meaning the capacity to control borders, manage threats, define endangered identities, and define areas of order. Thus, it shifts our attention in three ways. First, instead of analyzing security as a fundamental concept, the Paris School proposes to consider security as a "governmentality." Second, this approach focuses on the effects of power games rather than investigating the intentions behind the use of power. Third, rather than focusing on "speech acts," the Paris School emphasizes the practices, audiences, and contexts that enable and constrain the production of certain forms of government.[25]

WHOSE SECURITY AND AGAINST WHOM: CONSTRUCTING INSECURITY

The Paris School, like other critical security theories, assumes that security/insecurity is socially constructed. Like other critical theories, it generally accepts a constructed reality rather than a given reality. In this context, just as critical approaches focus on subjective knowledge rather than objective knowledge, the Paris School also argues that security and insecurity are produced/constructed by (in)securitizing actors/security professionals for some purposes and concerns rather than being a given and unchanging reality.

> A common-sense answer would be to say that insecurity refers to threats or dangers to someone. Insecurity is a politically and socially constructed phenomenon. The problem for security knowledge is then first of all one of threat definition: what threatens whom? Insecurities differ depending on the nature

of the threat and the referent object that is threatened. It leads to the view that insecurities, at least for analytical purposes, can be organized into different security sectors. The key question of the former issue is whether the threat is real or perceived. It is based on the traditional distinction between objective and subjective security that has structured both security studies and security politics for a long time.[26]

However, human security and national security can sometimes be intertwined, and states may implement national security policies on humanitarian grounds. "One way of characterizing the difference between human security and national security is to highlight their distinct threat definition. The former refers to the protection of the individual from a wide range of dangers potentially threatening a sustainable form of life. The latter refers primarily to defending the national territory and the citizens of a state from external aggression."[27]

Huysmans also describes insecurity as a socially constructed policy. Security that excludes one or is defined through the other makes others insecure. The social construction of security/insecurity is not a very special situation; this always happens. Under normal circumstances, insecurity is the situation where there is a threat or danger to someone. Then, there will be a threat to whom and by whom. Insecurity may vary depending on the nature of the threat and the reference object whose security is threatened. While there could be a threat to identity in the social security sector, there may be a military attack on the security of the state in the military sector. Huysmans also points out, unlike traditional security approaches, that insecurity is a subjective and political concept. He points out that it has become an important tool in the formation of security policies, especially for governments. It is instrumentalized by selecting a danger and a threat for certain political purposes and activating certain security mechanisms. He points out that it has become an important tool in the formation of security policies, especially for governments. It is instrumentalized by choosing a threat and a threat for certain political purposes and activating certain security mechanisms. In this process, discourse is used not only to determine the threat but also to determine the instruments that are used.

Like some other non-traditional approaches to security, the Paris school treats security as a social construction as opposed to an objective reality. . . . All of Bigo's (and by extension the Paris school's) works are informed by the same key assumption, namely that there is a merger of—what he calls—"internal" and "external" security into a "field of security," whereby the border between the two ceases to exist. The border between "internal" and "external" here is tantamount to the borders of sovereign nation states. According to Bigo, the end of bipolarity and the rise of the European Union, both have contributed to the undoing of this distinction. Thus, the lapse of the more traditional threats to security have left both internal and external security agents desperate for a reason d'être.[28]

In this context, ontologically, it depends on subjective rather than objective ontology and draws attention to the role of language, discourse, and inter-subjective interactions in producing reality. Both social realities and material realities are constructed through a linguistic process. However, the Paris School differs from both the Copenhagen School and the constructivist theory at this point. It draws attention to the fact that non-linguistic technological instruments are also used effectively in this process. "That is, language plays a central role in the modulation of security domains. But, the development and implementation of technological artifacts and knowledge, such as diagrams, computer networks, scientific data, and even the specific forms that need filling in, do more than simply implementing a policy decision that arose from a particular discursive framing of events."[29]

The (in)securitization process requires an extraordinary threat, while many problems can be defined as extraordinary threats to internal security recently. Terrorism, uncontrolled labor migration, asylum, human trafficking, and cross-border criminal activity have been integrated into an internal security field.[30]

The Paris School and IPS ask who, under what conditions, and against whom, and what consequences there are in the attempt of insecurity. According to the Copenhagen School, security is provided by securitization and requires a discursive process. This is called speech act in language theory and is based on Carl Schmitt and reflects a somewhat constructivist understanding. Successful speech act (securitization) also requires successful language and a society that will accept it. Of course, security seems to be a dialogical and intersubjective process. Those who initiate the discourse also decide what an existential threat is because the speech act is essential in presenting a security issue as a vital threat. For successful securitization, the audience must be convinced of it; otherwise, it will remain an attempt of securitization.[31]

On the other hand, Bigo emphasizes that securitization is not just a successful speech act. This also reveals the insecurity process of the Paris School. (In)securitization is not only done through a speech act but rather develops in a multidimensional process involving many different security actors. Therefore, someone who analyzes the securitization process does not only focus on the discursive process but also uses very different methods. Also, they are not interested in concepts such as the deepening and expansion of security because insecurity is a phenomenon we can encounter almost all the time.

Discursive formations and speech acts are not enough to understand how security works; As much as scholars focus on the quality of the spoken word, they need to look at both its perlocutionary nature and the conditions of security practices. While these conditions are undoubtedly mental (social), they also include physical, technical, material, and historical elements. Therefore, security includes discursive and non-discursive practices. The Paris School argues that this process cannot be limited to just speech acts, and that its sociological dimension should also be considered. Thus, the sociological approach differs from the Copenhagen school, which focuses on discursive and non-discursive practices (one does not have priority over the other) and treats security as a purely linguistic process.[32]

SPEECH ACT, SURVEILLANCE, BAN-OPTICON, GOVERNMENTALITY, AND DISPOSITIVE

For the Paris school, (in)securitization is not just a speech act that legitimizes the extraordinary and the exception, as the Copenhagen School expresses. Many different methods are used in this process. Surveillance includes technology and sometimes a process in which many different methods are used although it works like an ordinary process. In fact, ignoring them is due to the fact that they see internal and external security as two different fields. However, internally, the security elements and the police force use very different methods and manage the process with a Foucauldian understanding, using concepts such as the survival of the state and public order. On the other hand, the Paris school does not ignore the fact that the speech act is a fundamental concept in this process, but it is taken into account that other security professionals are involved in this process by different means, apart from the political elite. In fact, actors and groups directly or indirectly related to this security may present the issue as a daily issue to create the exceptional infrastructure in question. Generally, these measures are not presented as a matter of survival; for example, immigration and border control are carried out within the framework of a routine that protects freedom. Therefore, society does not see it as an extraordinary situation. The best example of this is Frontex. Although the first establishment of the European border and coast guard institution was in 2005, it became effective during the 2015–2016 period and aimed to protect the Schengen borders against migration. Therefore, this process is quite normal and does not appear to be anything extraordinary but there is a process of (in)securitization.[33]

On the other hand, instead of Foucault's concept of the panopticon, which expresses the surveillance of modern society, Didier Bigo uses the term "ban-opticon," which states that whoever is identified as a security problem will be put under surveillance. Therefore, instead of panopticon surveillance, which is in question due to the principle of governmentality in postmodern societies, he prefers the concept of ban-opticon, which indicates a situation in which the securitized segment is monitored by the development of technology.[34]

> The notion of "ban" originates from international relations (IR) and critical security studies and is on a parallel track with surveillance studies. The ban-opticon deconstructs some of the post–September 11 analysis as a "permanent state of emergency" or as a "generalized state of exception," which reinstates the question of who decides about the exception in the heart of the IR debate: who is sovereign, and who can legitimately name the public enemy. The ban-opticon dispositif is established in relation to a state of unease created by the United States and its allies. The United States has propagated the idea that there is a global "in-security," which is attributed to the development of threats of mass destruction, thought to be derived from terrorist and other criminal organizations and governments that support them.[35]

As noted above, the Paris school or (in)securitization theory or sociological approach considers security with (in)securitization. It is not separated from the characters and stances of the actors involved in the (in)securitization process. In addition, this process cannot be understood by looking at the intention of the securitizing actor; it is necessary to look at the practices that come into play in this process. Finally, it is not enough to look only at the speech act; therefore, according to the sociological approach, it is necessary to look at the concepts of dispositif, habitus, and field.[36] While the concepts of habitus and field are taken from Bourdieu, the concept of dispositif is taken from Foucault. According to Foucault, the concept of dispositif includes discourses, institutions, architectural forms, regulatory decisions, laws, administrative measures, scientific expressions, and philosophical, moral, and philanthropic/humanistic propositions; in short, many things are said and unsaid. On the other hand, the concept of field is a conceptualization with three basic features, referring to Bourdieu. It is the field of power, the field of struggle, and the field of domination. To these, Bigo adds the cross-power field. Although this is an area where transnational professional security actors are also involved, the most well-known actors are the police and soldiers.[37]

    First of all, if we describe the qualities of the concept of field, Bourdieu states that it is an order based on the existence of struggles. It is possible to say that these struggles take place between the new "players" who try to gain the right to enter the established order and the "dominant player or players" who try to hold the monopoly of power in this order and push the new "players" out of the competition. According to Bourdieu, the common point of those who play the game within the field is nothing but the continuation of the field; therefore, playing a certain game in the field means mutual recognition by all actors of the values on which the field is built. Based on these general expressions, it is possible to summarize the characteristics of a field as follows: there are actors in the field; a game they are ready to play; the existence of power relations within the field; the existence of the elements (material or symbolic) that will be the subject of struggle in the field; and finally the existence of the rules that are accepted by the actors and enable the continuation of the game in the field.[38]

DIDIER BIGO, MIGRATION PROBLEM, AND (IN)SECURITY

According to Didier Bigo, the issue of migration is generally seen as a security problem, and this point of view is also accepted for security forces, gendarmerie, military staff, intelligence service personnel, customs officers, border guards, and some social services (hospitals, schools). This is undoubtedly the case for healthcare organizations. It is even the case for organizations providing surveillance services for private security companies, for the visual and printed media, most of which are after sensational news, and for a certain segment of society. It is a situation where different actors constantly create and spread an atmosphere of fear and try to portray society in danger. This transformation of security naturally makes it difficult to determine what is internal security and what is international security. The fact that immigration has become a security issue in this way also brings about the issue of which methods to be used and what measures to be taken against the problem, and naturally, it leads to the introduction of many methods/measures.[39]

Bigo notes that the securitization of immigration has become a propaganda instrument for right-wing parties. In this regard, the perception of threat has been created by intimidating societies through racism and performing a successful "speech act" in this regard. With the securitization of immigration, politicians do not realize that they are losing control over their own borders. It is an event of securitization that is formed over the habitus of security professionals and their interests and the concepts of foreign and immigrant. These interests have reached a global dimension by crossing borders with the development of surveillance technologies. This situation is what causes the emergence of a risk society in which societies live in constant fear and unease, and it is actually a structural situation related to the association of freedom with security in a neoliberal society. According to Didier Bigo, securitization of migration is a process of securitization carried out by the successful speech act of political leaders against and to mobilize certain groups (security professionals).[40] Therefore, according to Bigo, the securitization of migration is

purely political. The expressions used in this process are certainly not innocent. The language used between the concepts of immigration and security
is a political language used to mobilize the masses. Therefore, migration is
problematized in Western societies, and it is an abuse of a situation rather than
a legal one and has evolved into a concept used to spread evil. This process
paves the way for resorting to extraordinary means, that is, illegal means,
regarding immigration, which has become a national threat.

According to Didier Bigo, security professionals are like professional
unease managers who decide to make a security problem instead of solving
it. In a sense, they behave like a specialist in deciding what is to be defined
as a security (issue). So, is there really a security issue or is security a matter decided by them? So, in a sense, they operate as professionals who focus
on prioritizing what is security. Some amateur security elements (associations, churches, parties not integrated in the decision-making process, ad hoc
spokesmen of social movements) may also be included in this game field.
They are not actually in the decision-making structure, but in a sense they can
be included in this game field. However, professionals are in a more advanta-
geous position in determining and managing the process. As a result, it can
be said that the field effect determines the result to an incredible degree.[41]
According to Bigo, security professionals "share a certain type of game
sense." They have something in common. They believe and act/react similarly, even if they are always in competition. Security professionals have all
become managers of uneasiness. They have created considerable autonomy
for their domain—the management of fear. They have succeeded in creating
"security," which is their goal (rather than the goal of national politicians).

However, Bello points out in her study that Bigo treats the securitization
process as a one-sided process and ignores the desecuritization process.
Stating that securitization of immigration is a process of social construction, Bello points out that the prejudices of different groups are effective in
their view of immigration, and that securitization and desecuritization can be
experienced at the same time.[42] "Our approach actually considers prejudice
as a cognition that informs the social construction of migration as a threat.
Prejudice is consequently the main qualifier of a perspective of the nation
that ties a society through the discrimination of specific groups of individuals, who are thus socially constructed as outer threats. . . . The reason for
which a variety of actors either socially construct or help deconstruct the
migration-security nexus depends on whether the upholding cognition of the
nation is a prejudicial or an inclusive one."[43] Moreover, Bello thinks that it is
not possible to end the securitization of migration as long as the negative prejudices of individuals and institutions against the migration continue to exist.[44]

CONCLUSION

The Paris School, which is considered among the critical security theories together with the Copenhagen School and the Welsh School, is also called the (in)securitization theory. The Paris School, based on the work of Bigo and Huysmans in particular, has actually developed with the work of authors gathered around the *International Journal of Political Sociology*, which started its publication in 2007. The aim of the school is to develop an inter-disciplinary study by developing the sociological perspective that they think is not given a necessary place in international relations studies. Therefore, the school's approaches are skeptical of the Copenhagen School's approach to dividing security into sectors because according to the members of the School, the entire securitization process is a social one. The most important feature of the school is that they show that the concepts of internal and external security or the concepts of inside and outside are intertwined, and they even use the concept of the Mobius strip to express that the border between the two has become unclear. According to the school, since the concepts of security and insecurity are not easily separated from each other, this situation also resembles the Mobius strip. According to the school, every attempt at security is also an attempt at insecurity. Since the security defined through the other makes both the other and itself insecure, the concept of security is essentially insecurity.

The Paris School is accepted among the critical theories because it sees security as a subjective phenomenon, considers the process of (in)securitization as an intersubjective process, focuses on the performative function of language, makes a social analysis, and emphasizes individual security. Moreover, it is a reflexive theory that must be regarded as a constructivist and constitutive theory. However, it has been distinguished from the Copenhagen school in terms of focusing on non-linguistic processes and tools, drawing attention to other securitizing actors, and focusing on the concept of security professionals in this context.

Bigo tries to show that the process is abused, and all security problems are tried to be solved through immigration and immigrants, mostly on the securitization of immigration in Europe. Therefore, securitization is a highly subjective process.

REFERENCES

Adler, Emanuel. "Constructivism in International Relations: Sources, Contributions, and Debates," *Handbook of International Relations*, edited by Walter Carlsnaes, Thomas Risse, and Beth A. Simmons, 112–44. London: Sage Publications, 2012.

Aradau, Claudia et al. "Critical Approaches to Security in Europe: A Networked Manifesto," *Security Dialogue* 37, no. 4 (2006): 457, https://doi.org/10.1177/0967010606073085.

Arı, Tayyar and Elif Toprak. *Theories of International Relations II.* Eskişehir: Anadolu University, 2019.

Balzacq, Thierry. "The 'Essence' of Securitization: Theory, Ideal Type, and a Sociological Science of Security," *International Relations* 29, no. 1 (2015): 103–13, https://doi.org/10.1177/0047117814526606b.

Balzacq, Thierry. "A Theory of Securitization: Origins, Core Assumptions, and Variants," in *Securitization Theory: How Security Problems Emerge and Dissolve,* edited by Thierry Balzacq, 1–30. London: Routledge, 2010.

Balzacq, Thierry. "The Three Faces of Securitization: Political Agency, Audience and Context," *European Journal of International Relations* 11, no. 2 (2005): 171–201, https://doi.org/10.1177/1354066105052960.

Balzacq, Thierry, Sarah Léonard, and Jan Ruzicka, "'Securitization' Revisited: Theory and Cases," *International Relations* 30, no. 4 (2015): 1–38, DOI: 10.1177/0047117815596590.

Balzacq, Thierry et al. "What Kind of Theory—If Any—Is Securitization?," *International Relations* 29, no. 1 (2015): 97–102, https://doi.org/10.1177/0047117814526606.

Balzacq, Thierry, Tugba Basaran, Didier Bigo, Emmanuel-Pierre Guittet, and Christian Olsson. "Security Practices," International Studies Encyclopedia Online. edited by Robert A. Denemark. Blackwell Publishing. Blackwell Reference Online, accessed March 18, 2010, DOI: 10.1111/b.9781444336597.2010.

Bello, Valeria. "The Spiralling of the Securitisation of Migration in the EU: From the Management of a 'Crisis' to a Governance of Human Mobility?," *Journal of Ethnic and Migration Studies* 48, no. 6 (2022): 1327–44, DOI: 10.1080/1369183X.2020.1851464 p. 1331.

Bigo, Didier. "Security, exception, ban and surveillance," *Theorizing Surveillance: The panopticon and beyond,* edited by David Lyon, 46–68. Portland, OR: Willan Publishing, 2006.

Bigo, Didier. "Globalized (in)security: The field and the ban-opticon," in *Terror, Insecurity and Liberty: Illiberal practices of liberal regimes after 9/11,* edited by Didier Bigo and Anastassia Tsoukala. 24–30. New York, NY: Routledge, 2008.

Bigo, Didier. "Security and Immigration: Toward a Critique of the Governmentality of Unease," *Alternatives* 27, no. 1 (2002), 74. https://doi.org/10.1177/03043754020270S105.

Bigo, Didier. "International Political Sociology," in *Security studies: Aan introduction,* edited by Paul D. Williams, 118–22. New York: Routledge, 2008.

Bigo, Didier. "When Two Become One: Internal and external securitisations in Europe," in *International Relations Theory and The Politics of European Integration: Power, Security and Community,* edited by Morten Kelstrup and Michael Williams. New York: Routledge, 2000.

Bigo, Didier. "The (in)Securitization Practices of the Three Universes of EU Border Control: Military/Navy - Border Guards/Police - Database Analysts," *Security Dialogue* 45, no. 3 (2014): 214, https://doi.org/10.1177/0967010614530459.

Bigo, Didier. Philippe Bonditti, and Christian Olsson. "Mapping the European Field of Security Professionals," in *Europe's 21st Century Challenge*, edited by Didier Bigo, Sergio Carrera, and R. B. J. Walker, 49–63. London; New York: Routledge, 2016.

Bigo, Didier and Emma McCluskey. "What Is a PARIS Approach to (In) securitization? Political Anthropological Research for International Sociology," in *The Oxford Handbook of International Security*, Oxford Handbooks, edited by Alexandra Gheciu and William C. Wohlforth. Oxford: Oxford University, Online March 2018, DOI: 10.1093/oxfordhb/9780198777854.013.9.

Bigo, Didier and R. B. J. Walker, "International, Political, Sociology," *International Political Sociology* 1, no. 1 (March 2007), 3–4. https://doi.org/10.1111/j.1749-5687 .2007.00001.x

Bigo, Didier and R. B. J. Walker, "Political Sociology and the Problem of the International," *Millennium: Journal of International Studies* 35, no. 3 (2007): 734–35. https://doi.org/10.1177/03058298070350030401.

Bigo, Didier. "The (in)Securitization Practices of the Three Universes of EU Border Control: Military/Navy - Border Guards/Police - Database Analysts," *Security Dialogue* 45, no. 3 (2014): 214, https://doi.org/10.1177/0967010614530459.

Booth, Ken. "Security and Emancipation," *Review of International Studies* 17, no. 4 (1991): 313–26, https://doi.org/10.1017/S0260210500112033.

Brandão, Ana Paula. "The Internal-External Nexus in the Security Narrative of the European Union," Janus.Net 6, no. 1 (2015): 1–19.

Burr, Vivien. *An Introduction to Social Constructionism*. London: Routledge, 1995.

Buzan, Barry. "People, States, and Fear: The National Security Problem in International Relations," *International Journal* 40 (1985), https://doi.org/10.2307 /40202323.

Eriksson, Johan. "Observers and advocates: On the political role of Security Analysts," *Cooperation and Conflict*, 34, no. 3 (2015): 314–15.

Floyd, Rita. "Framework: The Meaning of Securitization and the Method of JST," *The Morality of Security*, 2019, 49–73, https://doi.org/10.1017/9781108667814 .004.

Floyd, Rita. "Extraordinary or Ordinary Emergency Measures: What, and Who, Defines the 'Success' of Securitization?," *Cambridge Review of International Affairs* 29, no. 2 (2016): 677–94, https://doi.org/10.1080/09557571.2015.1077651.

Floyd, Rita. "Securitisation and the Function of Functional Actors," *Critical Studies on Security* 9, no. 2 (2021): 81–97, https://doi.org/10.1080/21624887.2020 .1827590.

Floyd, Rita. "Can Securitization Theory Be Used in Normative Analysis? Towards a Just Securitization Theory," *Security Dialogue* 42, no. 4–5 (2011): 427–39, https:// doi.org/10.1177/0967010611418712.

Floyd, Rita. "Towards a Consequentialist Evaluation of Security: Bringing Together the Copenhagen and the Welsh Schools of Security Studies," *Review of International Studies* 33, no. 2 (2007): 327–50, https://doi.org/10.1017/S026021050700753X.

Floyd, Rita. "When Foucault met security studies: A critique of the 'Paris school' of security studies." Paper presented at the 2006 BISA annual conference 18–20 December at the University of Cork, Ireland.

Floyd, Rita and Stuart Croft. "European Non-Traditional Security Theory: From Theory To Practice," *Geopolitics, History, and International Relations* 3, no. 2 (2011): 153.

Guzzini, Stefano. "The Concept of Power: A Constructivist Analysis," *Millennium: Journal of International Studies* 33, no.3 (2005): 495–521

Guzzini, Stefano and Anna Leander (eds.). *Constructivism and International Relations: Alexander Wendt and His Critics.* London: Routledge, 2006. https://doi .org/10.4324/9780203401880.

Hansen, Lene. "Reconstructing Desecuritisation: The Normative-Political in the Copenhagen School and Directions for How to Apply It," *Review of International Studies* 38, no. 3 (2012): 525–46, https://doi.org/10.1017/S0260210511000581.

Held, David and John B. Thompson (eds.). *Social Theory of Modern Societies: Anthony Giddens and His Critics.* Cambridge: Cambridge University Press, 1994.

Henig, Stanley. "Widening and Deepening," in *The Uniting of Europe*, 2nd ed., edited by Stanley Henig, 63–76. London: Routledge, 2002.

Huysmans, Jef. *The politics of insecurity: Fear, migration, and asylum in the EU.* London; New York: Routledge, 2006.

Jones, Richard Wyn. *Security, Strategy, and Critical Theory.* Colorado: Lynne Rienner Publishers, 1999, https://doi.org/10.1515/9781685857110.

Krause, Keith. "Critical Theory and Security Studies: The Research Programme of 'Critical Security Studies,'" *Cooperation and Conflict* 33, no. 3 (1998): 298–333, https://doi.org/10.1177/0010836798033003004.

Krause, Keith and Michael C. Williams. "Broadening the Agenda of Security Studies: Politics and Methods," *Mershon International Studies Review* 40, no. 2 (1996): 229–54, https://doi.org/10.2307/222776.

Lisle, Debbie. Vicki Squire, and Roxanne Doty. "Editorial: International Political Sociology: Critical and Collective Adventures," *International Political Sociology* 11, no. 1 (2017): 2, https://doi.org/10.1093/ips/olw030.

McDonald, Matt. "Securitization and the Construction of Security," *European Journal of International Relations* 14, no. 4 (2008): 563–87, https://doi.org/10 .1177/1354066108097553

McSweeney, Bill. "Identity and Security: Buzan and the Copenhagen School," *Review of International Studies* 22, no. 1 (1996): 81–93, https://doi.org/10.1017/ S0260210500118467.

Nabers, Dirk and Frank A. Stengel. "International/Global Political Sociology," in *Oxford Research Encyclopedia of International Studies*, ed. Renee Marlin-Bennett, 3–9, Oxford: Oxford University Press, 2019, https://doi.org/10.1093/acrefore /9780190846626.013.371.

Saleh, Alam. "Archive of SID Broadening the Concept of Security: Identity and Societal Security Archive of SID," *Geopolitics Quarterly* 6, no. 4 (2010): 228–41.

Sevim, Hüseyin. "Pierre Bourdieu'nun Uluslararası İlişkiler Kuramlarına Olası Katkıları," *Uluslararası İlişkiler* 11, no 43 (Güz 2014): 25.

Wæver, Ole. "New 'Schools' in Security Theory and Their Origins between Core and Periphery," *Journal of Physics A: Mathematical and Theoretical* 44, no. 8 (2011): 23. Paper presented at the annual meeting of the International Studies Association, Montreal, March 17–20, 2004.

Waever, Ole. "Security, the Speech Act Analysing the Politics of a Word," *Research Training Seminar* 7 (1989): 1–68.

Wendt, Alexander. "Constructing International Politics," *International Security* 20, no. 1 (1995): 71–81, https://doi.org/10.2307/2539217

Wendt, Alexander. "Anarchy Is What States Make of It: The Social Construction of Power Politics," *International Organization*, 46, no. 2 (1992): 391–425, https://doi.org/10.1017/S0020818300027764

Wendt, Alexander. *Social Theory of International Politics*. Cambridge: Cambridge University Press, 1999.

Williams, Michael C. "Words, Images, Enemies: Securitization and International Politics," *International Studies Quarterly* 47 (2003): 511–31.

NOTES

1. Rita Floyd and Stuart Croft, "European Non-Traditional Security Theory: From Theory To Practice," *Geopolitics, History, and International Relations* 3, no. 2 (2011): 153.

2. Alexander Wendt, "Constructing International Politics," *International Security* 20, no. 1 (1995): 71–81, https://doi.org/10.2307/2539217; Alexander Wendt, "Anarchy Is What States Make of It: The Social Construction of Power Politics," *International Organization*, 46, no.2 (1992): 391–425, https://doi.org/10.1017/S0020818300027764; Alexander Wendt, *Social Theory of International Politics* (Cambridge: Cambridge University Press, 1999); Emanuel Adler, "Constructivism in International Relations: Sources, Contributions, and Debates," *Handbook of International Relations*, eds. Walter Carlsnaes, Thomas Risse, and Beth A. Simmons (London: Sage Publications, 2012), 112–44.

3. For more details, see Stefano Guzzini and Anna Leander (eds.), *Constructivism and International Relations: Alexander Wendt and His Critics* (London: Routledge, 2006), 1–247, https://doi.org/10.4324/9780203401880; Stefano Guzzini, "The Concept of Power: A Constructivist Analysis," *Millennium: Journal of International Studies* 33, no. 3 (2005): 495–521; Vivien Burr, *An Introduction to Social Constructionism* (London: Routledge, 1995); David Held and John B. Thompson (eds.), *Social Theory of Modern Societies: Anthony Giddens and His Critics* (Cambridge: Cambridge University Press, 1994); Tayyar Arı and Elif Toprak, eds., *Theories of International Relations II*. Eskişehir: Anadolu University, 2019.

4. Barry Buzan, "People, States, and Fear: The National Security Problem in International Relations," *International Journal* 40 (1985), https://doi.org/10.2307/40202323; Michael C. Williams, "Words, Images, Enemies: Securitization and International Politics," *International Studies Quarterly* 47 (2003): 511–31; Bill McSweeney, "Identity and Security: Buzan and the Copenhagen School," *Review of International Studies* 22, no. 1 (1996): 81–93, https://doi.org/10.1017/s0260210500118467; Ole Waever, "Security, the Speech Act Analysing the Politics of a Word," *Research Training Seminar* 7 (1989): 1–68; Floyd and Croft, "European Non-Traditional Security Theory," 152–79.

5. Thierry Balzacq, "A Theory of Securitization: Origins, Core Assumptions, and Variants," in *Securitization Theory: How Security Problems Emerge and Dissolve*, ed. Thierry Balzacq (London: Routledge, 2010), 1–30; Thierry Balzacq, "The Three Faces of Securitization: Political Agency, Audience and Context," *European Journal of International Relations* 11, no. 2 (2005): 171–201, https://doi.org/10.1177/1354066105052960; Thierry Balzacq, Sarah Léonard, and Jan Ruzicka, "'Securitization' Revisited: Theory and Cases," *International Relations* 30, no. 4 (2015): 1–38, DOI: 10.1177/0047117815596590; Thierry Balzacq et al., "What Kind of Theory—If Any—Is Securitization?," *International Relations* 29, no. 1 (2015): 97–102, https://doi.org/10.1177/0047117814526606; Thierry Balzacq, "The 'Essence' of Securitization: Theory, Ideal Type, and a Sociological Science of Security," *International Relations* 29, no. 1 (2015): 103–13, https://doi.org/10.1177/0047117814526606b; Lene Hansen, "Reconstructing Desecuritisation: The Normative-Political in the Copenhagen School and Directions for How to Apply It," *Review of International Studies* 38, no. 3 (2012): 525–46, https://doi.org/10.1017/S0260210511000581; Matt McDonald, "Securitization and the Construction of Security," *European Journal of International Relations* 14, no. 4 (2008): 563–87, https://doi.org/10.1177/1354066108097553; Rita Floyd, "Framework: The Meaning of Securitization and the Method of JST," *The Morality of Security*, 2019, 49–73, https://doi.org/10.1017/9781108667814.004; Rita Floyd, "Extraordinary or Ordinary Emergency Measures: What, and Who, Defines the 'Success' of Securitization?," *Cambridge Review of International Affairs* 29, no. 2 (2016): 677–94, https://doi.org/10.1080/09557571.2015.1077651; Rita Floyd, "Securitisation and the Function of Functional Actors," *Critical Studies on Security* 9, no. 2 (2021): 81–97, https://doi.org/10.1080/21624887.2020.1827590; Rita Floyd, "Can Securitization Theory Be Used in Normative Analysis? Towards a Just Securitization Theory," *Security Dialogue* 42, no. 4–5 (2011): 427–39, https://doi.org/10.1177/0967010611418712.

6. Floyd and Croft, "European Non-Traditional Security Theory," 154–56.

7. For more detail see, Ole Wæver, "New 'Schools' in Security Theory and Their Origins between Core and Periphery," *Journal of Physics A: Mathematical and Theoretical* 44, no. 8 (2011): 23, paper presented at the annual meeting of the International Studies Association, Montreal, March 17–20, 2004.

8. Johan Eriksson, "Observers and advocates: On the political role of Security Analysts," *Cooperation and Conflict*, 34, no. 3 (2015): 314–15.

9. Rita Floyd, "Towards a Consequentialist Evaluation of Security: Bringing Together the Copenhagen and the Welsh Schools of Security Studies,"

Review of International Studies 33, no. 2 (2007): 327–50, https://doi.org/10.1017 /S026021050700753X; Keith Krause and Michael C. Williams, "Broadening the Agenda of Security Studies: Politics and Methods," *Mershon International Studies Review* 40, no. 2 (1996): 229–54, https://doi.org/10.2307/222776; Richard Wyn Jones, *Security, Strategy, and Critical Theory* (Colorado: Lynne Rienner Publishers, 1999), https://doi.org/10.1515/9781685857110; Keith Krause, "Critical Theory and Security Studies: The Research Programme of 'Critical Security Studies,'" *Cooperation and Conflict* 33, no. 3 (1998): 298–333, https://doi.org/10.1177/0010836798033003004.

10. Ken Booth, "Security and Emancipation," *Review of International Studies* 17, no. 4 (1991): 313–26, https://doi.org/10.1017/S0260210500112033.

11. Floyd and Croft, "European Non-Traditional Security Theory," 156.

12. Eriksson, "Observers and advocates," 311–330.

13. Krause and Williams, "Broadening the Agenda"; Stanley Henig, "Widening and Deepening," in *The Uniting of Europe*, 2nd ed. (London: Routledge, 2002), 63– 76; Alam Saleh, "Archive of SID Broadening the Concept of Security: Identity and Societal Security Archive of SID," *Geopolitics Quarterly* 6, no. 4 (2010): 228–41.

14. For more detail see, Ana Paula Brandão, "The Internal-External Nexus in the Security Narrative of the European Union," *Janus.Net* 6, no. 1 (2015): 1–19.

15. Didier Bigo and Emma McCluskey, "What Is a PARIS Approach to (In) securitization? Political Anthropological Research for International Sociology," in *The Oxford Handbook of International Security, Oxford Handbooks*, eds. Alexandra Gheciu and William C. Wohlforth (Oxford: Oxford University, Online March 2018), 1, DOI: 10.1093/oxfordhb/9780198777854.013.9.

16. Dirk Nabers and Frank A. Stengel, "International/Global Political Sociology," in *Oxford Research Encyclopedia of International Studies*, ed. Renee Marlin-Bennett (Oxford: Oxford University Press, 2019), 3–9, https://doi.org/10.1093/acrefore /9780190846626.013.371.

17. Debbie Lisle, Vicki Squire, and Roxanne Doty, "Editorial: International Political Sociology: Critical and Collective Adventures," *International Political Sociology* 11, no. 1 (2017): 2, https://doi.org/10.1093/ips/olw030.

18. Didier Bigo, "International Political Sociology," in *Security studies: An introduction*, ed. Paul D. Williams (New York: Routledge, 2008), 118–22.

19. Bigo, "International Political Sociology," 123.

20. Thierry Balzacq, Tugba Basaran, Didier Bigo, Emmanuel-Pierre Guittet, and Christian Olsson, "Security Practices," *International Studies Encyclopedia Online*, ed. Robert A. Denemark (Blackwell Publishing, Blackwell Reference Online, accessed March 18, 2010), 3, DOI: 10.1111/b.9781444336597.2010.x

21. Didier Bigo and R. B. J. Walker, "International, Political, Sociology," *International Political Sociology*, 1, no. 1 (March 2007), 3–4. https://doi.org/10.1111/j .1749–5687.2007.00001.x

22. Didier Bigo, "When Two Become One: Internal and external securitisations in Europe," in *International Relations Theory and The Politics of European Integration: Power, Security and Community*, eds. Morten Kelstrup and Michael Williams (New York: Routledge, 2000), 171.

23. Didier Bigo and R. B. J. Walker, "Political Sociology and the Problem of the International," *Millennium: Journal of International Studies* 35, no. 3 (2007): 734–35. https://doi.org/10.1177/03058298070350030401.

24. Didier Bigo, "The (in)Securitization Practices of the Three Universes of EU Border Control: Military/Navy - Border Guards/Police - Database Analysts," *Security Dialogue* 45, no. 3 (2014): 214, https://doi.org/10.1177/0967010614530459.

25. Claudia Aradau et al., "Critical Approaches to Security in Europe: A Networked Manifesto," *Security Dialogue* 37, no. 4 (2006): 457, https://doi.org/10.1177/0967010606073085.

26. Jef Huysmans, *The politics of insecurity: Fear, migration, and asylum in the EU* (London; New York: Routledge, 2006), 2–3.

27. Jef Huysmans, *The politics of insecurity*, 4.

28. Rita Floyd, "When Foucault met security studies: A critique of the 'Paris school' of security studies," paper presented at the 2006 BISA annual conference 18–20 December at the University of Cork, Ireland, p. 11.

29. Jef Huysmans, *The politics of insecurity*, 8.

30. Jef Huysmans, *The politics of insecurity*, 148.

31. Bigo and Walker, "International, Political, Sociology."

32. Thierry Balzacq, Tugba Basaran, Didier Bigo, Emmanuel-Pierre Guittet, and Christian Olsson, "Security Practices," *International Studies Encyclopedia Online*, ed. Robert A. Denemark (Blackwell Publishing, Blackwell Reference Online, accessed March 18, 2010), 4, DOI: 10.1111/b.9781444336597.2010.x

33. Didier Bigo, "International Political Sociology," 126–28.

34. Didier Bigo, "Security and Immigration: Toward a Critique of the Governmentality of Unease," *Alternatives* no. 27 (January 2002): 63–92, https://doi.org/10.1177/03043754020270s105, p. 82.

35. Didier Bigo, "Security, exception, ban and surveillance," *Theorizing Surveillance: The panopticon and beyond*, edited by David Lyon (Portland, OR: Willan Publishing, 2006), 46–68 (47).

36. Balzacq, Basaran, Bigo, Guittet, and Olsson, "Security Practices," 4.

37. Balzacq, Basaran, Bigo, Guittet, and Olsson, "Security Practices," 4; Didier Bigo, "Globalized (in)security: the field and the ban-opticon," in *Terror, Insecurity and Liberty: Illiberal practices of liberal regimes after 9/11*, eds. Didier Bigo and Anastassia Tsoukala (New York, NY: Routledge, 2008), 24–30.

38. Hüseyin Sevim, "Pierre Bourdieu'nun Uluslararası İlişkiler Kuramlarına Olası Katkıları," *Uluslararası İlişkiler* 11, no. 43 (Güz 2014): 25.

39. Didier Bigo, "Security and Immigration: Toward A Critique of the Governmentality of Unease," *Alternatives* no. 27 (January 2002): 63.

40. Didier Bigo, Philippe Bonditti, and Christian Olsson, "Mapping the European Field of Security Professionals," in *Europe's 21st Century Challenge*, eds. Didier Bigo, Sergio Carrera, and R. B. J. Walker (London; New York: Routledge, 2016), 49–63.

41. Didier Bigo, "Security and Immigration: Toward a Critique of the Governmentality of Unease," *Alternatives* 27, no. 1 (2002), 74. https://doi.org/10.1177/03043754020270S105

42. Valeria Bello, "The Spiralling of the Securitisation of Migration in the EU: From the Management of a 'Crisis' to a Governance of Human Mobility?," *Journal of Ethnic and Migration Studies* 48, no. 6 (2022): 1327–44, DOI: 10.1080/1369183X.2020.1851464 p.1331.

43. Bello, "The Spiralling of the Securitisation," 1335.

44. Bello, "The Spiralling of the Securitisation," 1335.

Chapter 8

Ontological Security Theory and the Security of Self

Tayyar Arı and Mehmet Ali Ak

INTRODUCTION

The ontological security theory, a part of critical security studies, describes security as including all intangible manifestations of interior existence and security in the physical or material sense. Ontological security comprises the security of one's existence, identity, and self.[1] At the state level, it is a securitization process in the framework of identity/security connections against potential existential threats to the state. The self-identity of the actors, as well as their interactions with other actors, must be solid and lasting for them to provide their ontological security.[2] Although ontological security theory is accepted among critical security studies, some significant distinctions exist. CSS encompasses persons, the environment, identity, and other factors besides physical security. Ontological security and CSS share comparable ideas on the identity-security link since they have epistemologically more interpretative and subjective aspects. However, when it is evaluated in terms of ontological and level of analysis, CSS focuses on human security; it opposes a state-centered approach and even views the state as a threat to individual security. In the ontological security theory, in the framework of the state-identity connection, state existential characteristics are tried to be safeguarded. Therefore, the state is not a threat but a formal structure that must be preserved. Individual and global security are less essential than national security. Ontological security theory prioritizes freedom, not emancipation, concerning the social memory of the state.[3]

In the 1990s, the ontological security idea was adapted from psychology and sociology and employed in the literature of international relations. In

1998, Jef Huysmans applied the idea for the first time in the field of IR. International relations ideas of the 2000s were influenced by writers including McSweeney, Jennifer Mitzen, Catarina Kinnvall, J. Brent Steele, Bahar Rumelili, and Ayşe Zarakol. They made contributions to the discipline by introducing ideas like the dichotomy between ontological and physical security, the link between identity and security, the extent of state survival, narratives, routines, conflict resolution, shame, and uncertainty. R.D. Laing, who was initially motivated by existentialism, combined existence and security in psychology in the 1960s; A. Giddens adopted the concept in sociology in the 1980s.[4] The authors viewed the link between security and self-identity in processes of social formation at the individual level. They emphasized how important it was to get rid of the tension that contributed to habitual consistency. They concluded that only in a situation where a person was relieved of their anxiety could they feel comfortable, act appropriately, and continue with their routines. Inspired by existentialism in the 1960s, R.D. Laing linked existence and security in psychology; in the 1980s, A. Giddens expanded the concept to sociology.[5] When ontological security is evaluated at the state level, some questions arise about the function and access of the state. According to Weber, the modern state is capable of working in harmony with society, recognizing friends and foes, as well as being a sovereign institution that confers legal power, controls the allocation of values, and makes laws. Therefore, it is also the provider of ontological security. After this basic introduction, it is important to discuss which circumstances led to the formation and development of ontological security and which differences exist on the basis of definition and practice of ontological security at the individual and state level, as well as how foreign policy behaviors are formed and implemented in the context of the identity-security relationship. Also, the context in which the relationship between biographical narratives and routines is constructed and its contribution to crisis resolution should be emphasized. It will be discussed where the ontological insecurity and anxiety phases emerge during foreign policy processes. All these questions and assumptions will be analyzed and debated through their evaluation with examples.

SUBJECTIVITY AND ONTOLOGICAL SECURITY

States, like individuals, are concerned about their ontological security in identity construction processes and try to preserve their "self" norms in order to maintain their stable status. Every state produces socially and politically specific objects of fear. The main reason for this is the cognitive separation of the concept of friend and foe, the establishment of certain meaning systems, and the creation of clear boundaries based on the necessity of survival.[6] Giddens defines ontological security as the expectation of continuity in a life that never ends and in which events take place in a predictable way. To achieve this, all fundamental existential queries must be addressed with precision. Clarifying the difference between "me" and "other" will therefore ensure coherence and order. By fending off objectified threats, Huysmans argues that physical security seeks to delay death. Ontological security, on the other hand, is a tactic to control the effects of these threats and to guard against the unpredictability of death.[7] According to Rumelili, states need biographical narratives to get rid of the anxiety of maintaining their existence stemming from physical dangers. Rumelili emphasizes that only ideas created in this way are capable of creating an existential security space. In addition, Rumelili questions the conditions of change and transformation in these narratives and all the facts that support the politics of survival based on physical security.

According to Mitzen, subjective principles are more important than objective rules in security comprehension. In terms of ontological security, long-term stability can ensure self-security although distinct political regions can change across time and space. Relationships developed with such external elements as the dominant ideology of the international system, regional power relations, social norms, global population migrations, and fight with non-state organizations construct new existential reflexes. Thus, the self-protected territories must re-create stability by reacting to the ever-changing world politics in their language.[8] David Campbell describes it as follows: Some subjects result from subjective circumstances and have been through various building processes instead of being a universal human character applicable to all eras. Its positioning, such as West/East, North/South, Civilized/Bedouin, and Native/Foreign, results from this subjectivity. Because every identity recognizes oneself as a subject and rejects objectification, every civilization attempts to establish its identity on these dichotomies. Due to the meaning values that make up its ontological security, each subject reacts to the global risks securitized in international politics. According to Campbell, discourse poses a challenge to US foreign policy. Discourse creates a persistent enemy. For special reasons, all states must secure this enemy created by the USA.[9]

According to Zarakol, ontological security has two sources: institutional and non-institutional. In the former, the person asks himself/herself some existential questions in order to define "self": What will happen after death? What is the purpose of life? How is the knowledge of truth obtained? Thus, he/she attempts to preserve internal stability. The latter is related to everyday contacts, relationships, and practices in a stable, safe environment. Throughout history, institutional sources have been divided into religious and secular. Societies that rely their legitimacy on religion have made it easier to build safe zones by addressing queries about their institutional ontological stability with information from the holy texts. Religion has been recognized as the "other" by secular institutional ontological security.[10] As a result, governments can construct various ontological conceptions of security. In this respect, ontological security theory does not contradict the view that anarchy is a phenomenon created by states. States are given identity in the international system and act accordingly. The content of ontological security changes in the context of the global system as states are dominated by more liberal or nationalist norms. For example, a state linked to EU identity may be more sensitive to global or regional concerns due to identification with EU identity. At the same time, more conservative governments primarily use stricter rules to develop and maintain their stability and order.

INDIVIDUAL AND SOCIETY LEVEL
IN ONTOLOGICAL SECURITY

In the 1960s, Laing used the concept of ontological security at the individual level. According to Laing, a person's self-identity and freedom in psychoanalysis can only be secured when they are free from uncertainty, fear, and disorder.[11] Krolikowski states that the search for ontological security should be examined at the individual level because individuals are actors that provide ontological security.[12] Croft also reduces ontological security to the individual and society rather than the state level. Croft states that putting the state in the individual's place reinforces the state's personality further. The individual has observed that s/he acts consistently as long as s/he can explain what it is and for what purpose s/he lives.[13] The ontologically secure individual, according to Laing, "is a natural, living, full, internally consistent, and continuous entity." As a result, maintaining ontological security allows the individual to integrate with his identity and society. Therefore, ontological security is regarded as one of the most fundamental requirements of a human in the post–Cold War era. Threats have evolved in areas other than the military, including economic collapse, political persecution, shortages, environmental issues, ethnic strife, terrorism, and diseases. Conditions that must be met to guarantee an individual's ontological security have grown more challenging. According to Laing, these threats have a negative impact on the individual's mental health and make them feel as though their own existence is threatened. As a means of removing these threats through continuities, narratives, and perceptions that exist in life, s/he attempts to take part in identity-creation processes. Ontological security is founded, at the individual level, on the consistency of biographical narratives, established behavioral patterns, and social networks created by daily routines.[14]

Giddens interprets the ontological security concept through the individual, adapts it to society, and introduces it to sociology. Giddens states that any uncertain and discontinuous progress will lead to ontological insecurity. The continuity of biographical narratives creates a secure presence. Thus, an unoriented and obscurity sense produced by modernity disappears, and a conscious individual emerges. Giddens says this will reduce anxiety and build a more stable situation. Societies with ontological security can cope with life's risks because they have a strong sense of their own identity.[15] Modern values have spread to the world through globalization, forming a supra-identity. Many communities are concerned that shared global rules will annihilate local identities. As a result, the global civil society movement erased borders and shattered the concept of "self." Consequently, civilizations viewed international norms as a threat to their ontological security in developing and sustaining biographical narratives. Nation-state movements were constrained during crises as liberal democratic institutions expanded, and intergovernmental and non-governmental groups grew more open to activism and humanitarian action.[16] According to McSweeney, daily routines are intimately tied to ontological security. He claims that because every reality and event have an essential component, uncertainty will result from shifting possibilities.[17] Routines create continuity in daily life; since biographical narratives and social interactions are predictable and foreseeable, they offer a sense of security. Giddens claims that routinization is a cognitive process exposed, shielded, or altered by actors in social settings. In the face of psychologically traumatizing events, routines are one of the most crucial processes that decision-makers should be aware of since they give rise to conceptions like friend, enemy, home, and foreign. Reconstructing historical or identity positions is necessary for regular transformation.[18]

The individual-society interaction, according to Kinnvall, has a framework that supports each other in the context of ontological security because ontological security has a reflexive structure; the person and society may modify each other. Maintaining ongoing awareness of the issue results in more peaceful and cautious communities. Order is rapidly formed in these cultures and anxieties are alleviated; self-esteem becomes steady and assumes a systematic structure.[19]

IDENTITY-SECURITY CONTEXT IN FOREIGN POLICY ANALYSIS

States are founded on three fundamental components, according to Weber's understanding of the modern state: country (land), nation (community), and sovereignty. In addition to these three key factors, states also consider other actors' recognition within an existential context that goes beyond their physical existence.[20] At the state level, ontological security means that all internal components the state considers crucial to its survival are completely secure and certain. What identity do states possess? What tradition does a state adhere to? To what extent does it resemble historical accounts? What ethnicity, religion, language, and cultural components does it have? How liberal or nationalist is it? These questions define its critical features in the global system. According to national identity, nature, and character in international politics, foreign policy behaviors can alter, transform, or remain unchanged. The fundamental components of identity are connected to states' needs for ontological security.[21] By using the word "self," identity expresses the existence of the subject defined by the "other." According to Derrida, "all identities can only exist with their differences," and every identity is in some ways the other and opposite of its own other. Calhoun sees identity as the component that distinguishes a "thing" as "the thing." The identity factor has directed nations in recognizing their "self" and "other" in the international system, as well as in deciding around which rules and phenomena to determine their strategy.[22] For instance, the Republic of Turkey was established as a nation-state based on Western standards and ideals within the context of Turkish identity. The Republic of Turkey had to rewrite its biographical narratives to find a new position following the fall of the Ottoman Empire. What does a Turk mean in this context? What kind of government governs the Republic of Turkey? What is the Republic of Turkey's ontological security areas? These issues had to be reframed in light of history, geography, and identity. Thus, new routines were constructed by decisions made in accordance with ontological security in the face of threats or others in the period's international system. Indeed, according to Subotic, the development of national identity develops future strategies and routines based on memory.[23]

According to Mitzen and Kinnvall, deep uncertainties present a risk to identity security because they provide a steady cognitive environment for subjectivity to survive. When an actor does not understand what to expect, he cannot determine the most appropriate link between aims, and how he will attain his goals becomes unpredictable. Deep uncertain situations make the actor's identity insecure since objectives are fundamental to identity. As a result, states serve as routines for pushing people to establish cognitive and behavioral certainty. Identity drives the state toward a specific goal, which must be consistent with national interests because the lack of physical death differentiates states from persons in terms of ontological security; therefore, the state must disclose its "self" to maintain continuity and stability. In other words, the security of the identity is more significant than the security of the body at the level of state analysis.[24] However, this perspective may not consistently demonstrate rational foreign policy action. According to Steele, nations might disregard realpolitik principles to avoid ontological insecurity. In the Serbia-EU relationship, for instance, even though Serbia had to meet many of the EU's social, economic, and political criteria, the membership process was prolonged because Serbia refused to compromise on issues related to its existence, such as the Kosovo issue, the problems in the Republika Srpska of Bosnia and Herzegovina, border disputes, and the Russia effect. Ontological security, meanwhile, views these obstacles as routines and believes that altering this will induce anxiety. Therefore, realpolitik requires rational thought but ontological security considers it safer to live with unchanging, untransformed, and stable difficulties.

The security dilemma is an example of this in realist theory. The security dilemma indicates that the state's security initiatives increase insecurity in an anarchic system. Consequently, when states arm themselves for security, other states, particularly bordering states, interpret this as a threat and arm themselves. Thus, nations feel more vulnerable due to the unending cycle of armament. This dilemma is not considered a risk to ontological security since arming for protection in response to a threat from another actor is a characteristic of the identity of that state. The security dilemma's recurring interaction and role allocation eliminate the uncertainty. Therefore, the resolution of the issue results in the absence of routines and ontological insecurity.[25]

According to the identity features of states, Steele identifies four important ontological security-seeking behaviors: reflective and material capacities, crisis resolutions, biographical narratives, and discourses of other actors. First, material capabilities contribute to identity formation. In the international system, governments prioritize behaving more freely and use deterrence above their material capabilities. However, Steele believes stronger governments are prone to more ontological mistrust due to increased international duties. When shared global crises, regional genocides, and systemic issues develop, it is assumed that actors with extensive material capability will build a control mechanism.[26] Their routines are disrupted as a result of these crisis-related interventions. This circumstance undermines their foreign policy behavior because in accordance with the ontological security theory, the international system has a flexible structure as opposed to a fixed and predetermined one. The prevalence of these developments and the deadlock lead strong governments to respond to crises differently. As a consequence, these governments' discourse is decisive, and their accomplishments are remarkable, given their recognized role as world leaders. In times of crisis, blaming and humiliating powerful governments lead to destabilization and cause strong states to transfer shame to other players and prioritize national interests. Consequently, problems progressively intensify and become uncontrollable.[27] Unfortunately, crises cannot be described by objective facts. Each state articulates its material and discursive responses to the crisis in accordance with its systemic position. Crises are anxiety-inducing circumstances; thus, they are processes that need immediate action so as not to generate ontological insecurity and, therefore, to prevent people from making poor judgments.

Steele characterizes biographical narratives as the performative assertion of the securitization process. Discourse is the last step before action in the performative speech process because facts such as words, discourses, and symbols impact behavior by constructing meaning. According to Austin, the performative utterance employs purpose-appropriate phrases and expressions, is real for the anticipated purpose, and is determined to meet the standards. Thus, nations' adherence to their biographical narratives and establishing a discursive foundation for their foreign policy actions enhance their capacity to behave according to self-identity beliefs.[28] The discourse methods of the co-actors describe a quest for new stability by demonstrating how faults and repercussions in the history of the international system cause anxieties and result in ontological insecurity. Co-actors are physically powerful and ontologically untrustworthy international actors, such as Nazi Germany and Mussolini's Italy. He says that comparable actors should act differently than they did during the era in question to avoid experiencing the same unfavorable outcomes. These activities constitute a perlocutionary term among actors. These words are performative; they have a relational effect that may also affect other actors. Therefore, the precaution mechanism against co-actors with large material capability that may cause ontological insecurity is essential for the stability of the international system and the reduction of anxieties.[29]

NARRATIVES, ROUTINES, CONFLICT RESOLUTIONS

The norms and values held by a state influence the states' policy-making practices. All practices generate a narrative and are crucial policy transformation and change instruments. As policy practitioners, leaders use some of these narratives in their foreign policy procedures; they are defined as active narratives. Unselected narratives are passive narratives that either do not reflect the policymaker's identity or are not beneficial to the international system. Narratives are critical to political life. We construct our identities and make sense of the world via narratives. The narratives are the most important construction elements of state continuity, and they must remain uninterrupted. The most significant characteristic of biographical narratives is that they serve as a basis for identity constructions.[30] Subotic argues that "biographical narratives constitute the basic framework for the practice of states." She asks existential questions like the following: Why do states conduct themselves in this manner? What changes have they made to their policies and practices?

How will the threats be deferred, and how will survival be guaranteed? She argues that a state's sense of ontological security is contingent upon the biographical narratives formed from the responses to these questions and its routines towards other states.

Narratives establish a picture of the self and a worldview based on collective interests. According to Flockhart, narratives give ontological security by establishing particular national values, fostering a feeling of unity, and serving as the uniting force of internal systems. In creating political texts from narratives, political actors might modify these narratives to convince their followers to adopt a specific policy. They capture and manipulate a collectively remembered past to arrange present-day political arguments.[31] For Wertsch, narratives do not exist independently and are not only interpretive instruments. They are ingrained in daily discourse, communication, and rhetoric and have a competitive relationship with one another. Because narratives are inherently normative, they serve as the foundation not just for what previously was but also for what should be.[32] Kinnvall discusses populism in India via the lenses of nationalism, religion, Hindu masculinity, and nativism. Kinnvall, who claims that these rules foster ontological mistrust within Hindu culture, explores how the narrative transformation of symbols, discourses, and collective identities in Hindu-style politics exerts ontological mistrust on minorities and immigrants.[33] Rumelili establishes a connection between the narratives and the state's existence. According to the ontological security approach, the concern for existence does not stem from tangible threats to physical security but rather from a narrative that requires continuity and is replicated in this manner. The objective of states is to build and maintain a lasting institutional presence. Therefore, dichotomies such as friend/enemy, local/foreigner, and self/other for the sake of survival are narrative definitions.[34] Subotic claimed that in the Serbia-Kosovo conflict, both parties pursued illogical policies in the area based on narratives.[35] Mitzen termed this circumstance as the ontological dilemma of security and insecurity.[36]

Routines are interactions that create more confidence and stability that eliminate unpredictable practices at the individual level. Routines are based on subjective judgments shaped by the distinction between "Self" and "Other." The individual resolves the anxieties against the phenomenon of existence with routines. Every crisis arises in a process where routines are broken and creates ontological insecurity.[37] According to Giddens, a new routine is required for the person or community to overcome this crisis. States and the anarchic system can only address insecurity via the maintenance of routines.[38] The identity repercussions of routines prevent breaking these connections, even if they are necessary for actual politics. An important part of Serbian society supported Russia's invasion of Ukraine even though this support was against the international community's views. These people supported maintaining their standard historical, social, and cultural practices[39] because conducting its regional and global policy under another uncertain process could result in worse outcomes. Routines, in Mitzen's opinion, help maintain identities. States might classify their daily activities as a topic in sociality when they act "anthropomorphically," like persons.[40]

Deborah Larson's examination of the persistence of routines will clarify the issue's background. Larson observed that when cognitive biases and mistakes were prevalent in US-Soviet interactions, even when desires and interests coincided, the likelihood of mutual misinterpretation rose, and cooperation prospects diminished. Although John Foster Dulles, John F. Kennedy, Richard Nixon, and Ronald Reagan had diverse personalities and management philosophies, all exhibited insecurity and irrational behavior. The persistence of such obstacles to rationality among people/decision makers in the study despite the identical behaviors of institutional states at the macro level demonstrates that ontological insecurity is more persistent at the state level, even if individuals' identities/routines vary.[41] Similarly, states generally adhere to the norms and principles of international law, regardless of regime type, leader personality, or power position. States neutralize micro-level variability in order to adopt the macro-level stability necessary for their ontological security.[42]

The ontological security requirements have a substantial effect on conflict resolution and peacemaking. Rumelili shows that the questioning of biographical narratives and behaviors based on a specific enemy in times of war, as well as in peace processes, causes ontological insecurity and that this insecurity may lead to the failure of these peace efforts. Rumelili underlines that a lasting feeling of peace can only be reached via the development of new biographical narratives and routines between the parties. For peace, she emphasizes that physical and ontological security should complement each other.[43] Contradictory biographical narratives and practices between Turkey and Greece, for instance, generate ontological mistrust. Throughout history, the Aegean conflicts and the status of the Western Thrace Turks have not been entirely resolved. They cannot be addressed owing to the routines and biographical narratives that foster mistrust since the parties feel insecure as a result of these routines.[44]

ONTOLOGICAL INSECURITIES, ANXIETIES, SHAME

According to Lacan, emotions and behaviors have a historical context. Their symbolic arrangement and systematization is the formation process of the subject. Subjectivity is a cognitive value in the stages of emotion and thought determined by other actors. The distinctions between nations in the international system result from a mix of historical events, crisis experiences, friend/enemy positioning, tradition, culture, language, religion, and other factors. Each state has a unique position in the international system, and this may vary according to the needs of the international system, not the character of the state.[45] According to the ontological security theory, negative historical events involving the subjectivity of states have a significant impact on their future strategies. Traumatic narratives and emotional anxieties in society generate a feeling of ontological insecurity and have the potential to alter the prevailing perspectives of foreign policy decision-makers, which is not a neutral process. Instead, actors and institutions centralize their authority by exploiting recognized threats, which may assume racist and sexist forms. The most plausible and accepted narrative includes widespread and deeply held emotional and symbolic codes. Therefore, the ideological perspective of policy-making elites influences the degree to which these narratives will be used. The anxiety and fear of trauma and negative experiences inside the state's identity are the origins of ontological insecurity. This circumstance may make states more conservative and independent. In her work "Ontological Insecurities and Postcolonial Imaginaries: The Emotional Appeal of Populism," Kinnvall describes this response via three concepts: populism, nativism, and racism.[46]

To comprehend how populist politicians and leaders use specific emotions as tools, we need to understand how anxieties and fears about a shifting political environment grow over time. During the European Union's (EU) enlargement process, the primary worries as new nations entered the union were the loss of jobs, fear of increased crime, and the likelihood of an economic crisis. However, beginning from 2014, Europe was more worried about immigration and terrorism at the state level, particularly following the assaults and subsequent attacks on the offices of *Charlie Hebdo*, producing ontological insecurity since it was regarded as an attack on self-identity values. In the former case, more conciliatory arrangements were made, but in the latter, severe and explicit policies were implemented. When examining the societal effects of ontological insecurity, the growth of the far right is particularly evident in EU nations. There are anti-immigrant inclinations, harsh foreign policy discourses, human rights abuses, and ethnic discrimination within the substance of far-right policies. Sixty-three percent in the United Kingdom, 64% in France, 69% in Italy and 69% in Spain, and 61% in Poland in 2019 endorsed this populist conduct, according to research from YouGov. Kinnval claims that these far-right activities are related to the discursive production of fear, anxiety, and threat, as opposed to economic and physical risks. In Europe, industrialization and globalization have contributed to increasing mistrust within the population. According to Kinnval, economic and political change, the restructuring of parties, the deterioration of the welfare state, legitimacy difficulties for ordinary parties, social marginalization, immigration, unemployment, and criminality may be potential causes. Nonetheless, the anxiety of identity loss is the leading cause of extremism.[47] Observing recent events in Europe and the West, we see various populist trends that correlate to the present far-right populism: nationalism and nativism, racism, xenophobia, new forms of democratic governance, the need for a powerful state, etc. In general, the focus is on reinstating national values and romanticized visions of the previous order. In the literature of the far right, ownership of the nation produces a conceptualization that produces the internal/external divide in society, such as nativism, which asserts that states should be inhabited only by members of the indigenous group ("nation") and that non-indigenous elements do not belong to these states. Islamophobia and xenophobia, which are antagonistic to religion and race, have, nonetheless, been consistent in all contemporary far-right populist appeals.[48]

The fundamental assumptions of traditional theories of international relations are based on the idea of fear, not anxiety. Fear is the main emotion aimed toward a specific item that triggers an adaptive reaction. Anarchy is both the outcome and the source of fear. Realists are afraid of anarchy due to the fact that states do not know the intentions of one another. This may result in war, conflict, or insecurity. Anxiety, on the other hand, is a psychological phenomenon and not an emotion; it is a sensation of unease or a persistent state of restlessness that may be described as "fear of fear."

In contrast to fear, anxiety lacks a clear empirical or tangible object, making it harder to comprehend and respond immediately to situations. While the condition of fear may be handled with the "fight or flight" method, the state of anxiety can be represented as enthusiasm, expectancy, threat, trust, friend/foe differentiation, etc. It fosters an environment in which a number of emotions or characteristics are analyzed concurrently, and it may be resolved by taking into account various aspects. The target of worry, according to Kierkegaard, is "nothing," and he compares it to the sensation of vertigo caused by staring down a cliff. In anxiety, a person focuses on the "possibility of the circumstance" rather than an actual threat or risk. According to Kierkegaard, anxiety emerges when a person is confronted with fundamental existential concerns and discovers that rational calculation cannot supply appropriate solutions. Then, individuals are compelled to make a decision. In the process of making a decision, emotions of indecision increase anxiety because the confidence that the consequences will be tolerated, regardless of whether they are favorable or unpleasant, is more consistent than a persistent sensation of vague anxiety. Ontologically, Heidegger also differentiates between dread and anxiety. According to Heidegger, fear is what we confront in every scenario in the world. Being absent from the world is a source of anxiety. While fear has an object, anxiety is nothing since it is a phenomenon that occurs as a result of being observed. Anxiety exacerbates preexisting issues, but a fixed and secure identity/presence lessens anxiety.[49]

The Hobbesian state eliminates the anarchic structure of the nature of the state by establishing an organized and regulated framework for the foreseeable future. The state has a system that decreases societal concerns by establishing laws and norms in the value distribution mechanism. The state plays the role of ontological security as the source of stability and continuity, and people submit to Leviathan to escape their anxieties in light of this security.[50]

According to the ontological security theory, the identity structures of the state and the social aspects of international anarchy create anxiety. Their anxieties grow or decrease depending on each circumstance's biographical narratives and routines. In the international system, governments may no longer anticipate the effects of previously acceptable actions if a crisis or shock disrupts typical foreign policy routines. States will feel helpless to defend their identities as they cannot respond appropriately to global concerns. The globalization trend most exacerbates this situation. According to the ontological security approach, frequent change and transition increase anxiety as it disrupts everyday patterns and requires adaptation. The nation-state either tried to adapt to this transformation or turned to a more protectionist approach. International marketization, immigration, communication, colonialism, and economic and cultural exchange eroded borders. States have become a framework in supranational organizations that are globalized in many ways, loosening their borders and failing to see the identity of their population.[51] Some state institutions have strengthened their identity policies, embraced historical narratives, formulated ambitious strategic objectives, compromised with globalization processes, and secured the state's self-defense through rigid boundaries. Even the United States of America and Europe have shown a defensive stance against globalization processes. US President Trump attempted to restrict the role of the United States in global processes and proposed a new US policy using phrases such as "America First," "Let's close the borders," "Let's increase customs taxes," and "Economic sanctions should be imposed." It reduced its support for NATO, withdrew from international organizations and arrangements like the Paris Climate Treaty, and chose to pursue a protectionist strategy.[52] The United Kingdom pursued a more conservative foreign policy in opposition to globalization by withdrawing from the European Union and boosting its populist rhetoric.[53]

One of the core notions of ontological security is shame. Giddens describes shame as "anxiety for the sufficiency of the story that permits the person to retain a cohesive biography." For Steele, the individual communicates shame in two ways; he displays regret for previous misdeeds and may apologize or attempt to alleviate feelings of shame by economic and strategic incentives. Inadequate US participation in the Rwanda massacre of the 1990s, for instance, is referred to as a "shame." Later, the Clinton administration apologized to Rwanda for the international community's apathy before NATO's action in Kosovo. In order to maintain its hegemon status, the United States engaged forcefully in Bosnia and Kosovo, with NATO, to eliminate this shame.[54]

CONCLUSION

Ontological Security theory has deconstructed physical security, which is included in the traditional security understanding in the international relations literature, and compared it with concepts such as internal/existence/self/identity security. Physical security is an objective defense mechanism, whereas ontological security extends the idea of security into the realm of subjectivity. Consequently, according to this view, self-identity/being security is more essential than physical security because ontological security assumes the permanence and stability of the individual and the state, whereas physical security is a transitory protective procedure. People living in certain states or communities participate in the international system by maintaining their own unique identities. All of their behaviors and strategies are dictated by the norms and values established by this identity. Therefore, the answers to the existential issues defining identity reveal the actions of persons and states. While individuals use these questions to establish their place in society, states create biographical narratives and become the sole actor of the international system, directing the policies they will implement in the future.

Even if physical security is provided in the discipline of international relations, the purposes of the states disappear, and the state may feel impersonal if the routines and biographical narratives required to ensure ontological security are not provided. These states are enslaved by the dominant ideology of the international system and feel the concern of survival in a constantly oriented position by not being able to govern themselves. Every threat that is encountered leads states to irrational policies. The primary determinants of more permanent and long-term strategies, biographical narratives, identity components, and routines—which are the sources of ontological security—also form the core of rational state policies. However, some processes could exhibit the reverse characteristic. States may favor implementing illogical procedures to safeguard ontological security. Even irrational behavior is viewed as a danger to the state's existence and is met with the utmost vigilance. Ontological security theory reveals a paradox in the relationship between rational and irrational behavior. To avoid facing this paradox, states problematize mechanisms that will perpetuate their presence in the international system and eliminate threats beforehand.

Ontological security is comprised of concepts such as biographical narratives, routines, stability, anxiety, and shame. Although these components were first applied to individuals in the fields of psychology and sociology, a theoretical framework was developed by applying them to states in international relations. According to this theoretical paradigm, biographical narratives are processes of identity creation comprised of responses to questions defining the presence of states. With these narratives, states both determine the distinction between "self" and "other" and create positioning in the international system. Routines are the whole of the practices that have become continuous for the protection of the daily/monthly/annual short-term order of the states. The existential certainties created by biographical narratives enable routines to form and continue. Stability is a safe space built by the process formed by the continuity of routines. Every stage that goes beyond this area creates ontological insecurity. Thus, uncertainties, threats, and risks create a world of anxiety for states. As a matter of fact, wrong decisions and practices made when acting with anxiety negatively affect the existence and position of the state. States initiate an ontological securitization process by seeking the object of shame to explain wrong decisions taken out of concern. Thus, it tries to put its existence into the process of rebuilding by postponing the concerns with the element of shame. The Ontological Security theory criticizes the realpolitik and security relationship created by concrete, given, precise, objective laws with this cycle and carries it to a more reflective, circular, interpretable, and subjective field.

REFERENCES

Anter, Andreas. *Max Weber's theory of the modern state: Origins, structure and significance.* Springer, 2014.

Arı, Tayyar. *Uluslararası İlişkilere Giriş.* 5. Baskı. Bursa: Aktüel, 2018.

Arı, Tayyar. *Uluslararası İlişkiler Teorileri.* 10. Baskı. Bursa: Aktüel, 2021.

Cash, John, and Catarina Kinnvall. "Postcolonial bordering and ontological insecurities." *Postcolonial Studies* 20, no. 3 (2017): 267–274.

Croft, Stuart, and Nick Vaughan-Williams. "Fit for purpose? Fitting ontological security studies 'into' the discipline of International Relations: Towards a vernacular turn." *Cooperation and Conflict* 52, no. 1 (2017): 12–30.

Della Sala, Vincent. "Narrating Europe: The EU's ontological security dilemma." *European Security* 27, no. 3 (2018): 266–279.

Ertem, Helin Sarı, and Aslı Nur Düzgün. "Uluslararası İlişkiler Disiplininde Ontolojik Güvenlik Teorisi: Kavram ve Literatür Odaklı Bir İnceleme." *Güvenlik Stratejileri Dergisi* 17, no. 37 (2021): 39–83.

Finnemore, Martha. "The purpose of intervention: Changing beliefs about the use of force." *Canadian Military Journal*, 2006.

Flockhart, Trine. "The problem of change in constructivist theory: Ontological security seeking and agent motivation." *Review of International Studies* 42, no. 5 (2016): 799–820.

Floyd, Rita. *Security and the environment: Securitisation theory and US environmental security policy*. Cambridge University Press, 2010.

García, Tomás Mena. "Donald J. Trump: A critical discourse analysis." *La Revista Estudios Institucionales* 5, no. 8 (2018): 47–73.

Giddens, Anthony. *The consequences of modernity*. Cambridge, MA: Polity, 1990.

Helbrecht, Ilse, Carolina Genz, and Lucas Pohl. "Ontological Security, Globalization, and Geographical Imagination." *Spatial Transformations*. Routledge (2021): 243–257.

Huysmans, Jef. "Security! What Do You Mean? From Concept to Thick Signifier." *European Journal of International Relations* 4, no. 2 (1998): 226–255.

Kenny, Michael. "Back to the populist future? Understanding nostalgia in contemporary ideological discourse." *Journal of Political Ideologies* 22, no. 3 (2017): 256–273.

Kinnvall, Catarina. "Ontological insecurities and postcolonial imaginaries: The emotional appeal of populism." *Humanity & Society* 42, no. 4 (2018): 523–543.

Kinnvall, Catarina. "Globalization and religious nationalism: Self, identity, and the search for ontological security." *Political Psychology* 25, no. 5 (2004): 741–767.

Kinnvall, Catarina. "Populism, ontological insecurity and Hindutva: Modi and the masculinization of Indian politics." *Cambridge Review of International Affairs* 32, no. 3 (2019): 283–302.

Kinnvall, Catarina, Ian Manners, and Jennifer Mitzen. "Introduction to 2018 special issue of European Security: Ontological (in)security in the European Union." *European Security* 27, no. 3 (2018): 249–265.

Kinnvall, Catarina, and Jennifer Mitzen. "Anxiety, fear, and ontological security in world politics: Thinking with and beyond Giddens." *International Theory* 12, no. 2 (2020): 240–256.

Krickel-Choi, Nina C. "The Concept of Anxiety in Ontological Security Studies." *International Studies Review* 24, no. 3 (2022): 1–20.

Krolikowski, Alanna. "State personhood in ontological security theories of international relations and Chinese nationalism: A sceptical view." *Chinese Journal of International Politics* 2, no. 1 (2008): 109–133.

Larson, Deborah Welch. *Anatomy of mistrust: US-Soviet relations during the Cold War*. Cornell University Press, 2000.

Mitzen, Jennifer, "Ontological security in world politics: State identity and the security dilemma." *European Journal of International Relations* 12, no. 3 (2006): 341–370.

Mitzen, Jennifer. "Anxious community: EU as (in) security community." *European Security* 27, no. 3 (2018): 393–413.

Mitzen, Jennifer, and Kyle Larson. "Ontological security and foreign policy." *Oxford Research Encyclopedia of Politics*, 2017.

Rumelili, Bahar. "Identity and desecuritisation: The pitfalls of conflating ontological and physical security." *Journal of International Relations and Development* 18, no. 1 (2015): 52–74.

Rumelili, Bahar. *Conflict resolution and ontological security.* Taylor & Francis, 2015.

Rumelili, Bahar. "Integrating anxiety into international relations theory: Hobbes, existentialism, and ontological security." *International Theory* 12, no. 2 (2020): 257–272.

Rumelili, Bahar, and Umut Can Adisönmez. "Uluslararası ilişkilerde kimlik-güvenlik ilişkisine dair yeni bir paradigma: Ontolojik güvenlik teorisi." *Uluslararası İlişkiler Dergisi* 17, no. 66 (2020): 23–39.

Solomon, Ty. "Ontological security, circulations of affect, and the Arab Spring." *Journal of International Relations and Development* 21, no. 4 (2018): 934–958.

Solomon, Ty. "Rethinking productive power through emotion." *International Studies Review* 19, no. 3 (2017): 481–508.

Steele, Brent J. *Ontological security in international relations: Self-identity and the IR state.* Routledge, 2008.

Subotić, Jelena. "Narrative, ontological security, and foreign policy change." *Foreign Policy Analysis* 12, no. 4 (2016): 610–627.

Tillich, Paul. *Courage to Be, with an introduction by Peter J. Gomes.* Yale University Press, 2000.

Wertsch, James V. "Narrative tools of history and identity." *Culture & Psychology* 3, no. 1 (1997): 5–20.

Wodak, Ruth. *The politics of fear: What right-wing populist discourses mean.* Sage, 2015.

Zarakol, Ayşe. "States and ontological security: A historical rethinking." *Cooperation and Conflict* 52, no. 1 (2017): 48–68.

NOTES

1. Jennifer Mitzen, "Ontological security in world politics: State identity and the security dilemma," *European Journal of International Relations* 12, no. 3 (2006): 342.

2. Anthony Giddens, *The consequences of modernity* (Cambridge, MA: Polity, 1990), 92.

3. Giddens, *The consequences of modernity*, 534.

4. Helim Sarı Ertem and Aslı Nur Düzgün, "Uluslararası İlişkiler Disiplininde Ontolojik Güvenlik Teorisi: Kavram ve Literatür Odaklı Bir İnceleme," *Security Strategies Journal* 17, no. 37 (2021): 42.

5. Jennifer Mitzen and Kyle Larson, "Ontological security and foreign policy," *Oxford Research Encyclopedia of Politics* (2017), 6.

6. Ayşe Zarakol, "States and ontological security: A historical rethinking," *Cooperation and Conflict* 52, no. 1 (2017): 49.

7. Jef Huysmans, "Security! What Do You Mean?: From Concept to Thick Signifier," *European Journal of International Relations* 4, no. 2 (1998): 242.

8. Mitzen, "Ontological security in world politics," 343.

9. Tayyar Arı, *Uluslararası İlişkiler Teorileri, 10. baskı* (Bursa: Aktuel, 2021), 580.

10. Zarakol, "States and ontological security," 55–57.

11. Catarina Kinnvall, "Ontological insecurities and postcolonial imaginaries: The emotional appeal of populism," *Humanity & Society* 42, no. 4 (2018): 530.

12. Alanna Krolikowski, "State personhood in ontological security theories of international relations," *Chinese Journal of International Politics* 2, no. 1 (2008): 111–113.

13. Stuart Croft and Nick Vaughan-Williams, "Fit for Purpose? Fitting Ontological Security Studies 'into' the Discipline of International Relations: Towards a Vernacular Turn," *Cooperation and Conflict* 52, no. 1 (2017): 16–17.

14. Nina C. Krickel-Choi, "The Concept of Anxiety in Ontological Security Studies," *International Studies Review* 24, no. 3 (2022): 6–7.

15. Ty Solomon, "Ontological security, circulations of effect, and the Arab Spring," *Journal of International Relations and Development* 21, no. 4 (2018): 938.

16. Catarina Kinnvall, *Globalization and religious nationalism in India: The search for ontological security* (London: Routledge, 2007), 19–20.

17. Ertem and Düzgün, "Uluslararası İlişkiler Disiplininde Ontolojik Güvenlik," 49.

18. Mitzen, "Ontological security in world politics," 346.

19. Catarina Kinnvall, "Globalization and religious nationalism: Self, identity, and the search for ontological security," *Political Psychology* 25, no. 5 (2004):748–749.

20. Andreas Anter, *Max Weber's modern state theory: Origins, structure, and significance* (New York: Springer Publishing, 2014), 153–155.

21. Brent J. Steele, *Ontological security in international relations: Self-identity and the IR state* (New York: Routledge, 2008).

22. Zarakol, "States and ontological security," 50–51.

23. Jelena Subotić, "Narrative, ontological security, and foreign policy change," *Foreign Policy Analysis* 12, no. 4 (2016): 611.

24. Bahar Rumelili, "Identity and Desecuritization: The Pitfalls of Conflating Ontological and Physical Security," *Journal of International Relations and Development,* 18, no. 1 (2015): 52–74.

25. Vincent Della Sala, "Narrating Europe: The EU's ontological security dilemma," *European Security* 27, no. 3 (2018): 267–269.

26. Rumelili, "Identity and Desecuritization," 53.

27. Rumelili, "Identity and Desecuritization," 72.

28. Rita Floyd, *Security and the environment: Securitisation theory and US environmental security policy* (Cambridge: Cambridge University Press, 2010), 10–12.

29. Rumelili, "Identity and Desecuritization," 68.

30. Nina C. Krickel-Choi, "The Concept of Anxiety in Ontological Security Studies," *International Studies Review* 24, no. 3 (2022): 4–7.

31. Trine Flockhart, "The problem of change in constructivist theory: Ontological security seeking and agent motivation," *Review of International Studies* 42, no. 5 (2016).

32. James V Wertsch, "Narrative tools of history and identity," *Culture & Psychology* 3, no. 1 (1997).

33. Catarina Kinnvall, "Populism, ontological insecurity and Hindutva: Modi and the masculinization of Indian politics," *Cambridge Review of International Affairs* 32, no. 3 (2019): 284–286.

34. Bahar Rumelili and Umut Can Adisönmez. "Uluslararası ilişkilerde kimlik-güvenlik ilişkisine dair yeni bir paradigma: Ontolojik güvenlik teorisi," *International Relations Journal* 17, no. 66 (2020): 25–26.

35. Subotić, "Narrative, ontological security," 620.

36. Jennifer Mitzen, "Anxious community: EU as (in)security community," *European Security* 27, no. 3 (2018).

37. John Cash and Catarina Kinnvall, "Postcolonial bordering and ontological insecurities," *Postcolonial Studies* 20, no. 3 (2017): 268.

38. Catarina Kinnvall, Ian Manners, and Jennifer Mitzen, "Introduction to 2018 special issue of European Security: Ontological (in)security in the European Union," *European Security* 27, no. 3 (2018): 250.

39. Bojan Brkic, "Russia's war in Ukraine leaves Serbia stuck between a rock and a hard place," *Euronews*, March 3, 2022, https://www.euronews.com/my-europe/2022/03/03/russia-s-war-in-ukraine-leaves-serbia-stuck-between-a-rock-and-a-hard-place

40. Mitzen, "Ontological security in world politics," 348.

41. Deborah Welch Larson, *Anatomy of mistrust: US-Soviet relations during the Cold War* (Ithaca: Cornell University Press, 2000).

42. Martha Finnemore, "The purpose of intervention: Changing beliefs about the use of force," *Canadian Military Journal* (2006): 157.

43. Bahar Rumelili, *Conflict resolution and ontological security* (Oxfordshire: Taylor & Francis, 2015).

44. Tayyar Arı, *Uluslararası İlişkilere Giriş*, 5. Baskı (Bursa: Aktuel, 2018).

45. Ty Solomon, "Rethinking productive power through emotion," *International Studies Review* 19, no. 3 (2017): 497.

46. Solomon, "Rethinking productive power through emotion," 534.

47. Solomon, "Rethinking productive power through emotion," 535.

48. Ruth Wodak, *The politics of fear: What right-wing populist discourses mean* (Washington: Sage Publications, 2015), 32.

49. Bahar Rumelili, "Integrating anxiety into international relations theory: Hobbes, existentialism, and ontological security," *International Theory* 12, no. 2 (2020): 259.

50. Paul Tillich, *Courage to Be, with an introduction by Peter J. Gomes* (New Haven: Yale University Press, 2000), 40–51.

51. Ilse Helbrecht, "Ontological Security, Globalization, and Geographical Imagination," *Spatial Transformations* (London: Routledge, 2021), 245–248.

52. Tomás Mena García, "Donald J. Trump: A critical discourse analysis," *La Revista Estudios Institucionales* 5, no. 8 (2018): 55–60.

53. Michael Kenny, "Back to the populist future?: Understanding nostalgia in contemporary ideological discourse," *Journal of Political Ideologies* 22, no. 3 (2017).

54. Steele, *Ontological security in international relations*, 13.

PART IV

Postmodern Theories

Critical International Relations

Chapter 9

Post-Colonial Perspectives in International Relations

Oktay Bingöl and Doğan Şafak Polat

INTRODUCTION

As it can be seen from the textbooks and scholarly articles, the postcolonial perspectives in the International Relations (IR) discipline have gone unheeded for a long time.[1] However, after almost a half century when IR emerged as a discipline, some textbooks and journals are seen to have been dedicated to postcolonial studies. Thus, one may argue that postcolonialism is being "decolonized" and categorized as a separate and distinct approach to IR. Postcolonialism focuses on identity construction in addition to many other different phenomena such as the consequences of imperialism, chauvinism, and self-determination, as well as on issues of nation/state creation, nationalism, and self-perception of societies established during the colonial period, which are of importance for both classical and neoclassical IR theories. Because of the widely contested utility of classical and neoclassical theories in the post–Cold War conditions, scholars desperately sought new paradigms in IR.

Postcolonial studies have put cogent arguments and contributed significantly to the study of "international" especially since the end of the Cold War. Accordingly, the "South" and "Third World" have become more visible in the discipline, and the Western-centric IR has been exposed to a foundational criticism. As postcolonial perspectives emerged mainly from experiences and struggles of the colonized others, the common philosophy underlying the different perspectives under the title "postcolonial" is to challenge the present realities which are regarded as the legacies of the colonial past. Contrary to the present IR, which is based on European history, events, and rhetoric, the scholars of this genre take the formerly colonized continents and their per-spectives as the focus of their study, and try to unveil the realities of knowl-edge production process and transform them. It is claimed by hat IR should also focus toward people, identities, and resistance together with traditional domain of states, militaries, and diplomacy.

This chapter is structured to achieve four aims. First is to discuss and clarify the frequently used terms and concepts in postcolonial studies. Second is to reveal the long process of the emergence of post-colonial theory, with its humanitarian, religious, economic, and political justifications from the "invent" of the Americas until present. In this historical survey, the interactions with non-traditional, non-constructive, critical, post-modern, post-structuralist perspectives are to be underlined. Third is to outline major strands such as colonial discourse theory, Orientalism, Eurocentrism, iden-tity and hybridity, and subaltern studies in it. Post-colonial theory is not exempt from criticism. Some scholars regard it as the re-construction of the West's domination over the former colonies and criticize the theory as being a new expression of the West's historical power and its alleged superiority over the rest of the world. In this respect, such criticism is also discussed in this chapter.

DEFINITIONS AND TERMS

In postcolonial literature, there are various terms and concepts such as colonialism, anti-colonialism, new colonialism, post-colonialism, postco-lonialism, postcolonial theory, and postcolonial perspectives that are often confused and used interchangeably. In this regard, this chapter concerns a definitional discussion.

In a chapter with the adjective "postcolonial," the concepts of imperialism and colonialism need clarification. Imperialism, in its simple meaning, is the process of establishing an empire. In this regard Michael Doyle argues that in empire, one state controls the political sovereignty of another state/society through force, dependency, and/or collaboration.[2] The term itself comes from the Latin word *imperium* to mean Roman dominance over the Mediterranean, part of North Africa, and Anatolian coasts.[3] *Imperialism* is regarded as a purposeful policy of obtaining colonies for economic, strategic, and political advantage. "Around the mid-nineteenth century, the term imperialism was used to describe the government and policies of Napoleon III."[4]

Imperialism is also defined with economic context. John A. Hobson, an English economist and a non-Marxist, conceptualized a well-accepted impe-rialism theory.[5] He argues that "as production at home exceeds the growth in consumption, and more goods are produced than can be sold at a profit, more capital exists than can be profitably invested. It is this economic condition of affairs that forms the taproot of imperialism."[6] Hobson believes that imperial expansion is preference not inevitability. Lenin, on the other hand, drawing on Hobson's concept, defines it as the highest stage and inevitable consequence of capitalism.[7] Lenin's work has influenced the international politics in the twentieth century.

The concepts "empire" and "imperialism" are interconnected, but vary in some aspects. An empire implies the "expansion of states outside their territory, a widening of geographical space, either by land or sea, extending boundaries of power and influence."[8] Other states are brought under direct control of the imperial power by "whatever means for whatever purpose."[9] In history several empires employed various methods such as taxation, political/ military administration, and use of slave labor.[10]

Colonialism, with its commonly accepted meaning, could be understood as expansion of Europe into the world between the sixteenth and twentieth centuries. In this expansion, European states dominated colonies beyond the European Continent and created an asymmetrical dependency relationship. This was not a simple relationship of economic exploitation and extended to social, political, and cultural dimensions, creating a complex domination. Basically, the colonizer and the colonized constitute two sides of such relationships.

Colonialism took various forms over history and in different spatial settings. Some colonies were predominantly established for settlement such as British colonies in North America and the Pacific. Some other colonies were founded for their resources. Since economic exploitation was the main motive for this type, they are not settled by colonizers and are administered directly and indirectly.[11]

As this discussion reveals, the terms "colonialism" and "imperialism" are interlinked but they hold differences. Edward Said argues that "imperialism means the practice, the theory, and the attitudes of a dominating metropolitan center ruling a distant territory; colonialism, which is almost always a consequence of imperialism, is the implanting of settlements on distant territory."[12] In short, it is physical occupation of a state. The main motivation for colonial endeavor is almost always to gain access to resources and land. In most cases this included natural resources, but there might also be a desire to gain access to land which offers some strategic military or economic advantage over rivals.[13] Bush, in support of this, states that "informal imperialism can exist without colonialism but colonialism cannot exist without imperialism."[14] More precisely, colonial domination is defined as "the political control, physical occupation, and domination of people over another people and their land for purposes of extraction and settlement to benefit the occupiers."[15]

Colonialism and slavery are frequently used together. Slavery is the control of one person by another. The former is the slave, the latter is the slaveholder. "The control is supported and exercised through violence and its threat. The aim of this control is primarily economic exploitation, but may include sexual use or psychological benefit."[16] Its history goes back to the early settlements in Mesopotamia and extends to all parts of the world. However, the European transatlantic slave trade opened a new chapter in the process and later coincided with colonialism.

Anti-colonialism which emerged and gained momentum in the process of colonialism is the political struggle of colonized peoples against the specific ideology and practice of colonialism. It "signifies the point at which the various forms of opposition become articulated as a resistance to the operations of colonialism in political, economic and cultural institutions."[17] The inevitable end of colonialism and anti-colonialism was decolonization. It is the process of revealing and breaking down colonialist dominance in all its forms. This includes liberating colonized territories from overt and physical domination, and destroying the covert aspects of institutional and cultural dominations. The latter is significant to be disposed of persisting legacies of colonialism after political independence.[18]

As the discussion on the link between imperialism and colonialism reveals, colonialism has continued in new forms after decolonization. In this regard, Kwame Nkrumah, the revolutionary leader of Ghana, described this new type as neo-colonialism or new colonialism. He argued that, although countries like Ghana had gained political independence, the former colonial powers as old imperialists and new imperialist states continued to control politics and economies of former colonized countries through new instruments of international political economy created after the Second World War and dependency relations.[19] In fact, Nkrumah "argued that neocolonialism was more insidious and more difficult to detect and resist than the direct control exercised by classic colonialism."[20] Later this term has been used to describe the former colonizers' policies, strategies, and interventions in ex-colonized countries after political independence. Instead of neo-colonialism, the neo-imperialism is widely used to distinguish the globalized capitalist economy relations from earlier neo-colonialism.[21]

However, a new term and concept emerged and was put in circulation: post colonialism, but its definitions vary. It is simply regarded as "the tradition of the oppressed."[22] Post-colonialism (post- with hyphen or often postcolonialism without it) deals with the legacies and impacts of colonization on cultures and societies. Before the term "postcolonialism," "post-colonial state" was first used after the Second World War. "Post-colonial had a clearly chronological meaning, designating the post-independence period. However, from the late 1970s the term has been used by literary critics to discuss the various cultural effects of colonization."[23] It has now various meanings as broad as covering the study of the European colonial history, the forms of European colonialisms, discursive practices of colonialism and new colonialism, complex natures of resistance movements, and new colonial legacies and impacts on societies. There are three stages that constitute post-colonialism: an awareness of the socio-economic, political, psychological, and cultural inferiority enforced on colonized society; the resistance to colonizers and upheavals for independence; and a growing awareness of cultural overlap and hybridity.

Despite the suffix "ism," it is not a coherent theory or image in IR with certain assumptions, epistemology, and methodology such as realism and liberalism. When the suffix "ism" is dropped it is used as an adjective (post-colonial) which is attached to nouns as a qualifier, and new terms appear such as "post-colonial state," "post-colonial theory," "post-colonial people." It can also be used as a noun "both in the singular (postcolonial) and the plural (postcolonials), designating the subjects of the postcolonial condition."[24] The hyphen from post-colonialism is often erased, and postcolonialism and postcolonial are used. On the other hand, "the prefix 'post' aligns 'postcolonialism' with a series of other 'posts'—'post-structuralism,' 'postmodernism,' 'post-Marxism,' 'post-feminism,' 'post-deconstructionism.'"[25] However, "the 'post' is not a periodization that signals the beginning of an era where colonialism remained in the past. It does not also mark the period after the colonial era, but rather the effects of this era in shaping the world that is ours."[26]

HISTORICAL BACKGROUND AND POSTCOLONIALISM INTERACTIONS WITH IR THEORIES

In this section, the origin and evolution of postcolonial perspectives are traced with a temporal approach. In history, empires such as the Romans, Arabs, Ottomans, China, and Russia among others conquered several territories in their neighboring and remote areas and expanded considerably. They established mainly a tributary system rather than colonies. They, thus, are not regarded as colonizers in this chapter, and therefore European colonization is the focus. European colonization of America, Africa, and Asia are divided into three periods: 15th and 16th centuries; 17th and 18th centuries; and the last 15 years of the 19th century and early 20th century after the Berlin Conference of 1885. These periods are interlinked to transformation from feudalism into capitalism in Europe. Despite the overlaps between periods, Portugal, Spain, Netherlands, Britain, and France, to a limited extent, were the main colonizers of America in the first period. In the second, these states turned their main colonization efforts to Asia. The Berlin Conference of 1885 marks the beginning of the third period and is defined as "Scramble for Africa." In general, European slavery went hand in hand with colonization but ended earlier.

When early European slavery and colonialism began in the fifteenth and sixteenth centuries it also gave birth to anti-slavery and anti-colonialist opposition.[27] In Africa, some societies resisted the arrival of transatlantic slavery and the domination established by Europeans. Resistance and rebellion badly affected the trade, causing losses and raising costs. Although the resistance usually failed in all cases to secure the enslaved Africans' freedom, it reduced the slave trade and increased the awareness in European countries.[28] During resistance, Africans used several forms of rebellion and contention such as trying to flee, damaging machinery, working slowly, or fighting. "They could also resist in subtler ways, for example, by keeping alive their African religious beliefs, names, language, music and stories."[29]

European acknowledgement of "sins of slavery" began with religious enlightenment. Bishop Bartolomé Las Casas's (1484–1566) objections to slavery is accepted as the first example of an anti-colonial campaign. He "informed the world about the genocide that had been practiced under the blessing of the Spanish king and that through him, the Pope had initially permitted missionaries from Spain and Portugal to undertake expeditions to America."[30] Several Latin American religious scholars were inspired by Las Casas's views on slavery and colonialism. In Latin America a liberation theology emerged in favor of humanism, equality, and the victims of discrimination, slavery practices, and oppression. These early struggles gave birth to a decolonization process which occurred in three broad phases from 1776 to 1975.

In the first stage (1776–1839), the liberal anti-slavery campaign developed alongside moral and religious justification as well as economic considerations. Regarding economic objection to colonialism, Adam Smith argued that colonies are consequences of the capitalists' greed and injustice. He also opposed slavery for being more expensive and less efficient for the economy. Edmund Burke, born in 1729, is known as being one of the campaigners of the eighteenth century for equal rights in colonies. He objected to the abuses of British domination in colonies and criticized the oppression of local societies by colonial administrations.[31] This coincided with the French Revolution's principles such as liberty, equality, and fraternity without discrimination of any kind. At the end of the eighteenth century and the early nineteenth century, another insider, Jeremy Bentham, criticized British colonialism and challenged European countries to liberate their colonies. The anticolonial awareness in Europe inspired Latin American revolutionaries. Simon Bolivar (1783–1830), for instance, stating that slavery is the worst human indignity, is the pioneer in Latin America. He either led or inspired all revolutions and independence movements in Latin America during the first quarter of the nineteenth century. Several European colonies in North and South America such as the USA (1776), Colombia (1810), Chile (1810), Mexico (1810), Venezuela (1811), Argentina (1816), Brazil (1821), and Peru (1821) among others gained their independence.

The second wave of decolonization was a long process from 1839 to 1931. "The numerous colonial wars and rebellions in different time periods in the various regions of the world are clear proof of strong resistance to European domination."[32] This period included further theoretical studies regarding colonialism. Karl Marx discussed colonial expansion in relation to the economic effects of capitalism, but he ignored any liberation program for colonial revolution. This period, on the other hand, witnessed the increased awareness in Africa. Simon Kimbangu (1889–1952), a former local Baptist Church evangelist, led the way against Belgian colonialism in the Democratic Republic of Congo. His followers founded the Kimbanguist movement. African independent churches and other religious movements also played a great role in fighting against colonialism.

The third phase refers to the end of European colonial rule between 1945 and 1975. Almost all colonies gained their political independence either through violent struggle or peaceful methods. The intensity of anti-colonial struggles had also produced theoretical and philosophical texts. In the early years of this period, the Commonwealth literature studies in national contexts turned to a separate "Commonwealth Literature" disciplinary area within English in the United States and England. Later colonial discourse theory and Commonwealth literary studies intersected in postcolonial studies and initial interventions on postcolonialism were formulated by scholars of former colonies working in English Literature departments of Great Britain.[33] On the other hand, Civil Rights activism during the 1960s inspired Black Studies.[34]

Beginning with the late 1950s, former colonized countries (named as Third World countries) initiated a series of conferences and groupings. In this regard the Nonaligned Movement was established at the Bandung Conference in 1958. The Conference was described as the beginning of "the postcolonial" and the marker of a change in the type of imperial confrontation postcolonial states had to face.[35] This movement spread throughout three colonized continents in 1966, and the Tricontinental Conference in Havana was convened. These conferences increased the demands of former colonized countries on the colonizers such as technology transfer, debt forgiveness, etc.[36] in addition to their impacts on postcolonial thinking. Later, such activism of former colonies turned to neo-colonial and postcolonial struggles challenging ongoing legacies of colonialism in new forms.[37]

Anti-colonial and liberationist writings of scholars such as du Bois[38] and Fanon[39] among others in this stage inspired postcolonial perspectives to challenge and oppose neo-colonial realities and illusions. Particularly Frantz Fanon's writings have stimulated numerous people across the globe in struggles for freedom from oppression and racially motivated violence. Ghana's independence in 1961 was a critical point, and with his experience of the anti-colonial movement, Kwame Nkrumah introduced the term "neo-colonialism" in 1965.[40] Frantz Fanon, on the other hand, conceptualized the psychological and sociological aspects of neo-colonialism.

As analyzed in proceeding chapters, the roots of postcolonial studies go back to slavery, colonialism, and struggles against them, and span across centuries. When IR emerged as a separate field after WWII, its mainstream theories, realism and liberalism, began to analyze high political issues such as stability of international systems, wars, and armaments among others. IR theory was Eurocentric and under domination of positivism. Post-positivist writings were mostly ignored. However, post-positivist understanding heavily influenced postcolonial studies during the later period. Postcolonialism was influenced by theories such as economic structuralism (Dependency School and World System Theory), constructivist turn, critical theory, post-modernism, and post-structuralism of the IR field. In broad meaning, several disciplinary fields like anthropology, history, cultural studies, or art contributed to postcolonial theory.[41] Antonio Gramsci's views on hegemony, Alexander Wendt's constructivism, and Michel Foucault's discourse theory inspired the first postcolonial scholars during the 1970s and 1980s.[42] Postcolonial studies have used social constructivist understandings in their interpretations of colonialism, neocolonialism, and postcolonialism and produced new concepts.

Postcolonial studies are rich, and there are several scholars in this genre. Among them, Edward Said is regarded as the pioneer of postcolonial writers, with his book *Orientalism*. Gayatri Chakravorty Spivak, inspired by Gramsci, gave meaning to the term "subaltern" in postcolonial perspectives and elaborated the role of "subaltern" and subaltern practice.[43] Homi Bhabha, on the other hand, provided a broad understanding of the postcolonial field, and "framed the parameters of postcolonial studies arguing that the theory has emerged from the colonial testimony of Third World countries and the discourses of minorities within the geopolitical divisions of East and West, North and South."[44] Bhabha's other concepts such as "mimicry" and "hybrid identities" have played important roles to understand colonialism and afterwards. Subaltern studies gained momentum during the 1990s and 2000s with contributions of subaltern scholars such as Ranajid Guha, Partha Chatterjee, and Dipesh Chakrabarty, among others who also adopted postmodernist and poststructuralist criticism.[45] In the following section, four postcolonial scholars—Said, Spivak, Bhabha, and Chakrabaty will be discussed in detail.

POSTCOLONIAL PERSPECTIVES AND CONCEPTS

Edward Said: Orientalism, Self, and Other

In his book *Orientalism*, Edward Said describes the term "postcolonial" as the "distribution of geopolitical awareness into scholarly, aesthetic, economic, sociological, historical and philological texts."[46] He emphasizes the importance of timing in the construction of dichotomy of "Orient"/"Occident." The concept has gained a greater importance with the "Age of Exploration" which has been led by Europeans and North Americans. Despite this commitment to the representational production of Orient and Occident, however, Said did not deny the material reality of Eastern or Western places. Rather, he stressed that which makes them seem Eastern (Oriental) or Western (Occidental) to us is the extensive repertoire of categorization made through discourse. From an Orientalist point of view, these civilized and anti-civilized positions are so contradictory that the latter can only be described with expressions such as "backwardness, inclination to laziness whereas the civilized position represents the values like progress, science, liberty, individualism and tolerance."[47]

The concept of "Orientalism" proves an imaginative effort by which all creations of a given region in the world are enclosed with a code of knowledge, which is constructed or reproduced endlessly by some dominant parties. For Said, "this construction is established on an ontological distinction between the Orient and mostly the Occident."[48] At the same time, this construction made it possible for both of the regions and their inhabitants to resemble (a homogenization) and differentiate (a stereotypization). This distinction defines Europe or the West as progressive and rational against the opposite backward and irrational Orient. This distinction also allows the liberal West, a contrasting image of a despotic East, to gain a positional superiority over the East.

In academic studies, the concept of "orientalism" has been widely accepted as the synonym of Western imperialism and racism.[49] It is also argued that there is "nothing of the sort as a delivered presence; there is just a representation."[50] Western representations of Orientalism do not give enough information about the Orient, but they set forth "the efforts of the West to impose itself on peoples and cultures under Western hegemony."[51] According to Said, "the West's representations of the Orient are distorted" and an undistorted representation of the Orient is attainable but "this charge conflicts with his poststructuralist insistence that the Orient is nothing more than a discursive phantasm."[52] Said described Orientalism as "a discourse created with different types of power namely power political, power intellectual, power cultural and power moral."[53]

The political misdeed of Orientalism was primarily because "it legitimized colonial sovereignty" over the Orient's territories, so Said also characterizes it as a "style for dominating" and "having authority over" the Orient.[54] In his view, the concept of Orientalism can be defined as the production of culturally defined information about the Other that helps to establish the Self's identity. "Otherness and identity are two inseparable sides of the same coin. The Other only exists relative to the Self, and vice versa."[55] "It may be in the nature of the production of an identity itself to have a dual opposition between familiar (Western/Self) and strange (Orient/Other)."[56] "The West constructs the East in both real and imagined terms, as monolithic, ahistorical, inherently not modern, and unable to change."[57] The Orient is "the geographical fiction and Orientalism is the discourse through which the West constructs the otherness and thus gives itself an identity."[58] In this way, the West obtains the right to dominate the Orient, "to save it from despotism, superstition, misery, slavery, etc."[59]

"Othering" is often used for "the domination of the colonized through representation which denies autonomy, agency, creative thought, and the ability of resistance to those living under colonial powers or in postcolonial contexts."[60] That is to say, much of Said's effect and the criticism against him is concerned with "the question of representation through which postcolonial people or 'subalterns' living under oppressive and exploitative regimes are represented."[61] Since the notions of Orientalism and the Other represent negativity, "both are very much related to the problems of Subalternity."[62]

Gayatri Chakravorty Spivak: Subalternity and Representation/Articulation

In his essay "Notes on Italian History," Gramsci first referred to the Subaltern, a military term meaning "of lower rank."[63] Subaltern is "a term used to draw attention within Western discourse to the portrayal of the Third World."[64] This term is used to refer to workers, peasants, and other groups exposed to the hegemony of the ruling classes in society. Their access to hegemonic power is denied. However, even "subaltern" is a notion to describe postcolonial or the member of an ethnic minority, and "it is used for the sheer heterogeneity of decolonized space."[65] Gramsci developed a plan consisting of six measures to study the history of the subalterns, which are explained in depth in his book.

He aims to study "firstly, their objective creation through shifts in economic production; secondly, their active or passive association with the dominant political forces and their trials to affect their programs; thirdly, the emergence of new parties and dominant organizations, produced primarily to subjugate and retain the subordinates; fourthly, the formations created by the subaltern community itself to uphold limited rights; fifthly, new formations that preserve the independence of the subalterns within old frameworks; sixthly, those formations that can help to demonstrate their autonomy as a whole."[66]

The notion of Subaltern gained eminence with Spivak's 1985 article, "Can the Subaltern Speak? Speculations on Widow-Sacrifice."[67] Her article was "the commentary on the work of the Subaltern Studies Group, questioning and exposing their patronizing attitude."[68] Spivak stresses that the subaltern's fundamental subjectivity is limited to the discourses in which it is constructed as a subaltern. In this sense, it would be deceptive to argue that allowing subaltern forces to speak was a simple matter. "Spivak reconsidered in new historical trends the problems of subalternity posed by capitalist politics of undermining the revolutionary voice and inequalities of labor in a globalized world."[69] She did not approve "the first place of Gramsci's claim of the autonomy of the subaltern groups."[70] The reason why she rejected "this Gramscian view is based on the view that this autonomy results in subaltern group homogeneity and subaltern subjective identity."[71] "Spivak's second critique of Subaltern Studies Group is about her belief that no methodology, even the most ambitious Marxist one, can escape a kind of essentialism in its attempt to define who or what may constitute the subaltern group."[72] In her article, Spivak shows that "the earliest political historiography changed the voice of subaltern groups (women, tribal people, Third World, orient)."[73] In her article, she also reveals the paradox that the subalterns have awakened by rendering realistic utterances against unfair oppression and injustice to a consciousness of their own rights. Spivak points out that by continuing construction and historical silencing, Western discourses created the subaltern.[74] Therefore as Spivak pointed out in her book, subaltern cannot speak or be silent.[75] She wants to give voice to the subaltern. She criticizes Eurocentric attitudes of the West, claiming that knowledge is never innocent, and is always driven by the economic interests and power of the West. According to Spivak, knowledge is like any product or commodity exported from the West to the Third World.

Homi K. Bhabha: Hybridity, Mimicry, Stereotype, and Ambivalence

Bhabha deals with various mechanisms "that threaten colonial domination, including sly civility, fetishism and paranoia."[76] The adversarial discourse of Bhabha comes about "by playing different kinds of ambivalence against a fixity that he rightly accredits to the conceptualization of Said."[77] While Bhabha criticizes "the oversimplification of East and West distinctions and colonizer and colonized in the early work of Said (because both 'poles' are hybrid and entangled in each other), their academic roles can be perceived similar as they both explore mechanisms that separate, classify, and dominate the world."[78]

Bhabha and Said's "approaches differ in focus: while Said focuses on differences and oppositions between colonized and colonizer, Bhabha generally examines points of similarities."[79]

In order to explain the problems that hybridity can create, Bhabha presents a relatively different and creative political character, particularly from the work of Said and Spivak. Because discursive uncertainty can be contradictory and ambivalent to the master's narratives, it can also motivate the subaltern to resist and interrupt it. "Uncertainty about authority expressed in traditional discourses make a form of subversion possible, founded on the undecidability that turns the discursive conditions of dominance into the justification of intervention."[80]

Bhabha made "a crucial and essential intervention when he suggested a weakness in the account of Said, namely that there is always the possibility that colonial power and discourse were solely owned by the colonizer."[81] In response, Bhabha suggested that the Orientalization effort should always fail as the colonial subject is constructed in a repertoire of conflict positions which make him or her "the source of both fixity and fantasy"[82] in a cycle that can only be uneven, divided, incomplete, and thus potentially resistant. Although there is an inclination to describe an overly unifying and monolithic understanding of Western cultural imperialism, the result is reduced to the influence of the imperialist discourse, as the following declaration: "East was/is not a free topic of thought and action."[83] Being aware of this, Bhabha emphasizes the discursive instability of Orientalism and underlines that it needs not be homogenous to be hegemonic. As a matter of fact, Bhabha pointed out a passage from Said's book *Orientalism* and stated that Said was also aware of this instability but did not emphasize this issue sufficiently.[84]

Bhabha analyzes the colonial "stereotype," an example of the application of colonial authority, to better explain the problem. The stereotypes like "cleverly oriental" and "noble savage" allow colonial power to stabilize the colonized subject and justify the superiority and authority of the colonizer. However, Bhabha has shown that such constructions are infinitely repetitive: "the colonized is both savage and yet the most obedient and dignified servant; he is mystical, primitive, and simple-minded and yet the most worldly and accomplished liar."[85] It is assumed that a "cultural distance/cultural difference" exists between the West and the East that helped legitimize the idea of civilizing the colonies.[86]

Within "his essay 'Of Mimicry and Man,' Bhabha points out the attempt by the colonizer to promote a civilizing mission by creating mimic men, that is, recognizable others who are nearly the same, but not quite."[87] Nonetheless, the same, but not quite ambivalence is exploitable. Mimicry effectively fills in as a disguise for threat or mockery, with the local taking steps to deny the desire for recognition or imitation of their master.

The concept of "ambivalence," at the heart of Bhabha's work, provides "a framework for understanding how stereotypes and identities are constructed in a complex relational process and how they relate to the concept of cultural superiority."[88] Ambivalence is conceptualized in Bhabha's work as "a complex mix of attraction and repulsion that characterizes the relationship between colonizer and colonized."[89] The implication is that "as much as the colonizer is repulsed by and repressive towards the colonized, the colonizer is also attracted to, influenced by, and opens to the claims of the colonized."[90] This desire "to create copies that are 'almost the same, but not quite' compels colonial discourse to be ambivalent."[91] "As the colonizer perceives the possibility of the equality of the colonized, he simultaneously seeks to eliminate this possibility as a means of maintaining control over the colonized and, therefore, maintaining the colonial difference, which guarantees his perceived supremacy."[92]

Dipesh Chakrabarty: Provincializing Europe, Postcolonial Thought, and Historical Difference

Chakrabarty's "influential *Provincializing Europe: Postcolonial Thought and Historical Difference* tackles Europe's mythical figure, frequently taken as the original site of modernity in many histories of capitalist transition in non-Western countries."[93] Chakrabarty argues that "this imaginary Europe is built into the social sciences. The very idea of historicizing carries with it some peculiarly European assumptions about disenchanted space, secular time, and sovereignty."[94] Chakrabarty explores how postcolonial discourse affects the writing of history and criticizes not only the authors, but also the authors of the subalterns, for not representing them well enough.[95]

Chakrabarty criticizes postcolonial writers and especially Indian historians for failing to write their own history. While there are so many studies on the history of Europe, the histories of regions outside Europe, including India, were in subalternity. Chakrabarty considers postcolonial thought as the practice of "incorporating into the universals, such as the abstract figure of man or the reason underlying human science in Europe of the 18th century."[96] In other words, Chakrabarty finds it problematic in the Enlightenment philosophy to accept human as an abstract figure.

As Chakrabarty puts it, postcolonial thinking helps to understand the different conditions of existence that somehow recognize the diversity of human experiences. This forces Chakrabarty, as distinct from Europe, to define the visions and experiences of India's political modernity. This recognition of historical difference allows him to question historiography as an idea suggesting that he understands everything that should be seen both in unity and in historical development. For this reason, Chakrabarty chooses to change the temporal structure represented by historiography as a way of think-ing. He argues that historicism, modernity, capitalism, and civilization that "first emerged in Europe, then elsewhere" represent a temporal framework. In problematizing this linear temporal framework, Chakrabarty suggests an alternative reading of global modernity processes by interacting with antinomies. As Chakrabarty deals with the different histories of the capital's life processes, he leads the way for a precise reading of the subject. He also addresses the problem of understanding history as a secular issue.

Chakrabarty sees secular history as inadequate when it comes to explain-ing the conditions of postcolonial existence. In the particular case of India, it is difficult to conceptualize political modernity as apparently non-modern, rural, nonsensical relations and practices of life that constantly affect modern state institutions. In the context of colonialism, since the task of concep-tualization is heavily imposed by such anachronisms, Chakrabarty seeks to develop a conceptual framework that takes into account other pasts he encounters as pioneers of capital. Chakrabarty's desire to combine other past forms reinforces the critique of secular histories.

CRITICISM OF POST-COLONIAL THEORY

Postcolonialism is criticized on the ground that the concept itself is highly contested and it is not advancing a specific methodology.[97] Its coherency as a well-developed image of IR is also questioned. In fact, postcolonialism is not a substantive theory in the international relations (IR) discipline. Scholars of this genre use different methodologies. Postcolonial theory does not have relatively powerful internal logics of IR, which is constituted of various epistemological and ontological images and paradigms allowing scholars to apply any of them to the emerging situation and events.[98] On the contrary, postcolonial studies are characterized as a loosely related set of approaches. It is a question mark whether such loosely linked perspectives could be turned into a more flexible and fast-adapting paradigm.

It is argued that postcolonial theory is problematic for researchers because of its lack of consensus and clarity and its language seems impenetrable.[99] In this regard, Christian "contends that the language employed mystifies instead of clarifies the condition of the marginalized, making it possible for a few people who know that particular language."[100]

Another challenge of postcolonial theory is its contextual framework, as it is linked to race, culture, and gender, settler and native. The questions about the processes and conditions of being settler, colonizer, colonized, and post-colonial pose difficulties. "The answers to these questions make postcolonial theory problematic."[101]

Postcolonial scholars are criticized for their tendency towards homogenization of slavery and colonial practices. In this regard, Robert Young sees Sartre and Frantz Fanon as the origins of such homogenization. He argues that "postcolonial theory is predominantly based on the work of Frantz Fanon who developed the analysis of colonialism as a single formation."[102] Fanon and Sartre conceptualized colonialism based on French practices which differed from British colonialism. While the former was direct and systemic, the latter was indirect and comparatively less systematic. Subsequently Edward Said, drawing on Fanon and Sartre, developed a theory that "was so inclusive as to make no distinction between colonialism and imperialism, or the different forms that they took, or, within the theoretical model elaborated, to make an opening for the impact of anti-colonial resistance."[103] Such homogenization leads postcolonial authors to take European colonialism "as a way to organize the experience of more than three-quarters of the people living in the world today."[104] By doing this way, it fails to explain the similarities between non-colonized societies as well as the differences in colonization process and anti-colonial struggles.[105] Homogenization and totalization make the essence of colonialism ambiguous, and the analysis of the dynamics of world politics gets difficult.[106]

In the postcolonial literature, slavery is also homogenized and restricted to the European slavery trade although the history of slavery includes various types. Over the history, it was practiced in several places on the globe such as Mesopotamian civilizations, Arabian empires, and inside Africa long before the European slave trade. The legacies of such historical slavery practices certainly influenced the European slavery process. They, however, are mostly ignored in postcolonial literature.

Although postcolonial perspectives criticize Eurocentrism in the discipline, its "historiography runs the risk of paradoxically reunifying the diversity and alterity of the colonized world under the sign and spectra of Europe—forcing all temporalities and cultures into a hyphenated relationship with colonialism. In other words, postcolonialism semantically delivers the idea of a world historicized through the single category of colonialism."[107]

Another criticism is that the "postcolonial academics actually reinforce neo-imperial imperatives of political domination in making the subaltern its subject, and thus contributing to a discourse whose reproduction it ultimately seeks to break down."[108] It is accused of reinforcing the "Self" and "Other" dichotomy. It is also argued that "postcolonial analysis lacks the methodological structure, thus totalize rather than analyze similar to mainstream theories in IR."[109]

"Postcolonial studies are also criticized for ignoring development and neglecting material practices in favor of mere representations."[110] This is true in part since they are seen as "critiques of the production of knowledge about the Other and their focus is on discourse analysis."[111] This is partly true since studies on development are inaccurate, superficial, or incomplete regarding international political economy and its institutions. However, there are various postcolonial studies which criticize the theory and practice of development.[112] Postcolonial theory's "systematic application in the area of development has only just started."[113]

Last but not least, while postcolonial scholars criticize Eurocentrism in IR, the great majority of them are educated in Western academia, studied there, still work at American and European universities. Their works are written in Western languages, mostly in English. In fact, postcolonial scholarship academic language is very difficult for the people of once colonized countries to understand. Whether this is a weakness or strength needs to be further discussed.

CONCLUSION

The postcolonial studies, which emerged as a critique of Western enlightenment, have critically examined the relationship between the colonizers and colonized from the beginning of colonization. These studies deal mostly with the subaltern part of society, and bring together a deep concern about the history of colonialism and imperialism. The West began to dominate the world with its knowledge and established colonies in order to exploit them not only economically but also culturally and politically. The postcolonial studies question a world order dominated by the West as well as its dominant interests and ways of looking at the world. They also mention international relations' understanding of inequalities and pressures in race, class, and gender relations around the world. These studies draw attention to how global problems play an important role in the international system, and try to find the underlying reasons for the imperial and colonial ideologies that legitimize the Western superiority in the international arena. In this sense, they are trying to reconstruct the society and raise awareness.

These studies constitute the framework of concepts or discourses with which the thinkers or writers strive to explain the problems of postcolonial people or subalterns. Postcolonialism studies focus on the colonial issues or texts by using some notions such as the "orientalism" of Said, "subaltern" of Spivak, "discourse" of Foucault, "hegemony" of Gramsci, "deconstruction" of Derrida. Although Postcolonialism began when colonialism was over, colonialism is still ruling the psyche of the people of some independent countries like India. The main goal of Postcolonial theory is fighting against the negative effects of colonialism. It's not just about saving the post-worlds, but about learning how the world can move together towards a place of mutual respect beyond this period.

To sum up, the Postcolonial theory is like a conceptual lens that provides us with an alternative set of theoretical tools to unfold the complexities of this world. At the same time, it offers a unique approach focusing on the exploitation of mind, consciousness, language, and religion of indigenous people. In this sense, the Postcolonial theory not only provides information about what represents the real, but is also used as a powerful tool for shaping the "Other."

REFERENCES

Abrahamsen, Rita. "Postcolonialism." In *International Relations Theory for the Twenty-First Century: An Introduction*, edited by Martin Griffiths, 111–123. New York: Routledge. 2007.

Abu El-Haj, Nadia. "Edward Said and the Political Present." *American Ethnologist* 32, no. 4 (2005): 538–555.

Ahmad, Aijaz. "The Politics of Literary Postcoloniality." *Race & Class* 36, no. 3 (1995): 1–20.

Andreotti Vanessa. "Homi Bhabha's Contribution and Critics." In *Actionable Postcolonial Theory in Education*. Postcolonial Studies in Education, 25–35. New York: Palgrave Macmillan, 2011.

Arı, Tayyar. *Uluslararası İlişkiler Teorileri*. Bursa: Aktuel Press, 2018.

Ashcroft, Bill, Gareth Griffiths, and Helen Tiffin. *The Empire Writes Back: Theory and Practice in Post-Colonial Literatures*. New York: Routledge, 2002.

Ashcroft, Bill, Gareth Griffiths, and Helen Tiffin. *Post-Colonial Studies: The Key Concepts*. New York: Routledge, 2013.

Bales, Kevin. *Understanding Global Slavery: A Reader*. Berkeley and Los Angeles: University of California Press, 2005.

Baylis, John, Steve Smith, and Patricia Owens. *Globalization of World Politics: An Introduction to International Relations*. New York: Oxford University Press, 2006.

Bell, Richard. "Slave Suicide, Abolition and the Problem of Resistance." *Slavery & Abolition* 33 no. 4 (December, 2012): 525–549.

Benjamin, Walter. "On the Concept of History." In *Selected Writings 1938–1940 Vol. 4*, edited by Howard Eiland and Michael W. Jennings. Cambridge, MA: Harvard University Press, 2003.

Bhabha, Homi. *The Location of Culture*. London: Routledge, 1994.

Bhabha, Homi. "Remembering Fanon: Self, Psyche and the Colonial Condition." In *Colonial Discourse and Postcolonial Theory: A Reader*, edited by Patrick Williams and Laura Chrisman, 112–123. New York: Columbia University Press, 1994.

Bhabha, Homi. "Difference, Discrimination and the Discourse of Colonialism." In *The Politics of Theory*, edited by Francis Barker, Peter Hulme, Margaret Iversen, and Diana Loxley, 194–211. Colchester: University of Essex, 1983.

Buchowski, Michal. "Social Thought & Commentary: The Specter of Orientalism in Europe: From Exotic Other to Stigmatized Brother." _Anthropological Quarterly_ 79, no. 3 (Summer 2006): 463–482.

Burke, Edmund. _On Empire, Liberty and Reform: Speeches and Letters_, edited by David Bromwich. New Haven: Yale University Press, 2000.

Bush, Barbara. _Imperialism and Postcolonialism_. Harlow: Pearson Education Limited, 2006.

Cain, Peter J. "Bentham and the Development of the British Critique of Colonialism." _Utilitas_ 23, no. 1 (2011): 1–24.

Chakrabarti, Sumit. "Moving Beyond Edward Said: Homi Bhabha and the Problem of Postcolonial Representation." _International Studies Interdiciplinary Political and Cultural Journal_ 14, no. 1 (2012): 5–21.

Chakrabarty, Dipesh. _Provincializing Europe: Postcolonial Thought and Historical Difference_. Princeton: Princeton University Press, 2000.

Chatterjee, Partha. _The Nation and Its Fragments: Colonial and Postcolonial Histories_. New Jersey: Princeton University Press, 1993.

Christian, Barbara. "The Race For Theory." In _The Post-Colonial Studies Reader_, edited by Bill Ashcroft, Gareth Griffiths, and Helen Tiffin, 457–460. London: Routledge, 1995.

Dirlik, Arif. "The Postcolonial Aura: Third World Criticism in the Age of Global Capitalism." _Critical Inquiry_ 20, no. 2 (1994): 328–356.

Doyle, Michael W. _Empires_. Ithaca: Cornell University Press, 1986.

Du Bois, William E. B. _The World and Africa: An Inquiry Into the Part which Africa Has Played in World History_. New York: International Publishers, 1965.

Dunne, Tim, Milja Kurki, and Steve Smith. _International Relations Theories: Discipline and Diversity_. New York: Oxford University Press, 2010.

Easthope, Antony. "Homi Bhabha, Hybridity and Identity, or Derrida Versus Lacan." _Hungarian Journal of English and American Studies_ 4, no. 1/2 (1998): 145–151.

Evans, Tony. "The Limits of Tolerance: Islam As Counter-Hegemony?" _Review of International Studies_ 37, no. 4 (2011): 1751–1773.

Fanon, Frantz. 1967. _Black Skin, White Masks_. New York: Grove Press, 1967.

Fieldhouse, David K. _Colonialism 1870–1945: An Introduction_. London: Weidenfeld and Nicholson, 1981.

Gandhi, Leela. _Postcolonial Theory: A Critical Introduction_. Edinburgh: Edinburgh University Press, 1998.

Gramsci, Antonio. _Selections from the Prison Notebooks_. Edited and translated by Quintin Hoare and Geoffrey Nowell Smith. London: Lawrence and Wishart, 1971.

Green, Marcus E. "On the postcolonial image of Gramsci." _Postcolonial Studies_ 16, no. 1 (2013): 90–101.

Guha, Ranajit. _Dominance Without Hegemony: History and Power in Colonial India_. London: Harvard University Press, 1998.

Hobson, J. Allan. _Imperialism_. Ann Arbor: University of Michigan Press, 1902.

Huse, Daen. "Mapping Postcolonial Worlds: A Critique of International Relations Theory, Latin American scholarship reviewed." MSc. diss., University of Birmingham, 2011.

Kapoor, Ilan. *Politics: The Postcolonial Politics of Development*. London and New York: Routledge, 2008.

Kennedy, Dane. "Imperial History and Post-Colonial Theory." *Journal of Imperial and Commonwealth History* 24, no. 3 (1996): 345–363.

Lenin, Vladimir I. *Imperialism: The Highest Stage of Capitalism, in Collected Works of V. I. Lenin*. Moscow: Foreign Language House, 1916.

Louai, El Habib. "Retracing the Concept of the Subaltern from Gramsci to Spivak: Historical Developments and New Applications." *African Journal of History and Culture (AJHC)* 4, no. 1 (2012): 4–8.

McGowan, Winston. "African Resistance to the Atlantic Slave Trade in West Africa." *Slavery & Abolition* 11, no. 1 (2008): 5–29.

Morton, Stephen. *Gayatri Chakravorty Spivak*. London & New York: Routledge, 2003.

Morton, Stephen. "Terrorism, Orientalism and Imperialism." *Wasafiri* 22, no. 2 (2007): 36–42.

Nederveen Pieterse, Jan. *Development Theory: Deconstructions/Reconstructions*. London: Sage, 2001.

Nkrumah, Kwame. *Neo-Colonialism: The Last Stage of Imperialism*. International Publishers Co. Inc., 1966.

Pasha, M. Kamal. "Western Nihilism and Dialogue: Prelude to an Uncanny Encounter in International Relations." *Millennium: Journal of International Studies* 39, no. 3 (2011): 683–699.

Port Cities Bristol. "Black Resistance Against Slavery." Accessed November 17, 2022. http://www.discoveringbristol.org.uk/slavery/against-slavery/black-resistance-against-slavery/.

Rathbone, Richard. "Some Thoughts on Resistance to Enslavement in West Africa." *Slavery & Abolition* 6, no. 3 (1985): 11–22.

Rattansi, Ali. "Postcolonialism and Its Discontents." *Economy and Society* 26, no. 4 (1997): 480–500.

Rice, Allan. "The Fight: African Resistance." *Revealing Histories*. Accessed November 17, 2022. http://revealinghistories.org.uk/who-resisted-and-campaigned-for-abolition/articles/the-fight-african-resistance.html.

Royal College of Surgeons. "Geographies of Colonialism and Slavery." Accessed November 17, 2022. https://www.rcseng.ac.uk/-/media/files/rcs/museums-and-shop/hunterian/exhibition-archive/exhibiting-difference/geographies-of-colonialism-and-slavery.pdf.

Rukundwa, Lazare S. and Andries G. van Aarde. "The Formation of Postcolonial Theory." *HTS Teologiese Studies/Theological Studies* 63, no. 3 (2007): 1171–1194.

Said, Edward. *Culture and Imperialism*. New York: Alfred A. Knopf, 1993.

Said, Edward. *Orientalism: Western conceptions of the Orient*. London: Penguin Books Limited, 2003.

Sax, William S. "The Hall of Mirrors: Orientalism, Anthropology, and the Other." *American Anthropologist* 100, no. 2 (1998): 292–298.

Seidman, Steven and Jeffrey C. Alexander. *The New Social Theory Reader: Contemporary Debates*. London and New York: Routledge, 2001.

Seth, Sanjay, ed. *Postcolonial Theory and International Relations: A critical introduction*. London: Routledge, 2013.

Shohat, Ella. "Notes on the Post-Colonial." *Social Text*. Third World and Post-Colonial Issues, no. 31/32 (1992): 99–113.

Slemon, Stephen. "Post-colonial Critical Theory." In *Postcolonial Studies Reader*, edited by Bill Ashcroft, Gareth Griffiths, and Helen Tiffin, 99–116. London: Routledge, 1995.

Spivak, Gayatri Chakravorty. "Can the Subaltern Speak? Speculations on Widow-Sacrifice." *Wedge* 7/8 (Winter/Spring 1985): 120–130.

Spivak, Gayatri Chakravorty. *In Other Worlds: Essays in Cultural Politics*. London: Routledge, 1987.

Spivak, Gayatri Chakravorty. "Can the Subaltern Speak?" In *Marxism and the Interpretation of Culture*, edited by Cary Nelson and Lawrence Grossberg, 271–313. Chicago: University of Illinois Press, 1988.

Spivak, Gayatri Chakravorty. "Theory in the Margin: Coetzee's Foe Reading Defoe's Crusoe/Roxana." In *Consequences of Theory: Selected Papers of the English Institute, 1987–1988*, edited by Jonathan Arac and Barbara Johnson, 154–180. Baltimore: Johns Hopkins University Press, 1991.

Spivak, Gayatri Chakravorty. "Can the Subaltern Speak?" In *Colonial Discourse and Postcolonial Theory: A Reader*, edited by Patrick Williams and Laura Chrisman, 66–111. New York: Columbia University Press, 1994.

Spivak, Gayatri Chakravorty. *A Critique of Postcolonial Reason: Toward a History of the Vanishing Present*. Cambridge: Harvard University Press, 1999.

Staszak, Jean-François. "Other/Otherness." In *International Encyclopedia of Human Geography,* edited by Rob Kitchin and Nigel Thrift, 43–47. Oxford: Elsevier, 2008.

Viotti, Paul R. and Mark V. Kauppi. *International Relations Theory.* London: Pearson, 2012.

Williams, Patrick and Laura Chrisman. "Colonial Discourse and Post-Colonial Theory: An Introduction." In *Colonial Discourse and Post-Colonial Theory: A Reader*, 1–20. New York: Columbia University Press, 1994.

Young, Robert J. C. "Editorial: Ideologies of the Postcolonial." *International Journal of Postcolonial Studies* 1, no. 1 (1998): 4–8.

Young, Robert J. C. *Postcolonialism: An Historical Introduction*. West Sussex: John Wiley & Sons Ltd., 2016.

Ziai, Aram. "The Ambivalence of Post-development: Between Reactionary Populism and Radical Democracy." *Third World Quarterly* 25, no. 6 (2004): 1045–1061.

Ziai, Aram. *Exploring Post-Development: Theory and Practice, Problems and Perspectives*. London: Routledge, 2007.

Ziai, Aram. "Postcolonial Perspectives on Development." *ZEF Working Paper Series*, No. 103 (2012). Accessed November 17, 2022. http://hdl.handle.net/10419/88339

NOTES

1. John Baylis and Steve Smith, *Globalization of World Politics* (Oxford: Oxford University Press, 2006); Tim Dunne, Milja Kurki, and Steve Smith, *International Relations Theories: Discipline and Diversity* (New York: Oxford University Press, 2010); Paul R. Viotti and Mark V. Kauppi, *International Relations Theory* (London: Pearson, 2012).

2. Michael Doyle, *Empires* (Ithaca: Cornell University Press, 1986), 45.

3. Bill Ashcroft, Gareth Griffiths, and Helen Tiffin, *Post-Colonial Studies: The Key Concepts* (New York: Routledge, 2013), 112.

4. Ashcroft et al., *Post-Colonial Studies*, 111.

5. Viotti and Kauppi, *International Relations Theory*, 195.

6. J. Allan Hobson, *Imperialism* (Ann Arbor: University of Michigan Press, 1902), 7, quoted in Ashcroft et al., *Post-Colonial Studies*, 114.

7. Vladimir I. Lenin, *Imperialism, the Highest Stage of Capitalism, in Collected Works of V. I. Lenin* (Moscow: Foreign Language House, 1916), 1960–1969.

8. Barbara Bush, *Imperialism and Postcolonialism* (Harlow: Pearson Education Limited, 2006), 1–2.

9. David K. Fieldhouse, *Colonialism 1870–1945: An Introduction* (London: Weidenfeld and Nicholson, 1981), 1.

10. Robert J. C. Young, *Postcolonialism: An Historical Introduction* (West Sussex: John Wiley & Sons Ltd., 2016), 25–26.

11. Young, *Postcolonialism*, 17.

12. Edward Said, *Culture and Imperialism* (New York: Alfred A. Knopf, 1993), 9, quoted in Ashcroft et al., *Post-Colonial Studies,* 40.

13. "Geographies of Colonialism and Slavery," Royal College of Surgeons, November 17, 2022, https://www.rcseng.ac.uk/-/media/files/rcs/museums-and-shop/hunterian/exhibition-archive/exhibiting-difference/geographies-of-colonialism-and-slavery.pdf.

14. Bush, *Imperialism and Postcolonialism*, 55.

15. Baylis and Smith, *Globalization of World Politics*, 228.

16. Kevin Bales, *Understanding Global Slavery: A Reader* (Berkeley and Los Angeles: University of California Press, 2005), 91.

17. Ashcroft et al., *Post-Colonial Studies*, 11–12.

18. Ashcroft et al., *Post-Colonial Studies,* 56–57.

19. Kwame Nkrumah, *Neo-Colonialism: The Last Stage of Imperialism* (International Publishers Co. Inc., 1966).

20. Ashcroft et al., *Post-Colonial Studies*, 146.

21. Ashcroft et al., *Post-Colonial Studies*, 147.

22. Walter Benjamin, "On the Concept of History," in *Selected Writings 1938–1940 vol. 4*, ed. H. Eiland and M. W. Jennings (Cambridge, MA: Harvard University Press, 2003), 392.

23. Ashcroft et al., *Post-Colonial Studies*, 168.

24. Ella Shohat, "Notes on the Post-Colonial," *Third World and Post-Colonial Issues* 31, no. 32 (1992): 101.

25. Shohat, "Notes on the Post-Colonial," 101.

26. Sanjay Seth, *Postcolonial Theory and International Relations: A critical Introduction* (London: Routledge, 2013), 20.

27. Winston McGowan, "African Resistance to the Atlantic Slave Trade in West Africa," *Slavery & Abolition* 11, no. 1 (2008): 5–29; Richard Rathbone, "Some Thoughts On Resistance to Enslavement in West Africa," *Slavery & Abolition* 6, no. 3 (1985): 11–22; Richard Bell, "Slave Suicide, Abolition and the Problem of Resistance," *Slavery & Abolition* 33, no. 4 (December, 2012): 525–549.

28. Alan Rice, "The Fight: African Resistance," *Revealing Histories,* November 17, 2022, http://revealinghistories.org.uk/who-resisted-and-campaigned-for-abolition/articles/the-fight-african-resistance.html.

29. Port Cities Bristol, "Black Resistance Against Slavery," November 17, 2022, http://www.discoveringbristol.org.uk/slavery/against-slavery/black-resistance-against-slavery/.

30. Lazare S. Rukundwa and Andries G. van Aarde, "The Formation of Postcolonial Theory," *HTS Teologiese Studies/Theological Studies* 63, no. 3 (2007): 1176; Young, *Postcolonialism,* 75–82.

31. Edmund Burke, *On Empire, Liberty and Reform: Speeches and Letters,* David Bromwich (ed.) (New Haven: Yale University Press, 2000).

32. Klose, *Decolonization and Revolution,* 20.

33. Ashcroft et al., *Post-Colonial Studies,* 45; Ali Rattansi, "Postcolonialism and Its Discontents," *Economy and Society* 26, no. 4 (1997): 480–500.

34. Ashcroft et al., *Post-Colonial Studies,* 24.

35. Young, *Postcolonialism,* 191; Edward Said, *Orientalism: Western conceptions of the Orient* (London: Penguin Books, 2003), 104.

36. Viotti and Kauppi, *International Relations Theory,* 209.

37. Young, *Postcolonialism;* Bush, *Imperialism and Postcolonialism;* Leela Gandhi, *Postcolonial Theory: A Critical Introduction* (Edinburgh: Edinburgh University Press, 1998), quoted in Viotti and Kauppi, *International Relations Theory,* 209.

38. William E. B. Du Bois, *The World and Africa; An Inquiry Into the Part which Africa Has Played in World History* (New York: International Publishers, 1965).

39. Frantz Fanon, *Black Skin, White Masks* (New York: Grove Press, 1967).

40. Nkrumah, *Neo-Colonialism,* ix.

41. Daen Huse, "Mapping Postcolonial Worlds: A Critique of International Relations Theory, Latin American scholarship reviewed," MSc. diss., University of Birmingham, 2011, 7.

42. Marcus E. Green, "On the postcolonial image of Gramsci," *Postcolonial Studies* 16, no. 1 (2013): 90–101.

43. Gayatri Chakravorty Spivak, *In Other Worlds: Essays in Cultural Politics* (London: Routledge, 1987); Spivak, "Can the Subaltern Speak?" in *Marxism and the Interpretation of Culture,* edited by Cary Nelson and Lawrence Grossberg (Chicago: University of Illinois Press, 1988), 271–313.

44. Homi Bhabha, *The Location of Culture* (London: Routledge, 1994), 171.

45. Dipesh Chakrabarty, *Provincializing Europe: Postcolonial Thought and Historical Difference* (Princeton: Princeton University Press, 2000); Ranajit Guha,

Dominance Without Hegemony: History and Power in Colonial India (London: Harvard University Press, 1998); Partha Chatterjee, *The Nation and Its Fragments: Colonial and Postcolonial Histories* (New Jersey: Princeton University Press, 1993).

46. Stephen Morton, "Terrorism, Orientalism and Imperialism," *Wasafiri* 22, no. 2 (2007): 36–42.

47. Tony Evans, "The Limits of Tolerance: Islam As Counter-Hegemony?" *Review of International Studies* 37, no. 4 (2011): 1751–1773.

48. Said, *Orientalism*, 2.

49. Dane Kennedy, "Imperial History and Post-Colonial Theory," *Journal of Imperial and Commonwealth History* 24, no. 3 (1996): 347.

50. Said, *Orientalism*, 21.

51. Kennedy, "Imperial History and Post-Colonial Theory," 347.

52. Kennedy, "Imperial History and Post-Colonial Theory," 348.

53. Said, *Orientalism*, 2–12, 94.

54. Nadia Abu El-Haj, "Edward Said and the political present," *American Ethnologist* 32, no. 4 (2005): 540.

55. Jean-François Staszak, "Other/Otherness," in *International Encyclopedia of Human Geography,* eds. Kitchin and Thrift (Oxford: Elsevier, 2008), 43.

56. Michal Buchowski, "The Specter of Orientalism in Europe: From Exotic Other to Stigmatized Brother," *Anthropological Quarterly* 79, no. 3 (2006): 463; Nadia Abu El-Haj, "Edward Said and the Political Present," 544.

57. Buchowski, "The Specter of Orientalism," 463; El-Haj, "Edward Said and the Political Present," 544.

58. Staszak, "Other/Otherness," 1–7.

59. Staszak, "Other/Otherness," 1–7.

60. William S. Sax, "The Hall of Mirrors: Orientalism, Anthropology, and the Other," *American Anthropologist* 100, no. 2 (1998): 292–298.

61. Spivak, "Can the Subaltern Speak?" 271–275, 308.

62. Spivak, "Can the Subaltern Speak?" 271–275, 308.

63. Spivak, "Theory in the Margin: Coetzee's *Foe* Reading Defoe's Crusoe/ Roxana," in *Consequences of Theory: Selected Papers of the English Institute, 1987–1988,* eds. Jonathan Arac and Barbara Johnson, 154–180 (Baltimore: Johns Hopkins University Press, 1991).

64. Said, *Orientalism*, 334–353.

65. Spivak, *A Critique of Postcolonial Reason: Toward a History of the Vanishing Present* (London: Harvard University Press, 1999): 310.

66. Antonio Gramsci, *Selections from the Prison Notebooks*, edited and translated by Quintin Hoare and Geoffrey Nowell Smith (London: Lawrence and Wishart, 1971).

67. Spivak, "Can the Subaltern Speak? Speculations on Widow-Sacrifice," *Wedge* 7/8 (Winter/Spring, 1985): 120–130.

68. El Habib Louai, "Retracing the Concept of the Subaltern from Gramsci to Spivak: Historical Developments and New Applications," *African Journal of History and Culture (AJHC)* 4, no. 1 (2012): 4–8.

69. Louai, "Retracing the Concept," 4–8.

70. Louai, "Retracing the Concept," 4–8.

71. Louai, "Retracing the Concept," 4–8.

72. Louai, "Retracing the Concept," 4–8.

73. Stephen Morton, *Gayatri Chakravorty Spivak,* Routledge Critical Thinker Series (London & New York: Routledge).

74. Spivak, "Can the Subaltern Speak?" 271–275, 308.

75. Morton, *Gayatri Chakravorty Spivak.*

76. Antoni Easthope, "Homi Bhabha, Hybridity and Identity, or Derrida versus Lacan," *Hungarian Journal of English and American Studies* 4, no. 1–2 (1998): 145.

77. Easthope, "Homi Bhabha, Hybridity and Identity," 145.

78. Easthope, "Homi Bhabha, Hybridity and Identity," 145.

79. Vanessa Andreotti, "Homi Bhabha's Contribution and Critics," in *Actionable Postcolonial Theory in Education,* Postcolonial Studies in Education (New York: Palgrave Macmillan, 2011), 25.

80. Bhabha, *The Location of Culture,* 112.

81. Homi Bhabha, "Difference, Discrimination and the Discourse of Colonialism," eds. Francis Barker, Peter Hulme, Margaret Iversen, and Diana Loxley, *The Politics of Theory* (Colchester: University of Essex, 1983), 200. This essay is not reprinted in *The Location of Culture.*

82. Bhabha, "Difference, Discrimination and the Discourse of Colonialism," 200.

83. Edward W. Said, *Culture and Imperialism* (New York: Alfred A. Knopf, 1993), xiii.

84. Bhabha, *The Location of Culture,* 73.

85. Dipesh Chakrabarty, *Provincializing Europe: Postcolonial Thought and Historical Difference* (New Jersey: Princeton University Press, 2000), 7; Spivak, *A Critique of Postcolonial Reason,* 290.

86. Bhabha, *The Location of Culture,* 82, 66, 77, 85.

87. Bhabha, *The Location of Culture,* 86.

88. Sumit Chakrabarti, "Moving Beyond Edward Said: Homi Bhabha and the Problem of Postcolonial Representation," *International Studies Interdisciplinary Political and Cultural Journal* 14, no. 1 (2012): 13.

89. Ashcroft, et al., *The Empire Writes Back,* 12.

90. Steven Seidman and Jeffrey C. Alexander, *The New Social Theory Reader: Contemporary Debates* (London and New York: Routledge, 2001), 26.

91. Seidman and Alexander, *The New Social Theory Reader,* 26.

92. Andreotti, *Homi Bhabha's Contribution and Critics,* 26.

93. Chakrabarty, *Provincializing Europe,* 26.

94. Chakrabarty, *Provincializing Europe,* 30–37.

95. Chakrabarti, "Moving Beyond Edward Said," 15–29.

96. Chakrabarti, "Moving Beyond Edward Said," 15–29.

97. Robert J. C. Young, "Editorial: Ideologies of The Postcolonial," *International Journal of Postcolonial Studies* 1, no. 1 (1998): 5.

98. M. Kamal Pasha, "Western Nihilism and Dialogue: Prelude to an Uncanny Encounter in International Relations," *Millennium: Journal of International Studies* 39, no. 3 (2011): 683–700.

99. Stephen Slemon, "Post-Colonial Critical Theory," in *Postcolonial Studies Reader*, ed. Bill Ashcroft, Gareth Griffiths, and Helen Tiffin (London: Routledge, 1995), 100; Rukundwa and van Aarde, "The Formation of Postcolonial Theory," 172.

100. Barbara Christian, "The Race For Theory," in *The Post-Colonial Studies Reader*, ed. Ashcroft et al. (London: Routledge, 1995), 457–460.

101. Rukundwa and van Aarde, "The Formation of Postcolonial Theory," 173–174.

102. Young, *Postcolonialism*, 18.

103. Young, *Postcolonialism*, 18–19.

104. Gandhi, *Postcolonial Theory*, 168.

105. Gandhi, *Postcolonial Theory*, 168.

106. Aijaz Ahmad, "The Politics of Literary Postcoloniality," *Race and Class* 36, no. 3 (1995): 9.

107. Gandhi, *Postcolonial Theory*, 171.

108. Gandhi, *Postcolonial theory*, 167; Spivak, "Can the Subaltern Speak?" 271–313.

109. Gandhi, *Postcolonial theory*, 167.

110. Arif Dirlik, "The Postcolonial Aura: Third World Criticism in the Age of Global Capitalism," *Critical Inquiry* 20, no. 2 (1994): 328–356.

111. Patrick Williams and Laura Chrisman, "Colonial Discourse and Post-Colonial Theory: An Introduction," in *Colonial Discourse and Post-Colonial Theory: A Reader* (New York: Columbia University Press, 1994): 8.

112. Aram Ziai, "The Ambivalence of Post-Development: Between Reactionary Populism and Radical Democracy," *Third World Quarterly* 25, no. 6 (2004): 1045–1061; Aram Ziai, *Exploring Post-Development: Theory and Practice, Problems and Perspectives* (London: Routledge, 2007); Pieterse Nederveen, *Development Theory: Deconstructions/Reconstructions* (London: Sage, 2001).

113. Aram Ziai, "Postcolonial Perspectives on Development," ZEF Working Paper Series, no. 103 (2012): 21, December 3, 2019. http://hdl.handle.net/10419/88339

Chapter 10

Feminism and/or Gender Studies in International Relations

A New Language for Women's Studies?

Çiğdem Aydın Koyuncu

INTRODUCTION

Understanding the current gender relations established within the framework of men's superiority to women and questioning how these relations transform at every level of the global social, economic, and political aspects of life is at the core of feminist approaches in international relations. Based on the experiences, feelings, and thoughts of women who are oppressed, marginalized, and even considered invisible in the field of international relations, feminist approaches also challenge the epistemological and ontological foundations of traditional theories of international relations and argue that these theories should be revised/incorporated by including women's existence/experiences. In particular, feminists, who question the gender bias inherent in realism, have criticized the nature of international relations based on concepts and issues such as state, sovereignty, power, security, conflict/war, and global governance and tried to express their feminist alternatives openly for these issues over the past 20 years. However, despite this development and deepening of feminism, it is not possible to say that feminists are fully and truly involved in the field of international relations. Considering that the field of international relations has a very masculine nature, progresses based on traditional practices, and is not very open to changes, and keeping in mind that it is not so easy to accept the discourses of change in the perception of power, it will be easy to understand why feminism cannot be fully positioned in this field.[1]

As a normative approach, feminism seems to put gender as a basic structure at the center of its studies in the field of international relations. However, it should be noted that feminism does not have a single theoretical approach, despite this basic structure. Feminists agree on the current secondary status of women, the pressures they face, and the need for gender equality between women and men. Nevertheless, they have different views on the ways to liberate women in the field of international relations.[2] In other words, besides those with or without a feminist perspective, there are even people who adopt very opposing views among those who have adopted feminist approaches. At this point, the focus on gender and the invisibility and inequality of women constitutes their common ground.

Feminism has different perspectives on evaluating gender relations and changing the disadvantaged status of women based on these relations. In the context of these different perspectives, feminism in international relations does not appear as a single/unitary theory, but as many different and sometimes competing approaches. This is one of the criticisms of feminism. These criticisms are based on the fact that the existence of different types of feminism (such as liberal feminism, radical feminism, socialist feminism, postmodernist feminism, and poststructuralist feminism) can threaten feminism's integrity in international relations[3] and weakens it against other theories.

On the other hand, different feminist approaches create richness within the entirety of feminist theory by analyzing each topic in depth from their perspectives and developing criticisms towards each other when appropriate. For example, liberal feminists focus on ensuring equal rights for women and women's access to education and the economy, while Marxist feminists focus on transforming the oppressive socio-economic structures of capitalist society.[4] Standpoint feminists argue that women's knowledge comes from a perspective that has the potential to provide more complete insights into world politics.[5] On the other hand, post-modern feminists reject the claims that a theory can tell "one true story" about the human experience and present multi-faceted analyses.[6] Liberal feminists such as Cynthia Enloe attempt to highlight women's roles and engage them in public life. However, post-positivist and standpoint feminists go further and force international relations researchers to question the normative foundations of their theories by asking how gender biases and distortions are accepted in the discipline and why they have not been noticed until now.[7] To deconstruct this biased perspective, they examine the gender-constructed language used in mainstream theories, especially realism, and focus on the impact of traditionally used dichotomies such as objectivity/subjectivity, public/private, war/peace, and national/international in international relations.[8] This is because those in the first place in these groupings represent the masculine value that we subconsciously decide to be more valuable than the second.[9] Feminists argue that using this analysis to investigate key international relations texts will provide remarkable insights into the gendered nature of language and knowledge used by the traditional international relations theory and will enable new definitions of concepts such as the state, power, and security.

It is also evident from the examples above that feminist approaches have developed analyses from different perspectives on many topics in the field. It is understood that separate criticisms have been developed towards the perspectives put forward by the feminist approach, and it is also noteworthy that many of these criticisms are put forward by other feminist approaches. For example, despite their practical achievements (such as representation and women's rights), liberal feminists are criticized by other feminist approaches as the "add women and mix" approach and are accused of displaying a simplistic attitude towards the empowerment of women with their so-called discourses.[10] Again, it is seen that some post-positivist feminists are accused of imperialism on the grounds of masking the real face of war, because of the language they use while analyzing wars as "an opportunity for women's rights" or "women's liberation."[11] These debates among liberal feminists, standpoint feminists, and post-positivist feminists also show that there is a natural tension between women's desire to place their voices on the international stage and their goals to completely deconstruct gender.[12] Again, this point can be considered an example in the debates among radical feminism, liberal feminism, and post-modern feminism, especially on gender issues. Radical feminism highlights feminine structures from gender stereotypes, regards feminine structures as more valuable, and claims that women will be more effective than men in resolving conflicts through their human relations experiences in the social structure. Radical feminists suggest that war has a masculine base and that throughout history it has been started and carried out mostly, or even entirely, by men. They argue that gendered structures alone will not be sufficient in the analysis of the reasons for this situation, and an inquiry based on biological differences (such as the connection of men's testosterone/hormonal status with war) should be added. Liberal feminists, on the other hand, oppose radical feminists' overemphasis on gender and basically act from the point of equality between men and women. Although liberal feminists state that studies on women's participation in decision-making mechanisms should be increased, they are distant from the emphasis that women alone can change the nature of international relations. Post-modern feminists, on the other hand, criticize liberals for attempting to integrate women into a masculine understanding by underestimating gender and criticizing post-modern feminism for having an exaggerated understanding of gender.[13]

Despite the divided nature of feminism within the discipline, it seems that all feminist international relations researchers are united in terms of concerns about gender.[14] Gender not only creates inequalities in power relations and social structures but also has significant effects on the relevant experiences of men and women.[15] Feminists aim at explaining the role of gender in the theory and practice of international relations by positioning women in international politics in different ways and investigating how they are affected by the structures and behaviors in the international system. Additionally, the common aim of all feminists is to attempt to understand the secondary status of women in the field of international relations, whereas the differences between them arise in the reasons and analyses of this secondary position. Although there are so many feminist approaches in international relations, it is seen that all these approaches have the common interest/aim of "gender equality" or at least "ensuring women's freedom."[16]

Gender is defined as the social roles assigned to men and women, and it is different from "sex." Feminism has considered gender as a point of criticism. In other words, it criticizes a gender that has been formed in the social process over time and consists of discourses produced in favor of men, rather than a gender that is innate and based on biological differences. Therefore, feminism and gender intersect in this sense. However, there are recent analyses suggesting that unlike their own criticism, feminists fall into the same mistake as the groups they criticize do by completely excluding masculine values/men. The use of the term "gender studies" instead of "feminist studies" has increased recently due to the negative perspectives created/formed based on these points. In fact, although all fields of study such as women's studies, gender studies, and feminist studies address and analyze the same points in general, it is important to question the reasons for the occurrence of these spatial differences. On the one hand, considering that gender has negative repercussions for both women and men, these different usages can be understood and supported by the fact that men's issues can also be analyzed on the basis of gender issues. Women's studies, on the other hand, can be considered a more general framework (a field covering them all), as they do not have a usage covering a discussion on the basis of the concepts of feminine-masculine and sex-gender.

At this point, the main problem is why studies do not develop analyses around the concept of gender by avoiding the use of the expression of feminist approaches, despite the increased visibility of women and awareness of violence against women, the progress on securing women's rights, and the representation of women in the public sphere as a result of the birth of feminism and the rise of feminist movements and struggles. Is this really a new and useful language? Can the discourse of "gender studies," which avoids using feminism, create a negative feedback in the field of women's studies? These should be considered important points of discussion and analysis.

The number of analyses that use the term "gender" instead of "feminism" and question the distinction between sex and gender or the uncertainty in some studies has also increased in recent years.[17] Although these studies include many criticisms, they are important in terms of discussing every question related to women and women's issues across the world. However, within the framework of recent developments, a definition of "gender studies," in which gender and gender relations are centered, is more commonly and averagely used instead of "feminist women's studies," which reflect historical, chronological, and intellectual effects. It is important to analyze whether this is a deliberate use within the framework of the questions above or what the positive/negative contributions of this usage can be to determining women's issues in the field of international relations or recommending solutions to these issues. In this context, after presenting the development process of women's studies and feminist approaches in the field of international relations, this study aims to evaluate discourses on international relations based on feminist approaches and gender analyses through the questions raised above.

INTERNATIONAL RELATIONS
AND WOMEN'S STUDIES

Women's studies constitute an interdisciplinary academic field of study that focuses on issues such as the understanding of socially and culturally structured gender through women's lives and experiences, discrimination and oppression faced by women, relationships between power and gender, and women's identities intersecting with social positions including race, sexual orientation, belonging to social-economic classes, and disability. Women's studies have a more general content compared to feminism and gender studies. For example, this field includes not only feminist theory and gender analysis, but also theories and methods including standpoint theory,[18] multiculturalism, intersectionality,[19] transnational feminism, social justice, bio-politics, materialism, and even ethnography, community-based research/survey, discourse analysis, critical theory-based readings, and post-structuralism.[20] In the basic framework, the field explores and criticizes the different social norms of gender, race, sexuality, and other social inequalities. In short, women's studies are related to and include gender studies, feminist studies, sexuality studies, cultural studies in a broader sense, ethnic studies, African-American studies, and others.[21]

As one the first classes of women's studies, Madge Dawson, an Australian feminist, offered "Women in a Changing World" at the Department of Adult Education at the University of Sydney in 1956, focusing on the socio-economic and political status of women in Western Europe. Dawson is considered one of the founders of this field. The first unit of women's studies in the United States was opened in 1969 at Cornell University. The first program of women's studies, which was launched with an intensive work following the foundation of this unit, was planned as a course at San Diego State University.[22] The first scientific journal of women's studies, called *Feminist Studies*, was published in 1972.[23] The first association of women's studies, called the National Women's Studies Association, was founded in the US in 1979.

Initially, women's studies generally tried to develop analyses of women's invisibility by asking the question *"where are the women?"*[24] Nonetheless, they adopted a broad perspective over time, starting from the criticism of the male-centered nature of the social sciences in the analysis on women's roles and lives in the face of sexual policy and major power structures in society. Women's studies analyze women's contributions to both international relations and other social sciences, criticism points on discourses and practices about women, changes and transformations of women, and their problems.

FEMINISM AND INTERNATIONAL RELATIONS

Feminist approaches in international relations have not only a normative nature but also ethical commitments in the form of comprehensiveness, relationality, and self-reflexivity, which are the most important characteristics that distinguish them from other critical theories.[25] Despite the normative differences in feminist international relations approaches, these three commitments are widely shared and strongly followed by feminists in international relations in the context of epistemological, ontological, and methodological perspectives.[26] The form of comprehensiveness can be explained as follows: Feminist international relations scholars do not only study to understand and evaluate the upper framework, but also add sub-factors to their analyses in detail. For example, feminists who study globalization do not only evaluate neoliberal perspectives that promote the capital mobility of international organizations, government agencies, and elites, but also examine female immigrant housekeepers, women micro entrepreneurs, and every positive/negative area in which women play a role in the global structure.[27] Similarly, feminist international relations scholars try to find identity dynamics and alternative possibilities for a conflict resolution process on both sides of the conflict to understand the issue/problem while conducting their research on fields of conflict.[28]

The norms of both comprehensiveness and self-reflexivity also help feminists break down their inner marginalizing, elitizing, and excluding prejudices without using their own perspectives. The analysis of weapons of mass destruction by Carol Cohn and Sara Ruddick is a good example to understanding the relationality of feminism. Cohn and Ruddick argue that feminist positioning against war also opposes negative developments, for example, the use and proliferation of weapons of mass destruction. This is also against the structure that strengthens the dominant perspective of Western powerful states and denies the political and social realities of both women and men living in less powerful states. Additionally, Cohn and Ruddick state that feminists who are citizens of very powerful and armed states should both support disarmament efforts in their own countries and express the inequalities created by powerful states in the world. Self-reflexivity and comprehensiveness cannot be applied by considering one's own belongings well and denigrating others. An example of this can be given from third-world feminists. Another important view accepted by feminists is that the whole world cannot be understood only through the eyes of Western white feminist women, that besides Western realities, the third world also has realities, cultures, and lifestyles, and relationality analyses should be carried out within this scope.[29] For example, as post-colonial feminists suggest, just because Western feminist women wear skirts or jackets, African or Middle Eastern feminists do not need to dress like them. It is necessary to accept and respect the fact that every woman has her own culture and lifestyle.

Considering the course of development of feminist approaches in international relations, these feminists have basically ascended over the views of second-wave feminists who criticized social structures, and the mastery of the masculine nature in these structures. However, feminists started to do research in the field of international relations, especially after the 1980s. *Millennium* was one of the first journals in this field. A special issue on women and international relations was published in 1988, where Fred Halliday argued that international relations theories try to explain the reality of world politics with a biased and masculine perspective in which women's lives and experiences do not participate in these explanations.[30] In the special issue of *Millennium* in 1991, Grant and Newland[31] stated that the nature of international relations has been formulated as overly confrontational, security-anxious, and anarchic by current theories, especially realism, weakening the field of international relations. Grant and Newland also addressed the issues of structural violence in international relations such as poverty, environmental injustice, and socio-political inequality, which are considered feminine, that is, a soft policy area, and often neglected, as well as constitute the real causes of international conflict and problems. Ann Tickner, Cynthia Enloe, Spike Peterson, Jan Jindy Pettman, Ann Runyan, and Christine Sylvester, who are important advocates of feminist international relations, opposed the state-centered and positivist nature of international relations and tried to demolish the discipline's power- and realism-based approaches.[32]

Feminist schools of international relations argue that the main subjects and concepts of international relations such as power, security, and sovereignty are highly masculine. For example, Tickner, in her feminist analysis of Hans Morgenthau's Six Principles of Political Realism, criticizes realism, in which power is expressed to have a highly rational and masculine nature.[33] Additionally, Enloe criticizes the issue that security- and power-centered analyses are produced through a highly masculine state-centered perception of the international system that excludes both women and their experiences.[34]

In 1999, a new feminist journal, the *Feminist Journal of Politics*, was established to develop a dialogue between academics in international relations and politics. The period in which these journals and studies emerged is a period when traditional theories among international theories and their inability to make predictions about the future were subjected to intense criticism.[35] After the end of the Cold War, the process of change has also been introduced on a theoretical ground with the participation of non-state actors in the field of international politics and the entrance of more non-traditional issues (i.e., human rights, ethnic issues, environmental issues, excluding security and war/conflict) in global policy agendas. In this period, feminist movements began to attract attention and find a place in the agendas of the United Nations (UN) and other international institutions.[36] This was a process in which several international regulations have been adopted in the field of international law to both recognize women's rights and combat violence against women.[37] In fact, as of the end of the 1990s, feminists were more successful in being visible in international institutions than influencing the discipline of international relations. In this period, anti-war feminists, with their cooperation with the UN, encouraged the Security Council to take the resolution no. 1325, thus enabling women to participate in international peace negotiations and operations, especially in a decision-making position. Additionally, they drew the attention of the World Bank and other international development agencies to the negative effects of neoliberal globalization and structural development policies on poor women, and they encouraged the European Union to establish gender inequality policies officially.[38] Feminists who mostly dealt with structural inequalities, women's economic problems, and human rights until September 11, 2001, intensely analyzed international security issues after 2001. Unlike other critical international relations theorists, feminists have attempted to reveal the sexist origins of global insecurities and terrorism in the context of Western and non-Western masculine structures underlying political and economic inequalities.[39]

GENDER AND INTERNATIONAL RELATIONS

Gender studies are an interdisciplinary academic field focused on analyzing gender identity and representation. This area includes women's studies, men's studies, all non-heterosexual studies (queer studies),[40] and even studies based on sexual analyses. This is an interdisciplinary field because it gets support from several fields, including literature, language, geography, history, political science, sociology, anthropology, cinema, media, international relations, law, and medicine. Therefore, it does not only include analyses of women/women's issues but also analyzes the effects of gendered patterns on women, men, and non-heterosexual groups. This is where they intersect with feminism. This is because feminist theory uses gendered analysis as a building block in its criticism and inquiries about women/women's issues.

Some of the feminist approaches in international relations consider feminism and gender as synonymous concepts. A study of gender also includes feminist criticism inevitably and due to necessity. Therefore, it is useful to consider not only the relationship between gender and feminism, but also that between gender and sex to better analyze this process. Sex and gender are both independent and interrelated concepts. As mentioned earlier, sex difference refers to natural/innate physical differences, whereas gender has a post-socially structured context. Despite these differences, they are related to each other, at least because their origin arises from sex difference. Anne Fausto-Sterling, a biologist and a feminist scholar, rejects a biological and social determinist perspective and analyzes how the interaction between biological structures and the social environment profoundly affects the capacity of individuals.[41] As mentioned earlier, feminists analyze not only gender-related problems but also sex-related issues such as problems regarding the fertility and maternal characteristics of women. However, the most important problem is the restriction of women's innate childbirth-related and maternal characteristics on a sexist basis. Asking pregnant women not to participate too much in public spaces, expecting them to leave their jobs, and not allowing them to be involved in diplomacy, politics, and military fields by considering their desire to become mothers can be given as examples in this regard. Feminist Simone de Beauvoir also draws attention to the existence of a gender discourse expressed in social contexts via her famous quote *"one is not born, but rather becomes, a woman."*[42] Societies want to identify people as soon as they see them so that they can produce behavioral, thinking, and emotional patterns (meaning that these patterns may differ based on sex). Therefore, sexes' preferences of hairstyles, voice tone, walking styles, clothes, and even colors are made according to masculine and feminine patterns, whereby their behaviors that do not comply with these patterns are not accepted.

Of course, the field of international relations can be analyzed on the basis of gender, at which point it should be noted that the field has a highly masculine structure.[43] There are also discussions among feminists on the use of gender. Some feminists argue that it is sufficient to consider and criticize gender only on the basis of feminine roles assigned to women. This method shallows feminist analyses because gender also assigns some masculine roles to men, which should be questioned. For example, it is important to examine how voluntarily men accept these roles, whether they question them at all, and whether they ever complain about them. Feminist approaches that focus solely on the questioning of feminine values on a sexist basis are likely to make a big mistake. According to this view, feminists make mistakes by themselves regarding the points they criticize, as well as their neglect of the issues and contributions of both men and men. At this point of criticism, some state that it would be more appropriate to use the concept of gender instead of feminism. For example, Whitworth insists that using the term "gender" instead of "feminism" or using the term "gender studies" instead of "feminist studies" will create a more neutral working space.[44] She argues that this is because feminism focuses on developing one-sided/women-only analyses. In this context, Flax introduces a different inquiry. She states that if we limit the feminist discourse only to women's issues, we unknowingly and ironically give privileges to men who do not have problems.[45] This is because men are considered a proper/related universal category, whereas women are considered a feminine and separated/isolated special category in the private sphere.[46] This view, which provides privilege and hegemony to men, is of course completely rejected by feminists. However, a persistent discourse based on women's issues or views may also cause either the masculine structure to be repeatedly reproduced and strengthened or the contradictions to be pursued.

Feminists have differences in their normative views of how the gender category is complementary to the structure of international relations. They also have different views on how gender is considered/perceived by other categories such as race, ethnicity, or class, which are often included in international relations theories. The majority of international relations feminists consider gender a relational structure in which masculine identities are preferred to feminine ones.[47] They also emphasize gender as a category that is highly related to the field of international relations, covering all its aspects. For example, feminists use gender in their analyses to criticize the rhetoric of security in the context of the global "fight against terrorism" after 9/11. In addition to the US occupation of Iraq and Afghanistan, they criticize the socialist structures in the discourses used by Islamic fundamentalist groups. As an example of these discourses, a sense of country defense with masculinity was created in the US after 9/11 by using concepts such as "man enough" including the use of nuclear weapons.[48] It is a fact that these gendered and especially masculine discourses gradually increased in the Trump era.

Gender is a concept used in the field of international relations in the analysis of various research questions. Some feminists use gender as a variable to analyze the behaviors of states in an anarchic system. For example, some feminist studies show that states with high domestic violence and gender inequality rates are more likely to use war politics in their foreign policies.[49] On the other hand, they argue that states with gender equality are more likely to be peaceful and aligned toward international cooperation.[50] Unlike many international relations feminists who use gender as an analytical tool, the advocate of this "neo-feminist" approach, which explores the effect of gender inequality on state behaviors, use gender as a variable to theoretically challenge the state-centered and reductionist nature of realistic theory. Moreover, feminists use the gender variable to explain the inequalities among international actors and in the international economy.[51] As time has progressed, international relations feminists have gradually moved away from the dual understanding of gender to explore the masculine and the feminine in global politics. For example, they have started to use the concept of "hegemonic masculinity" to indicate the domination and obedience of men who have an impact on international relations, including international conflicts.[52]

The term "gender analysis" has become widespread instead of "feminist analysis" recently in the field of international relations. This approach, which is formulated using a gender perspective, suggests that it would not be explanatory to consider the status of women only from the central gender relations perspective within the framework of men's patriarchal domination, regardless of the race, ethnicity, and colonial hierarchy in society. According to Scott, feminists have started to use the word "gender" more seriously, in a more accurate sense, to mean the social organization of the relationship between the sexes.[53] With its most recent use, gender was first used by American feminists who insisted that gender-based distinctions are originally social. This word denotes the rejection of biological determinism implied in the use of terms such as sex or sexual differences. Gender also emphasizes the relational aspect of normative definitions of femininity. Those who are concerned about women's studies being very limited and distinctly focused on women have used the term "gender" to present a relational concept to our analytical vocabulary. According to this view, women and men are defined according to each other, and neither of them can be grasped by a completely separate field of study.[54] From this point of view, the use of gender studies in all areas of the social sciences, including international relations, will contribute to the literature.

Furthermore, gender is sometimes used synonymously with women in its simplest use. The term "gender" is preferred to the word "women" in the title of many books and articles on the history of women. In some cases, the main reason why this use is preferred to point out certain analytical concepts, albeit ambiguously, concerns the political acceptability of the field/study. This request or anxiety for acceptability is observed not only in the case of using "gender" instead of "women" but also in uses where "gender" is preferred to "feminism."

The use of gender in such cases is considered to increase the academic gravity of the study, because gender has a more *neutral* and *objective* perception than feminism or even woman. Gender seems to conform to the scientific terminology of social sciences, and therefore, is distinguished (allegedly sharply) from feminist politics. This use of gender neither gives essential feedback about inequality or power (as feminism does) nor mentions the side (women) victimized and made invisible so far. For example, the term "women's history," unlike traditional practices, declares its own policy by considering women as valid historical subjects, whereas the term "gender" encompasses women, but does not mention their names and thus does not appear to pose a serious threat. This use of gender in this manner also points to one side of what could be called the quest of feminist studies for academic legitimacy in the 1980s (Scott, 1986: 1056). Yet, the positive contributions of feminist thoughts and movements to both women and their rights/issues are clear today. Therefore, the awareness that feminism is *a theoretical framework* that is used to analyze women and women's issues should be settled in the present day when feminism has gone far beyond a search for legitimacy. Feminism already uses gender analysis as an *explanatory* and *supportive* element in its own theory. In other words, while one is a theoretical approach, the other is one of the focuses of analysis used in that theory. They are not contradictory to or different from each other, but they are intertwined. Using a title such as gender analysis can be supported if it is based on a criticism towards a unilateral analysis of feminism—the fact that feminism does not fall into such mistake is one of the most important criticisms among feminists. On the other hand, if excluding the contribution of feminism to women's studies due to the reaction to feminism is an effort to make it invisible, it is then necessary to reveal and criticize this effort.

CONCLUSION

The main purpose of feminist international relations approaches is to reveal women's invisible position in the field of international relations, criticize the previously established domains/concepts and theories of the discipline, and question the point of view of the social structures that exclude cooperation among structures, consider the international structure solely of states, and forget that states are made up of people.

Feminism especially emphasizes that new concepts, issues, and approaches should be used to ensure international relations, one of the main fields of the social sciences, to be more descriptive and inclusive towards women and women's issues. Today, there are studies with a feminist point of view in all areas of international relations, adding a new dynamism to the discipline. Therefore, the place of feminism in international relations can no longer be denied. However, the conceptual use of "gender analysis" has increased in the analyses of issues and domains of international relations. Although feminism is a bundle of theoretical approaches used in women's studies, gender analysis is one of the main explanatory/complementary parameters that are also used by feminism. Therefore, it is not an understandable to make such a conceptual differentiation and emphasize gender due to political concerns or reactions to feminism. On the contrary, the contribution of feminism and feminist movements to favorable processes such as increasing women's visibility in the field of international relations, addressing and resolving women's issues, and taking steps regarding women's rights is undeniable.

REFERENCES

Ackerly, B. A., and J. True. "An Intersectional Analysis of International Relations: Recasting the Discipline." *Politics and Gender* 4, no. 1 (2008): 1–18.

Ackerly, B., M. Stern, and J. True (eds.). *Feminist Methodologies for International Relations.* Cambridge: Cambridge University Press, 2006.

Agathangelou, A. M., and L. H. M. Ling. "Power, Borders, Security, Wealth: Lessons of Violence and Desire from September 11." *International Studies Quarterly* 48, no. 3 (2004): 517–538.

Antrobus, P. *The Global Women's Movement: Origins, Issues and Strategies.* London: Zed Books, 2005.

Beauvoir, Simone de. *İkinci Cinsiyet.* çev. Gülnur Acar-Savran. İstanbul: Koç Üniversitesi Yayınları, 2019.

Brown, Chris. "Turtles all the way down: Anti-foundationalism, Critical Theory and International Relations." *Millennium: Journal of International Studies* 23, no. 2 (1994): 213–236.

Caprioli, M. "Feminist IR Theory and Quantitative Methodology." *International Studies Review* 6, no. 2 (2004): 25–69.

Carastathis, Anna. "The Concept of Intersectionality in Feminist Theory." *Philosophy Compass* 9, no. 5 (2014): 304–314.

Chew, Hubin Amelia. "What's left? After 'imperial feminist' hijackings." In *Feminism and War: Confronting US Imperialism*, edited by Robin L. Riley, Chandra Talpade Mohanty, and Minnie Bruce Pratt, 75–91. London: Zed Books, 2008.

Chin, C. B. N. *In Service and In Servitude: Foreign Female Domestic Workers and the Malaysian Modernity Project*. New York: Columbia University Press, 1998.

Craft, Niki. "A Call on Feminists to Protest Against the War in Afghanistan." In *September 2001: Feminist Perspectives*, edited by Susan Hawthorne and Bronwyn Winter, 151–155. Melbourne: Spinifex, 2002.

Disch, Lisa Jane, and M. E. Hawkesworth. *The Oxford Handbook of Feminist Theory*. Oxford: Oxford University Press, 2016.

Enloe, C. *Bananas, Beaches and Bases: Making Feminist Sense of International Politics*. California: University of California Press, 1996.

Fausto-Sterling, Anne. *Myths of Gender: Biological Theories about Men and Women*. New York: Basic Books, 1992.

Feminist Studies. Accessed May 12, 2019. http://feministstudies.org/abouthfs/history .html.

Flax, J. "Postmodernism and gender relations in feminist theory." In *Feminism/ Postmodernism*, edited by Linda Nicholson, 39–62. New York: Routledge, Chapman & Hall, 1990.

Friedman, Susan Stanford. "Feminism, State Fictions and Violence: Gender, Geopolitics and Transnationalism." *Communal/Plural* 9, no. 1 (2001): 111–129.

Goldstein, J. *International Relations*. New York: Longman, 2001.

Goldstein, J. *War and Gender*. Cambridge: Cambridge University Press, 2002.

Gorney, Edna, and Hedva Eyal. "On Nuclear Weapons: A Feminist Perspective." *Isha L'Isha-Haifa Feminist Center*, 1989. Accessed February, 12, 2019, https://www .atomicheritage.org/location/marshall-islands

Grant, R., and K. Newland. *Gender and International Relations*. London: LSE Press, 1991.

Halliday, F. "Hidden from International Relations: Women and the International Arena." *Millennium* 17, no. 3 (1988): 419–428.

Harcourt, W. *The Global Women's Rights Movement: Power Politics around the United Nations and the World Social Forum*. UNRISD Working Paper 25. Geneva: United Nations Research Institute for Social Development, 2006.

Harding, Sandra. *The Feminist Standpoint Theory Reader: Intellectual and Political Controversies*. New York: Routledge, 2004.

Hesse-Biber, Sharlene Nagy. "The practice of feminist in-depth interviewing." In *Feminist Research Practice*, edited by S. N. Hesse-Biber and P. L. Leavy, 111–148. CA: Sage Publications, 2007.

Hoffman, John. *Gender and Sovereignty, Feminism, the State and International Relations*. New York: Palgrave, 2001.

Jacoby, T. "From the Trenches: Dilemmas of Feminist IR Fieldwork." In *Feminist Methodologies for International Relations*, edited by B. Ackerly, M. Stern, and J. True, 153–173. Cambridge: Cambridge University Press, 2006.

Jaggar, Alison M. *Feminist Politics and Human Nature.* Lanham, MD: Rowman & Littlefield Publishers, 1983.

Kaufman-Osborn, T. "Gender Trouble at Abu-Ghraib." *Politics and Gender* 1, no. 4 (2005): 597–619.

Khan, Ada P. *The Encyclopedia of Stress and Stress-Related Diseases.* New York: Facts on File, Inc., 2006.

Marchand, M., and A. S. Runyan (eds.). *Gender and Global Restructuring: Sites, Siting and Sightings.* New York: Routledge, 2000.

Peterson, V. S. *Gendered States: Revisions of International Relations Theory.* Boulder: Lynne Rienner Press, 1992.

Pettman, Jan Jindy. *Worlding Women: A Feminist International Politics.* Routledge: London, 2002.

Randall, Vicky, and Georgina Waylen. *Gender, Politics and the State.* London: Routledge, 1998.

Regan, P. M., and A. Paskeviciute. "Women's Access to Politics and Peaceful States." *Journal of Peace Research* 40, no. 3 (2003): 287–302.

Rothenberg, Paula. "Women's Studies—The Early Years: When Sisterhood Was Powerful." In *The Evolution of American Women's Studies*, edited by Alice E. Ginsberg. New York: Palgrave Macmillan, 2008.

Ruby, Jennie. "Is This a Feminist War?" In *September 2001: Feminist Perspectives*, edited by Susan Hawthorne and Bronwyn Winter. Melbourne: Spinifex, 2002.

Şaşman Kaylı, Derya. *Kadın Bedeni ve Özgürleşme.* İzmir: İlya İzmir Yayınevi, 2013.

The Sydney Morning Herald. "Ardent warrior for women's rights." July 31, 2003. http://smh.com.au/national/ardent-warrior-for-womens-rights-20030731-gdh6tb. html

Scott, J. W. "Gender: A Useful Category of Historical Analysis." *The American Historical Review* 91, no. 5 (1986): 1053–1075.

Shaw, Susan M., and Janet Lee. *Women's Voices, Feminist Visions: Classic and Contemporary Readings.* Sixth Edition. New York: McGraw-Hill, 2015.

Steans, Jill. *Gender and International Relations.* Cambridge: Polity Press, 1998.

Stern, M. "Racism, Sexism, Classism and Much More: Reading Security-Identity in Marginalized Sites." In *Feminist Methodologies for International Relations*, edited by B. Ackerly, M. Stern, and J. True, 174–197. Cambridge: Cambridge University Press, 2006.

Sweeney, S. "Government Respect for Women's Economic Rights: A Cross-National Analysis, 1981–2003." *The Human Rights Institute Conference: Economic Rights, Conceptual Measurement, and Policy Issues.* Connecticut: University of Connecticut, October 27–29, 2005.

Sylvester, C. *Feminist International Relations: An Unfinished Journey.* Cambridge: Cambridge University Press, 2000.

Sylvester, Christine. "The Contributions of Feminist Theory." In *International Relations Theory: Positivism and Beyond*, edited by Steve Smith, Ken Booth, and Marysia Zalewski, 254–278. Cambridge: Cambridge University Press, 1999.

Tickner, J. *Gender in International Relations: Feminist Approaches to Achieving Global Security.* New York: Columbia University Press, 1992.

Tickner, J. A. "Gender in World Politics." In *The Globalization of World Politics: An Introduction to International Relations,* edited by John Baylis, Steve Smith, and Patricia Owens, 262–277. Oxford: Oxford University Press, 2008.

Tickner, J. A. *Gendering World Politics: Issues and Approaches in the Post-Cold War Era.* New York: Columbia University Press, 2001.

Tickner, J. A. "Hans Morgenthau's Principles of Political Realism: A Feminist Reformulation." *Millennium* 17, no. 3 (1988): 429–440.

Tickner, J. A. "You Just Don't Understand: Troubled Engagements Between Feminists and IR Theorists." *International Studies Quarterly* 41, no. 4 (1997): 611–632.

Tickner, J. A., and Laura Sjoberg. "Feminism." In *International Relations Theories: Discipline and Diversity,* edited by Tim Dunne et al., 185–202. Oxford: Oxford University Press, 2007.

True, J. "Feminism and Gender Studies in International Relations Theory." 2010. Accessed September 23, 2020, https://oxfordre.com/internationalstudies/view/10.1093/acrefore/9780190846626.001.0001/acrefore-9780190846626-e-46?print=pdf.

True, J., and Mintrom, M. "Transnational Networks and Policy Diffusion: The Case of Gender Mainstreaming," *International Studies Quarterly* 45, no. 1 (2001): 27–57.

Tür, Özlem, and Çiğdem Aydın Koyuncu. "Feminist Uluslararası İlişkiler Yaklaşımı: Temelleri, Gelişimi, Katkı ve Sorunları." *Uluslararası İlişkiler* 7, no. 26 (2010): 3–24.

Weldon, L. "Inclusion and Understanding: A Collective Methodology for Feminist International Relations." In *Feminist Methodologies for International Relations,* edited by B. Ackerly, M. Stern, and J. True, 62–87. Cambridge: Cambridge University Press, 2006.

Whitworth, S. *Feminism and International Relations: Towards a Political Economy of Gender in Interstate and Non-Governmental Institutions.* London: Macmillan, 1994.

Wiegman, Robyn. *Women's Studies on Its Own: A Next Wave Reader in Institutional Change.* Durham: Duke University Press, 2002.

NOTES

1. Özlem Tür and Çiğdem Aydın Koyuncu, "Feminist Uluslararası İlişkiler Yaklaşımı: Temelleri, Gelişimi, Katkı ve Sorunları," *Uluslararası İlişkiler* 7, no. 26 (2010): 17–19.

2. Alison M. Jaggar, *Feminist Politics and Human Nature* (Lanham, MD: Rowman & Littlefield Publishers, 1983), 353.

3. Susan Stanford Friedman, "Feminism, State Fictions and Violence: Gender, Geopolitics and Transnationalism," *Communal/Plural* 9, no. 1 (2001): 125.

4. Jill Steans, *Gender and International Relations* (Cambridge: Polity Press, 1998), 16–19.

5. Chris Brown, "Turtles all the way down: Anti-foundationalism, Critical Theory and International Relations," *Millennium: Journal of International Studies* 23, no. 2 (1994): 231.

6. Steans, *Gender and International Relations,* 25–26.

7. J. A. Tickner, "You Just Don't Understand: Troubled Engagements Between Feminists and IR Theorists," *International Studies Quarterly* 41, no. 4 (1997): 619; Christine Sylvester, "The Contributions of Feminist Theory," in *International Relations Theory: Positivism and Beyond*, ed. Steve Smith, Ken Booth, and Marysia Zalewski (Cambridge: Cambridge University Press, 1999), 267.

8. Steans, *Gender and International Relations,* 57; Tickner, "You Just Don't Understand," 431.

9. Tickner, "You Just Don't Understand," 432.

10. Steans, *Gender and International Relations,* 161.

11. Hubin Amelia Chew, "What's left? After 'imperial feminist' hijackings," in *Feminism and War: Confronting US Imperialism*, eds. Robin L. Riley, Chandra Talpade Mohanty. and Minnie Bruce Pratt (London: Zed Books, 2008), 80–81; Jennie Ruby, "Is This a Feminist War?," in *September 2001: Feminist Perspectives*, eds. Susan Hawthorne and Bronwyn Winter (Melbourne: Spinifex, 2002), 149; Niki Craft, "A Call on Feminists to Protest Against the War in Afghanistan," in *September 2001: Feminist Perspectives*, eds. Susan Hawthorne and Bronwyn Winter (Melbourne: Spinifex, 2002), 152.

12. Sylvester, "The Contributions of Feminist Theory," 268.

13. J. Goldstein, *International Relations* (New York: Longman, 2001), 127.

14. Tickner, "You Just Don't Understand," 619; Jan Jindy Pettman, *Worlding Women: A Feminist International Politics* (Routledge: London, 2002).

15. Steans, *Gender and International Relations,* 10; J. A. Tickner, "Gender in World Politics," in *The Globalization of World Politics: An Introduction to International Relations*, eds. John Baylis, Steve Smith, and Patricia Owens (Oxford: Oxford University Press, 2008), 265.

16. J. A. Tickner and Laura Sjoberg, "Feminism," in *International Relations Theories: Discipline and Diversity*, ed. Tim Dunne et al. (Oxford: Oxford University Press, 2007), 188–192.

17. For example, the place of the fertility of women in women's issues is one of the issues discussed in this framework.

18. Standpoint Theory is a theoretical approach developed in the 1980s to examine the production of information and its effects on power practices. This theory is based on the idea that knowledge is created socially, whereby minorities and certain groups (such as women) who are not historically represented are neglected or marginalized in generating information. Based on Marxist thought, this approach is a challenge to those presented as political and social realities. See Sandra Harding, *The Feminist Standpoint Theory Reader: Intellectual and Political Controversies* (New York: Routledge, 2004), 2.

19. Intersectionality has emerged during the third wave of feminism. Kimberlé Williams Crenshaw is the most prominent representative of this concept. This theoretical approach seeks to understand how institutional structures shape an individual's gendered, racial, and social status. See Anna Carastathis, "The Concept of Intersectionality in Feminist Theory," *Philosophy Compass* 9, no. 5 (2014): 304–314.

20. Paula Rothenberg, "Women's Studies—The Early Years: When Sisterhood Was Powerful," in *The Evolution of American Women's Studies*, ed. Alice E. Ginsberg (New York: Palgrave Macmillan, 2008), 68.

21. Robyn Wiegman, *Women's Studies on Its Own: A Next Wave Reader in Institutional Change* (Durham: Duke University Press, 2002); Susan M. Shaw and Janet Lee, *Women's Voices, Feminist Visions: Classic and Contemporary Readings*, Sixth Edition (New York: McGraw-Hill, 2015); Lisa Jane Disch and M. E. Hawkesworth, *The Oxford Handbook of Feminist* Theory (Oxford: Oxford University Press, 2016), 1; Sharlene Nagy Hesse-Biber, "The practice of feminist in-depth interviewing," in *Feminist Research Practice*, eds. S. N. Hesse-Biber and P. L. Leavy (CA: Sage Publications, 2007), 111–148.

22. "Ardent warrior for women's rights," *The Sydney Morning Herald*, July 31, 2003, http://smh.com.au/national/ardent-warrior-for-womens-rights-20030731 -gdh6tb.html; Ada P. Khan, *The Encyclopedia of Stress and Stress-Related Diseases* (New York: Facts on File, Inc., 2006), 308.

23. Feminist Studies, accessed May 12, 2019, http://feministstudies.org/abouthfs/ history.html.

24. Paula Rothenberg, "Women's Studies—The Early Years," 68.

25. B. A. Ackerly and J. True, "An Intersectional Analysis of International Relations: Recasting the Discipline," *Politics and Gender* 4, no. 1 (2008): 1–18; B. Ackerly, M. Stern, and J. True (eds.), *Feminist Methodologies for International Relations* (Cambridge: Cambridge University Press, 2006).

26. J. True, "Feminism and Gender Studies in International Relations Theory," 2010, accessed September 23, 2020, https://oxfordre.com/internationalstudies/view /10.1093/acrefore/9780190846626.001.0001/acrefore-9780190846626-e-46?print =pdf.

27. C. B. N. Chin, *In Service and In Servitude: Foreign Female Domestic Workers and the Malaysian Modernity Project* (New York: Columbia University Press, 1998); M. Marchand and A. S. Runyan (eds.), *Gender and Global Restructuring: Sites, Siting and Sightings* (New York: Routledge, 2000).

28. T. Jacoby, "From the Trenches: Dilemmas of Feminist IR Fieldwork," in *Feminist Methodologies for International Relations*, eds. B. Ackerly, M. Stern, and J. True (Cambridge: Cambridge University Press, 2006), 153–173; M. Stern, "Racism, Sexism, Classism and Much More: Reading Security-Identity in Marginalized Sites," in *Feminist Methodologies for International Relations*, eds. B. Ackerly, M. Stern, and J. True (Cambridge: Cambridge University Press, 2006), 174–197.

29. C. Sylvester, *Feminist International Relations: An Unfinished Journey* (Cambridge: Cambridge University Press, 2000), 283; Tickner and Sjoberg, "Feminism," 191–192.

30. F. Halliday, "Hidden from International Relations: Women and the International Arena," *Millennium* 17, no. 3 (1988): 419–428.

31. R. Grant and K. Newland, *Gender and International Relations* (London: LSE Press, 1991), 5.

32. True, "Feminism and Gender Studies," 5.

33. J. A. Tickner, "Hans Morgenthau's Principles of Political Realism: A Feminist Reformulation," *Millennium* 17, no. 3 (1988): 429–440.

34. J. Tickner, *Gender in International Relations: Feminist Approaches to Achieving Global Security* (New York: Columbia University Press, 1992); C. Enloe, *Bananas, Beaches and Bases: Making Feminist Sense of International Politics* (California: University of California Press, 1996).

35. J. A. Tickner, *Gendering World Politics: Issues and Approaches in the Post-Cold War Era* (New York: Columbia University Press, 2001); True, "Feminism and Gender Studies," 5–6.

36. P. Antrobus, *The Global Women's Movement: Origins, Issues and Strategies* (London: Zed Books, 2005); W. Harcourt, *The Global Women's Rights Movement: Power Politics around the United Nations and the World Social Forum*, UNRISD Working Paper 25 (Geneva: United Nations Research Institute for Social Development, 2006).

37. L. Weldon, "Inclusion and Understanding: A Collective Methodology for Feminist International Relations," in *Feminist Methodologies for International Relations*, eds. B. Ackerly, M. Stern, and J. True (Cambridge: Cambridge University Press, 2006), 62–87.

38. True, "Feminism and Gender Studies," 6.

39. A. M. Agathangelou and L. H. M. Ling, "Power, Borders, Security, Wealth: Lessons of Violence and Desire from September 11," *International Studies Quarterly* 48, no. 3 (2004): 517–538; T. Kaufman-Osborn, "Gender Trouble at Abu-Ghraib," *Politics and Gender* 1, no. 4 (2005): 597–619.

40. *Queer* means deviation from the norm. In other words, it is considered a deviation from being a man or woman, which is accepted as the norm in terms of gender.

41. Anne Fausto-Sterling, *Myths of Gender: Biological Theories about Men and Women* (New York: Basic Books, 1992), 8.

42. Simone de Beauvoir, *İkinci Cinsiyet*, çev. Gülnur Acar-Savran (İstanbul: Koç Üniversitesi Yayınları, 2019).

43. John Hoffman, *Gender and Sovereignty, Feminism, the State and International Relations* (New York: Palgrave, 2001), 31.

44. S. Whitworth, *Feminism and International Relations: Towards a Political Economy of Gender in Interstate and Non-Governmental Institutions* (London: Macmillan, 1994), 25.

45. J. Flax, "Postmodernism and gender relations in feminist theory," in *Feminism/Postmodernism*, ed. Linda Nicholson (New York: Routledge, Chapman & Hall, 1990), 39–62.

46. Vicky Randall and Georgina Waylen, *Gender, Politics and the State* (London: Routledge, 1998), 19.

47. V. S. Peterson, *Gendered States: Revisions of International Relations Theory* (Boulder: Lynne Rienner Press, 1992), 8.

48. Edna Gorney and Hedva Eyal, "On Nuclear Weapons A Feminist Perspective," *Isha L'Isha-Haifa Feminist Center*, 1989, 14, accessed February, 12, 2019, https://www.atomicheritage.org/location/marshall-islands

49. M. Caprioli, "Feminist IR Theory and Quantitative Methodology," *International Studies Review* 6, no. 2 (2004): 25–69; J. Goldstein, *War and Gender* (Cambridge: Cambridge University Press, 2002).

50. P. M. Regan and A. Paskeviciute, "Women's Access to Politics and Peaceful States," *Journal of Peace Research* 40, no. 3 (2003): 287–302.

51. J. True and M. Mintrom, "Transnational Networks and Policy Diffusion: The Case of Gender Mainstreaming," *International Studies Quarterly* 45, no. 1 (2001): 27–57; S. Sweeney, "Government Respect for Women's Economic Rights: A Cross-National Analysis, 1981–2003," *The Human Rights Institute Conference: Economic Rights, Conceptual Measurement, and Policy Issues* (Connecticut: University of Connecticut, October 27–29, 2005).

52. J. Tickner, *Gender in International Relations: Feminist Approaches to Achieving Global Security* (New York: Columbia University Press, 1992).

53. Derya Şaşman Kaylı, *Kadın Bedeni ve Özgürleşme* (İzmir: İlya İzmir Yayınevi, 2013), 27.

54. J. W. Scott, "Gender: A Useful Category of Historical Analysis," *The American Historical Review* 91, no. 5 (1986): 1054.

Chapter 11

Critical Geopolitics in International Relations

Murat Yeşiltaş

INTRODUCTION

By the late 1980s, critical geopolitics had begun to take shape based on criticisms against the mainstream geopolitical thought, also known as classical or traditional geopolitics. The 1980s is a period where postmodern and critical theoretical discussions had intensified on a wider platform within the international relations discipline. Therefore, the establishing theoretical discussions for critical geopolitics had been formalized within the "dissident" tradition that rose with the postmodern and critical tendency in the International Relations Theories (IRT). However, it is controversial whether critical geopolitics is an IRT or not. It can be seen evidently that none of the leading textbooks gave a place for critical geopolitics.[1] This is mostly because critical geopolitics places itself within the Political Geography discipline on a wider platform to form a resistance against the well-established classical geopolitical paradigm.[2]

Despite being a sub-study field of Political Geography, it can be clearly seen that critical geopolitics provides a potent criticism against political realism. Since critical geopolitics, based on the social reality, is not a default or is not objective—that it corresponds to the system established discursively and historically—stipulates that world politics do not have a process separate from the discursive construct. In other words, critical geopolitics claims that defining the world means looking at it from a specific perspective and thus compressing international politics to a certain form. Most importantly, critical geopolitics suggests that the depicted stage, meaning the ability to visualize global politics in high quality (via maps), is a part of the struggle for the perspective of each political subject.[3] Such an assumption is a complementary quality to the post-structuralist global politic problematizing that we are familiar with in IRT and provides an important theoretical foundation in drawing attention to the spatial and geographical construction of global politics.[4] The goal here is to show that all kinds of initiatives trying to degrade the complex causality of global politics to a single essence via geographical representations and categories are produced from a certain hub and perspective.[5]

It has been argued that critical geopolitics can be best understood through a comparison with classical and mainstream realist geopolitics. This approach is accurate to a great degree. Both handle the relation between geography and politics. However, despite this insignificant common ground, they greatly differ from each other in the meta-theoretical foundation trying to understand the relation between the ideal side and the material side of the social world and the relation between the representation of the social reality and the actual reality itself. In other words, mainstream classical geopolitics engages with the *politics of geography* as it tries to show how the material factors constituting a background for politics aid the actor in taking the most optimal decision. Yet critical geopolitics, on the contrary, problematizes the geography itself and handles the *geographical politics*. So, critical geopolitics is interested in the *geo-politics of geopolitics*.

For understanding the theoretical and methodological basis of critical geopolitics, this section adopts three-level analysis. The first is the criticisms towards the classical geopolitics to understand the history of critical geopolitics. The second is the connection it establishes with the postmodern political theory to understand its political philosophy. The final is the method it uses to understand that the methodology of critical geopolitics should be analyzed in totality.

CLASSICAL GEOPOLITICS

Critical geopolitics is a "dissident" tradition resisting the hierarchical and culturalist distinction of the global politics via separating from the classical/traditional geopolitics emerging with the deterministic and essentialist characteristics via being imperialist, and racist in the last quarter of the 19th century. As said by Dalby, it has emerged as a "dissident" intellectual position criticizing the politics of geographical determination of politics" and trying to show that alternative political (geographical-geopolitical) envisagement forms are present.[6] According to critical geopolitics, geopolitics is not an innocent endeavor providing for the formation of knowledge via examining the "geographical" realities "naturally" but it is a highly ideological and politicized analysis method. This criticism rendered critical geopolitics as a study field engaging in understanding how international politics is envisaged spatially or geographically, and while so, how politics writes/interprets the global space.[7] Reviewing the opposing position taken by critical geopolitics more explicitly against classical geopolitics is also important to understand its fundamental propositions regarding the philosophy of politics. Therefore, looking at a brief history of geopolitics can help us understand what critical politics is opposing.

To understand the intellectual and theoretical concerns of critical geopolitics, the relation between academic geography and classical geopolitics as an academic field should be considered. Classical geopolitics is a paradigm that emerged and developed between 1870 and 1945 when the competition between the imperialist countries was most intense. The theories produced by the leading names of this paradigm had shaped significantly the subsequent geopolitical studies. Every one of the founders' names of classical geopolitics had not only produced texts trying to develop a theory within the geography discipline but also presented problem-solving approaches leading the ideas directly impacting the state governing philosophy and practices. Therefore, traditional geopolitics is a problem-solving thought tradition and theory. The fundamental goal of leading thinkers forming a source for the formation of the classical geopolitical paradigm is to find a geography-based existence regarding how the balance shall be provided between surviving via expansion outwards and the most effective restructuring for their countries during the age of cultural transformation and social revolutions. Therefore, their questions are related more to the state rather than geography directly. For example, while American Alfred T. Mahan engages with the "path to national perfection for the state," German Friedrich Ratzel theorized the "best relation between the state and geography" and thus searched for ways for expanding the state. Whereas Halford Mackinder was in search of reform for empowering and restructuring of British Empire. The common ground for all of them is they all suggest that geography is or should be functional in maximizing the power of the state.

In parallel to the dominant scientific discourse of the era, these founder names were after producing universal laws related to the formation, development, and expansion (land expansion or controlling faraway lands) of the states. Ratzel, in his works, suggests that a powerful and successful state shall never be satisfied with the existing borders; and shall be "in search for securing its living area" and expanding its borders. Therefore, according to Ratzel, the continuous "search for the living area" of the state is one of the most basic and unchanging geopolitical laws.[8] The contrary shall cause the state to disappear and be removed from the stage of history. This geopolitical law guided the emergence of a political strategy in the German geopolitics school that suggests that Germany should expand beyond its current lands (Lebensraum) and formed the main tendency of its foreign policy of Hitler. It is possible to identify this main vein of classical geopolitics as the geopolitical mindset fortified around the axis of the "organic state" paradigm.[9] Aforesaid geopolitical tradition adapts the natural conditions to the relations between states and handles the land expansion or conquest (capture) as a survival problem and legitimizes imperial politics with geographical arguments.[10]

For Halford Mackinder representing the English branch of classical geopolitics though, the problem is exactly to reorganize and restructure the British Empire in the international global struggle both ideologically and geographically. When compared to German organic state schools, Mackinder does not place much importance on why and how the state is formed. According to Mackinder, the British Empire being triumphant in this struggle can be primarily possible by changing the "envisagement of geography." In 1905, in his historical speech titled "Scope and Methods of Geography" given at the Royal Geography Society, he argued that "new geography" should from now on be under the service of the state (Kearns, 2009). "New geography," according to Mackinder, should be used not to gather useless information on the locations on the earth's surface but to produce practical benefits for the state in achieving political goals.

As the goal in classical geopolitics is to formulate the knowledge for the state and statesmen providing for restructuring their own country and for carrying them ahead in the imperial competition, geopolitics is most primarily structured as a "science of the state." Therefore, state-centricity manifests as one of the most fundamental characteristics of classical geopolitics. Other than this there are three distinctive properties of classical geopolitics.

Firstly, classical geopolitics is a thought system composed of solid assumptions related to what geography tells and why this is meaningful and where each analysis supports the other tautologically and is an essentialist thought form reducing the politics to unchanging spatial categories (central land, peripheral land, heartland, rimland, etc.). In other words, classical geopoliticians, while talking about geography and its physical properties, claim that they are also talking about reality. In this regard, classical geopolitics sees the world as a whole composed of nation-states and reduces the struggle and fight in international politics to a hierarchical essence as a derivative of the power struggle present among the different geographical spaces. In the said hierarchy, especially the essentialist, exotic, and ethnocentric spatial categories like West-East, undeveloped-developed are placed in a narrow problematic axis and the differences are transformed into a geographical essence containing certainty. Thus, in the classical geopolitical paradigm, there is a continuous search for a spatial *essence*. This spatial essence search constitutes the core of the theoretical approaches of all classical texts. English geopolitician Halford Mackinder's formula represents the most striking example in this regard. According to the geopolitical model of Mackinder also known as the Land Power Theory, from now on (1905), the real struggle shall progress between land forces and naval forces, and dominating the land shall facilitate the world domination for a state. According to Mackinder, "whoever gained control over Eastern Europe shall control the Heartland | *whoever controls the Heartland shall control the World Island | whoever controls the world island shall control the world.*"[11] Just like Mackinder, in the models of Haushofer, Spykman, and many other geopoliticians, a spatial center should be controlled to survive in world politics.[12]

Secondly, classical geopolitics has a geographical determinism (geographical determinism assumption) that sees all kinds of political and social existence as a derivative of spatial placement. In other words, in the classical geopolitical tradition, the determinism idea argues that the environment (space and geography) is a deterministic element in structuring the behaviors (political, cultural, and daily) of the states. This tendency includes space in the production of policy as an unchanging, always valid factor. According to this approach, as the special positioning shall not change, the politics is subject to the terms of geography. The space reflects the condition of the state taken on physicality. Here the world as a whole can be known and drawn objectively "as a self-proclaimed reality outside of us." In such a perspective, geography is considered the objective reality itself. In other words, a geopolitical construct suggesting that "testimony of the eye" (maps) is sufficient to comprehend the reality that had penetrated the soul of the entire policy production. There is no doubt here that nature determines the destiny of the states (nations).[13]

For the third one, classical geopolitical has an ideological essence and construct that places the nation-state at its core in a way not to be visualized as separate from imperialism, conservatism, nationalism, and racism idea and practices. All the geographical and special depictions, fixation, and separations that are claimed to be so-called scientific, are political and ideological. For example, on the world map representing the model of Haushofer, there is an ethnocentric hierarchy mapped as colonizing and colonized world, whereas the world politics construct of Mackinder centered on Eurasia (Siberia) has a political agenda for preventing a possible alliance between Germany and Russia. In addition, in all early period German, English, Italian, American, and Japanese (examples can be multiplied) geopolitical models, there is a dominant explicit imperialist and conservative ideology.[14] Moreover, economic nationalism emerges as a dominant construct in all classical geopolitical models.[15]

CRITICAL GEOPOLITICS

Critical geopolitics claims that geopolitics is a discourse produced socially, culturally, and politically and thus the assumptions claimed to be a geographical reality by the one who talks on geopolitics cannot be considered separate from this discourse.[16] The first point called to mind by such an approach is regarding that the conceptual foundation on which the geopolitics feeds is variable. Besides being mostly poststructuralist, also the critical and constructivist conceptual approaches provided a source for many studies in critical geopolitics. Such an eclectic structure primarily provides one studying critical geopolitics with a rich foundation to inquire about the linguistic structure of the concept. According to critical geopolitics, geopolitics is not an innocent endeavor discovered for contributing to the formation of knowledge via examining "naturally" the "geographical" realities but is a highly ideological and politicized analysis form. In other words, critical geopolitics engages in understanding how international politics is envisagement (read as thought) spatially or geographically and how politics, while doing so, writes/interprets global space. These arguments show us that critical geopolitics mainly fed on poststructuralist studies to build its conceptual basis. Especially thinkers like Michel Foucault, Jacques Derrida, and Edward Said provided a significant source for shaping the conceptual path of critical geopolitics.[17] Critical geopolitics collecting knowledge-power relation and discourse analysis from Foucault, linguistic decoding from Derrida, and spatial and imaginative representation forms of reality from Said, does not accept that the widespread opinion regarding that global politics can be understood through geographical justifications is a reality.[18]

Regarding the fields of research, problematized scales, and used methods, even though there are some differences among them, it is possible to understand critical geopolitics, focusing on especially the works of writers like Gerard Ó Tuathail, Simon Dalby, and John Agnew as being the founders of the field. The common property of all is defining geopolitics as a *discourse*. Where *discourse* for the ones studying critical geopolitics is "not the independent, innocent contributions made to the objective knowledge; on the contrary, it serves the benefits of certain groups in the society and facilitates the use and justification of certain views and interpretations, thus takes root in what [Foucault] calls 'power/knowledge.'"[19] In this regard, geopolitical discourse, differing from the *language* and the lingual performance, is a systematized political action forming with power relations. When considered in this manner, critical geopolitics claims that talking about geopolitical discourse practices cannot be independent of fundamental structural properties of the modern state, its corporate formative architecture, the construction process of state devices, and the sociopolitical power relations taking a founder role in this process.

When the names above are taken to the core, three basic founder texts are providing a source for the formation of the political philosophy of critical geopolitics. First of these is the book called *Critical Geopolitics: The Politics of Writing Global Space,* the doctoral thesis written in 1986 by Gerard Toal who undertook also the founder role of the field, published in 1996.[20] The second one is *Geopolitics: Revisioning World Politics* by John Agnew and his work called *Mastering Space* written together with Stuart Corbridge.[21] The third one is the work of Simon Dalby titled *Creating the Second Cold War: The Discourse of Politics.*[22] Both regarding their being founder works and regarding their being resources for future critical geopolitical studies, the critical geopolitical studies are divided again into three based on the fields they problematize. Considering the diversity of the studies conducted in this field, especially after the 1990s, this classification still maintains its validity.

Macro Scale: Geopolitics of International Order

First of these is the *macro-scale* approach seen in *Mastering Space* by Agnew and Corbridge (1995), acknowledged as one of the most important texts of critical geopolitics, and in other works of Agnew where geopolitics is handled in regard to modernity and international economic political discussion.[23] Despite that the critical works of Agnew against geopolitics covered earlier years (1982, 1983, 1984), we can say that conceptualizations like geopolitical discourse, geopolitical order, and geopolitical imagination are examined in more detail in the studies led by Agnew. Also, in an article Agnew wrote together with Ó Tuathail (1992), geopolitics is considered as a *structure* as much as a culture. Agnew's tendency is to consider geopolitics as a "structure" operating together with the political economy shaping global politics and the modernist paradigm. Agnew conceptualizes this structure itself as the geopolitical *order,* the phenomena rendering the geopolitical order as the geopolitical *discourse,* and the final visualization of the geopolitical discourses as the geopolitical *imagination.* According to Agnew and Corbridge, the order indicates the rules, institutions, activities, and strategies became routine, operating via the international political economy in different historical periods. Identifying the term together with "geopolitics" draws attention to the geographical elements of the world order.[24]

Agnew and Corbridge, in this regard, indicate the historical presence of three geopolitical orders. According to the periodization they performed based on international economic politics and international power distribution around the question of who dominates the economy worldwide, the first geopolitical order is the "British centered geopolitical order" (1815–1875).

England emerged in this order as the "hegemonic power" both directing and controlling the world economy. The second geopolitical order is defined as the "geopolitical order of competition between imperialists" where the imperialist competition was intensified (1895–1945) that destabilized the European power balance system (especially the challenge of Germany). The third order is the "Cold War geopolitical order" (1945–1990) representing the transformation of world politics into a system where it is fortified around two opposing paradigms.

According to Agnew and Corbridge, in each geopolitical order, different discourses are dominant. Here what is meant by the geopolitical discourse is the issue of how the geographical and spatial operation of the international economy politics is "written and read" in political actions at different geopolitical orders. In other words, the geopolitical discourses emerge as all kinds of practices creating *consent* in geopolitical orders becoming hegemonic. However, discourse is not composed simply of talks, texts, or writings; they are formal practices creating and affecting the body of rules enabling the geopolitical orders. In other words, the geopolitical discourse is the process where spatial representations guiding the spatial practices that are central to the geopolitical order are created.[25]

Agnew and Corbridge argue that three different *geopolitical discourses* and representations accompany the three different *geopolitical orders*. The first one is the "civilization-centered geopolitical discourse" (civilizational geopolitics) stating the transformation of the European geography, at the same time, into a cultural "region" and emphasizing the "uniqueness" and "noble" part of the European civilization. In this geopolitical discourse, international politics operates over cultural representations of geographical spaces claiming the supremacy of Europe. The second one is the "naturalized geopolitics" and had left its mark on the period as the geopolitical discourse was dominant in the imperial competition. Their most fundamental characteristics are the separation of the world between the colonialists and the colonialized, the claim that states need land expansion to meet their biological needs, and the geopolitical discourse where environmental determinism is dominant regarding that nature has a deterministic effect on the behavior of the states. The last geopolitical discourse is the "ideological geopolitics" where international politics is constructed over the ideologies as the representation of "two different worlds" in the Cold War era.

Mesoscale: Geopolitical Culture

Even if it is not theoretical, regarding the fields they examine, different from the geopolitical analyses of Agnew and Corbridge at the *macro* level, mesoscale studies constitute the second critical geopolitics category. These studies in general, instead of the geopolitics of interstate relations that examine the geopolitical discourses around the axis of concepts like *geopolitical culture* and *geopolitical vision,* work on how the governing elites or institutions of a certain state *position, think, and imagine* their country in a certain historical period. The top concept used most frequently in these studies, geopolitical imagination is composed of discourses related to "how" and "where" the different identity groups in a state or society position their country regarding their neighbors, within their region, and the international system.[26] In other words, the geopolitical imagination claims that geography is an imagined, i.e., established, reality at the same time instead of reflecting an objective reality. The importance of the concept for those who are studying critical geopolitics is that when different geopolitical cultures or traditions are examined in a country, it is necessary to consider that there can be more than one geopolitical imagination. In other words, the geopolitical imaginations can differ within any country for political and ideological positions of different social or class-based groups.[27]

Besides geopolitical imagination conceptualizing, Dijking, who also performs analyses on this scale, explains geopolitical discourses with the concept of "geopolitical vision." According to Dijking, the geopolitical vision is defined as "thoughts of someone that contain (in)securities and (dis)advantages regarding the relationship between their own country and the other countries and/or that activate their ideas related to a collective mission or foreign politics strategy." In other words, it is possible to define the geopolitical visions as the state of "national identity concepts transformed into geographical terms and symbols."[28] When engaged in this form, both the geopolitical imaginations and the geopolitical visions are significantly important in understanding how the geopolitical cultures present in a country have emerged and formed.

Micro-Scale: Geo-Political Power

Other than the mesoscale studies, the critical geopolitical studies of Ó Tuathail[29] are *micro-scale,* which problematizes the history of geopolitical narratives with a Foucauldian perspective and places geopolitical practices within knowledge/power-centered discursive processes. According to Ó Tuathail, since critical geopolitics cannot be considered independent from the dominant power relations of spatialization policies shaped by the power through geopolitical discourse and practices, it is in search of developing a new perspective aiming to reveal these relations. The said perspective takes geopolitics as a strategy of power and claims that this relation is not different from other power relations and defines geopolitics as geo-power. In studies by Ó Tuathail, especially with Agnew, Dalby, and Routledge, and one of the most important texts of critical geopolitics—*Critical Geopolitics*, he focuses on how our critical thinking regarding geopolitics can be deepened. Ó Tuathail placing modernity criticisms of thinkers like Foucault, Derrida, and Said at the center suggests taking a political position regarding the "removal of emphasis" on colonization and anti-democratic tendencies "embedded" within the epistemological and geopolitical thought in our re-fictionalization of power and space as a tool enabling the operation of ontological, global politics in re-problematizing of the time-space relation. In other words, Ó Tuathail's goal is to reverse the acknowledged hierarchies and to demolish the logo-centric narrative dominant in the spatial production of classical geopolitical tradition and international politics to show the difference between identity and breaking up against totality/unity. This theoretical foundation enables us to be aware of the knowledge/power/interest connection and to feel doubt against unifying and homogenizing super-narratives of classical geopolitics when discussing geopolitics and geography.[30]

This strategy is significantly important for those who study critical geopolitics in two aspects. Firstly, the ones studying critical geopolitics make it possible both to resist the theoretical practices based on *reality-claimed knowledge* and against the imposed borders forming a "reality" order in classical geopolitics and to reverse this tendency. Secondly, this strategy draws attention to the discursive operation and power establishment aspects of geopolitics. In this regard, the critical thought of Ó Tuathail, based on that reality, is not default or objective—it corresponds to a system established discursively and historically, argues that world politics does not have a separate process from the discursive construct. Such a postulate aids in problematizing the strength and power reflections embedded in the geopolitical discourses to the extent that it draws attention to the historicity of reality.[31]

In this scope, critical geopolitics aims both to *decentralize* the analytical focus of the biased and incomplete world politics construct of the political realism integrated with the geopolitical mentality and to direct our attention to alternatives of different state, power, and knowledge formations and thus to establish a practice opposing hegemony.[32] Thus critical geopolitics provides an analytic frame against the structuralist and determinist geographical perspective that examines the elements of geographical realities shaping the actors and that takes the side of the structure in structure-actor duality, that claims that there is a *transformative* reality examining the roles of social, historical, and linguistic uses of existing realities in painting, representing, and constructing the word, and that avoids assigning a mystic autonomy to the space. The said perspective places the inter-subjective aspect of the social world and knowledge, establishing the role of social thoughts, and mutual formation of the actor-structure relation to the core of the research.

Regarding the ones studying geopolitics at the micro-scale, there are four properties of geopolitics. The first one is that geopolitics is not an art of state management as described by the classical geopolitics tradition but is a cultural and political phenomenon. Geopolitics should be understood, in the best way, as the spatial practices both material and representative that are related to the state itself. Therefore, critically studying geopolitics can be possible primarily by instituting the state around a certain cultural narrative. Critical geopolitics, in this regard, analyzes the myths, geopolitical imaginations, and national exceptional foundations of the state or forms a resistance point against the narrative indicating these are simple descriptions. According to critical geopolitics, defining and establishing the state as a national society is a geopolitical action. This action includes selecting one among many national identities, drawing a border against the outside, and transforming the segregated locations (spaces) into a homogenous internal space (read as homeland). In this regard, geopolitics is a political, cultural, and social discourse born from the comprehension of national space and national time via producing from an *essence* exceeding the time (history)—space (geography) dialectic.[33]

The second one claims that the geopolitical space is multiple and then constructed as political and social in many forms and shapes. Therefore, it focuses on the aspects of geopolitics executed via border drawing practices and performances shaping the daily activities of the state. It fictionalizes both the conceptual borders and material borders (legal) of the state indicating the border between the "safe inside" and "anarchical outside" as the subject of the research. Thus, critical geopolitics is not interested in outside the state; it is interested in the construction processes, mechanisms, and forms of "in" and "out," "here" and "there," "domestic" and "foreign."[34] Accordingly, geopolitics is a border-producing political action, as Ashley defined foreign politics as an "ideocratic border producing political performance." Instead of placing the state in front of the traditional and *a priori* interstate foreign policy relations system, it handles it as a socio-cultural structure established via its actions related to *outside* continuously enabling itself. The border drawing practices of geopolitics are both conceptual and cartographic, both imaginary and real, and both social and esthetic.[35] Critical geopolitics is interested in analyzing how all these practices are entangled within a "discursive coil/totality."

For the third one, critical geopolitics argues that the geopolitical discourse and practices are executed not in a single field but different fields related to each other. This means that geopolitical discourses and representative practices have many ways to spread throughout society. In this regard, geopolitics, instead of being a total of centralized practices, consists of decentralized (dispersed) discourses and practices that also have elitist and popular forms of statements. In the critical geopolitics style, we see more in the studies of ÓTuathail, it is suggested that there are three geopolitics types. *Formal geopolitics* is defined as the geopolitical judgment forms produced by scientists, academicians, and strategy/thought institutions and in time transformed into tradition. (Geopolitical judgment, in the broadest sense, is conceptualizing of and representing forms or techniques of (world) politics by applying geographical categories.) *Practical geopolitics* is the geopolitical judgment forms established by the government representative and foreign politics bureaucrats and that find their meaning in the official foreign politics of the states. *Popular geopolitics* is the geopolitical judgment forms revealed in media, cinema, novels, and caricatures that gain a seat in popular culture.

The fourth, critical geopolitics that problematizes the handling methods of classical geopolitics for geography as a power affecting the intentional politics regarding cause and effect, rejects the "objectivity, scientific Ness and naturalness" of this tradition. Most importantly it tries to deposit the settled knowledge that is believed to be "God given," emerging as the dominant principle in classical geopolitics, and defends that the knowledge cannot be formed independently from interpretation. In this scope, the fundamental concern of geopolitics is not to understand generally the source and structure of power and strength but to reveal the power practices that penetrated the geography and geopolitical discourses and their political techniques. At the core of the analysis, there are not categorically fixed things like certain land, border, region, or space but the processes to understand how the said categories are produced.[36] In this regard, critical geopolitics must reveal the processes enabling the formation of geopolitical discourses and state that these are not the "view from nowhere" (i.e., against the claim of they being geographical realities) but the "view from somewhere" that is valid all the time.[37]

Text and Discourse in Critical Geopolitics

Text

Despite the differentiation of the focused and problematized areas, on a methodological level, there are also some nuances between the ones studying critical geopolitics. However, in any case, text and textual analysis lie at the core of critical geopolitics, methodologically. In this regard, critical geopolitics is based on the postulate revealing itself with "there is no non-text" judgment of Derrida, of the "linguistic transformation" of the 1980s, assuming that world politics can be read through texts.[38] This change termed "linguistic turn," while bringing forth the lingual structure of the reality, provides for the acceptance of a postulate regarding that there is no understanding or reality independent from language and requires that the text should be handled together with the concept of language. In this regard, critical geopolitics also claims that the text, more than being an exact copy of the political world, enables it. Therefore, the *text* in critical geopolitics establishes the geopolitical discourse. In the words of Müller, the text and the analysis of a text is just like "bread and butter" for critical geopolitics. The importance of the text is also placed at the bedside of the critical geopolitics project of Ó Tuathail as a metaphor: conceptualizations like "writing global space,"[39] "geopolitical scenario," and "geo-drawing"[40] as location-writing/definition are sufficient to show the importance of text in the critical geopolitical approach of Ó Tuathail.[41]

Accordingly, geopolitics is also the production and distribution of strategic texts and maps; and in such a way the geopolitical discourse is perceived as a type of geo-drawing action within global politics.[42] Critical geopolitics separates itself from the classical geopolitical paradigm by understanding the founder role of the text. In this regard, textuality on one side and discursiveness on the other become the indispensable take-off points of the critical geopolitical perspective. When considered as such, the concept of text is a field unifying the vocal and writing with discourse. This is important in two ways. First, it does not see the discourse as constituted only of text and enables us to see the materiality of the discourse. It shows the importance of this discursive formation as the network of rules operating as the distinctive aspect of the things thought, written, and said by the people. For the second, the discursiveness and textuality place the inclusion/exclusion practices of classical geopolitics to show its *logo-centric* characteristic within the borders of the philosophical discourse of modernity and forms a resistance point against the political technologies of geopolitical practices.

This approach presents itself basically within critical geopolitics at the conceptualization of geography. According to Ó Tuathail, geography is not "writing *about* the place" but the act of "place writing" on its own; i.e., writing action in fact is one of the fundamental tools enabling the place.[43] Therefore critical geopolitics, instead of reading geography as an academic discipline reflecting the reality, handles it, via various power relations, as the spatial social *construction* of the world (geographical construction of the space), a social institution/an institutional practice, and a field of social/intellectual practical thinking and knowledge production field.[44] This approach, on its own, presents to the agenda a basic postulate that the act of writing, before the text,[45] does not reflect reality. So, it becomes possible to ask the question: What exactly does the act of writing reflect, and what does it make possible? The responses to this question differ; however, ones studying critical geography and critical geopolitics had reached a consensus at the point that the act is an interpretation of the world.[46] In other words, within the logic of Derrida, the texts enabled by the writing can only present themselves as different texts in a way connected to the other texts/via other texts.[47] More explicitly, in the continuing interaction process, as in speeches and written texts, each subject or each text is affected by or affects the other subjects or other texts.

From critical geopolitics perspective, the relation between power and knowledge emerges in the process of establishing the text. In Dalby's words, critical geopolitics necessitates looking with doubt at the textual foundation of the Archimedean illusion regarding that the world can be apprehended.[48] This starting point somehow means to place a dual reading of the anarchy problematique of Ashley that made a significant impression on the critical perspective towards geopolitics in the geopolitical discourse. According to Ashley, anarchy as defined by realism—because geopolitics has also the same radicalism as political realism[49]—means an international government without the governor or order without the regulator. Ashley claims that this dominant founder discourse can be read in two ways. Anarchy leads to acceptance of the legitimacy of both different ways to establish order and the roles of different sovereign subjects in the construction of history.[50] The classical geopolitical texts like anarchy discourse of realism engage with anarchy as the permanent founder element of *outside,* and both position the state within the outside and reconstruct the anarchy problematique for the reorganization of inside. Thus anarchy, as a double-sided operating endless condition, becomes distinct in the geopolitical judgment. Therefore, the analysis of text, for critical geopolitics, reveals its role in performing the establishment of geopolitical discourses.

By the apprehension of the importance of text, the text analyses of critical geopolitics are presented in three fields as mentioned above. The first field is to consider the classical geopolitical tradition where critical geopolitics constructs itself over the deconstruction of classical geopolitics around the axis of knowledge/power and discourse. Here, there is the goal of "displacing" the founder texts in the intellectual history presented by the academic/official geopolitical thought. The second field where textual analysis is definitive is composed of speeches and political documents based on the dual reading of the practical geopolitical judgment.[51] The third one is the textual analyses of the popular geopolitical genre that is in the effort of disclosing the power establishing the language of the daily production of geopolitics that transcends to the popular culture level.[52] Here, especially through which tools the geopolitical discourse creates consent in popular culture is looked for.

Discourse

As in the text, the discourse and discourse analysis are also important bases within the critical geopolitical examinations. The difference between the two concepts is the discourse connecting text to politics.[53] As a theoretical strategy, from macro-scale analyses related to how the geopolitical imaginations frame world politics[54] to ethnographic micro-scale studies where border conflicts are reviewed, discourse within the geopolitical studies, in general, constitutes a central position. According to Ó Tuathail, the "geopolitical discourse" concept is perhaps referred to together with critical geopolitics more than in other study fields.[55] In this regard, discourse analysis is at a central position in reference to geopolitical examinations.

The discourse analysis is to construe critically the oral and signed texts, within their context of use, considering also the social, political, and cultural discourses they create, by the discourse analyzer based on the political agenda. Discourse is handled within a certain social, historical, and political context covering inter-textual and discursive events affected by and affecting the texts more than a sequence formed by the texts. The political agenda, as it is stipulated that the analyzer cannot approach the analysis unbiasedly, should be considered as the analysis direction towards a certain goal (generally liberating and equalizing). The criticism, in discourse, is made not only as an adverse reprehension as generally indicated by the word but more often with the goal to show what is not present, to deny the innocence of the present, and to disclose the present power relations.

In this regard, the discourses, as the ability sequences owned by the societies, can be conceptualized as the sociocultural source used by them to construct and structure the meaning of their words and actions. The discourses, in this manner, define meaningful writing, speaking, listening, and how to behave. As used by Ó Tuathail and Agnew, discourse is defined as the "sociocultural sources used by people in forming the meanings about their worlds and activities."[56] Thus, discourses are a series of ability and rules groups providing for the readers/audiences and speakers/viewers to form an ordered meaninÓgful whole via taking what they hear and read.[57] Therefore, critical geopolitics aims to shed light on operating schemes under geopolitical power through discourse analysis.

The geopolitical discourses, according to Agnew, emerge as the *consent* creator elements that enable the hegemony founder characteristics of geopolitical orders. In this regard, the geopolitical discourse is related to how geography is *written and read* in domestic and foreign politics and how they are made possible as different practices at different times. So, the geopolitical discourse indicates, via referring to the different historicity status of political elites and institutional contexts, how the politics is *spatialized,* and the use of this with systematic and dispersed rules and concepts.[58] Agnew and Corbridge emphasize four important points related to the said approach. *The first one* is that the geopolitical discourse is not a separate action trying to identify the effect of the geographical elements on a certain foreign policy construction.

Therefore, the geopolitical discourse should not be perceived as a simple *naming* performed with the condition of being linked to any geography. Instead, the geopolitical discourse indicates that defining and naming a space means activating various narratives, subjects, and perceptions. For example, naming a space as "Islamic" or "Western" is not just giving a name but on the contrary to render said conceptualization an object of any political strategy stipulated and planned within a political context.

For the second one, the geopolitical discourse is an action consisting of practical judgment instead of the planned spreading of a formal geopolitical model. Practical geopolitical intellectualization is based on common sense narratives and distinctions. In this regard, establishing a space within discourses containing oppositions (Western–Not Western, civilized-barbarian, democratic-despotic, etc.) provides for the emergence of complementary categories. *For the third one,* the geographical knowledge given in the geopolitical discourse generally has a reductionist nature. The information on space is filtered and oppressed to be fixed for the construction of a geopolitical category. In this regard, the geopolitical discourse and judgment progress over the maximum simplification of the complex geopolitical categories and thus produce controllable geopolitical categories. *For the fourth one,* the geopolitical discourse field, as a competitive field, represents the hegemony struggle of discourses in competition with one another and therefore, all political elites do not influence the geopolitical discourse at equal ratios. Regarding the ones studying critical geopolitics, it is to reveal which discourse is hegemonic or which other discourses are forming a resistance against this hegemonic discourse.

CONCLUSION

When considered as a whole, critical geopolitics provides an important foundation for us to develop a critical position against the classical geopolitical mindset that world politics can be drawn objectively. In this regard, the goal of critical geopolitics is to demolish the logo-centric (establishing doctrines like friend-foe, good-evil; thought system where the former is seen as superior to the latter) narrative that is dominant in the spatial production of the classical geopolitical tradition and international politics in order to show the difference as opposed to identity, breaking apart as opposed to totality/unity and to turn around the acknowledged hierarchies. This strategy is important for us in two aspects. Firstly, the ones studying critical geopolitics make it possible both to resist the theoretical practices based on reality claimed knowledge and against the imposed borders forming a "reality" order in classical geopolitics and to reverse this tendency. Secondly, this strategy draws our attention to the discursive operation and power-establishing aspects of geopolitics. In this regard, the state of being critical in critical geopolitics, based on reality being not default or objective, means that world politics does not have a process separate from discursive construct. Such a postulate aids in problematizing and forms a resistance mechanism against the strength and power reflections embedded in the geopolitical discourses to the extent that it draws attention to the historicity of reality.

As a result, critical geopolitics aims to "decentralize" the analytical focus of the biased and incomplete world politics construct of the political realism integrated with the classical geopolitical mentality and to direct our attention to alternatives of different states, power, and knowledge formations. Thus, it argues that it is possible to establish a practice opposing hegemony. In this scope, critical geopolitics provides an analytic frame against the structuralist and determinist geographical perspective that examines the roles of social, historical, and linguistic uses of existing realities in painting, representing, and constructing the word, and avoids assigning a mystic autonomy to the space. This perspective both deepens and differentiates the analytical focus of our understanding regarding the inter-subjective aspect of the social world and knowledge, establishing the role of social thoughts, and international relations regarding the emphasis on the mutual formation of the actor-structure relation.

REFERENCES

Agnew, John, and Corbridge, Stuart. *Mastering Space: Hegemony, Territory and International Political Economy*. London and New York: Routledge, 1995.

Agnew, John, and Muscara, Luca. *Making Political Geography*. Second Edition, Rowman & Littlefield Publishers, 2012.

Ashley, Richard K. "A Double Reading of the Anarchy Problematique," *Millennium: Journal of International Studies* 17, no. 2, (1988): 227–262.

Atkinson, David. "Geopolitical Imaginations in Modern Italy," in *Geopolitical Traditions: Critical Histories of a Century of Geopolitical Thought*, edited by K. Dodds & D. Atkinson. London: Routledge, 1998: 93–118.

Burchill, Scott et al. *Theories of International Relations*. Palgrave Macmillan, 2013.

Cohen, Saul Bernard. *Geopolitics: Geography of International Relations*. Rowman & Littlefield Publishers, 2009.

Dalby, Simon. *Creating the Second Cold War: The Discourse of Politics*. New York, London: Bloomsbury Academic, 2016.

Dear, Michael. "The Postmodern Challenge: Reconstructing Human Geography," *Progress in Human Geography* 31, no. 5, (2007): 262–74.

Derrida, Jacques. *Of Grammatology*. Baltimore: Johns Hopkins University Press, 1976.

Dijking, Gertjan. *National Identity and Geopolitical Vision: Maps of Pride and Pain.* Routledge, 1996.

Dittmer, Jason, and Sturm, T. *Mapping the End Times: American Evangelical Geopolitics and Apocalyptic Visions.* London: Ashgate, 2010.

Do d ods, Klaus. *Geopolitics: A Very Short Introduction.* Oxford University Press , . 2011.

Dodds, Klaus. "Geopolitics in the Foreign Office: British representations of Argentina 1945- 1961." *Transactions of the Institute of British Geographers* no. 19 (1994): 273–290.

Dodds, Klaus. *Global Geopolitics: A Critical Introduction.* Routledge, 2004.

Dodds, Klaus, and Atkinson, David (eds.). *Geopolitical Traditions: A Century of Political Thought.* London and New York: Routledge, 2000.

Dodds, Klaus, Merje Kuus, and Joanne Sharp. *The Ashgate Research Companion to Critical Geopolitics.* Ashgate, 2013.

Dodds, Klaus, and Sidaway, James. "Halford Mackinder and the 'Geographical Pivot of History': A Centennial Perspective," *The Geographical Journal* 170, no. 4 (2004): 292–297.

Häkli, J. "Discourse in the Production of Political Space: Decolonizing the Symbolism of Provinces in Finland," *Political Geography* 17, no. 3, (1998): 331–363.

Hansen, Lane. *Security as Practice: Discourse Analysis and Bosnian War.* Routledge, 2006.

Hepple, Leslie. "Metaphor, Geopolitical Discourse and the Military in South America," in *Writing Worlds: Discourse, Text & Metaphor in the Representation of Landscape*, edited by Barnes and Duncan. Routledge, 1992.

W. Hepple, Lesslie W., "The Revival of Geopolitics," *Political Geography Quarterly* 5, no. 4, (October 1986): 21–26.

Herb, Guntram. "The Politics of Political Geography," in *The Sage Handbook of Political Geography*, edited by Kevin R. Cox, Murray Low, and Jenny Robinson. Ashgate, 2008.

Kuus, Merje. "Europe's Eastern Expansion and the Reinscription of Otherness in East-Central Europe," *Progress in Human Geography* 28, no. 4, (2004): 472–489.

Livingtone, David. *The Geographical Tradition: Episodes in the History of a Contested Enterprise.* Oxford, UK: Blackwell Publishing, 2002, 28–29.

Mackinder, Halford. "The Geographical Pivot of History," *The Geographical Journal.* Vol. 23, No. 4, (April 1904): 421–437.

Megoran, N. "For ethnography in political geography: Experiencing and re-imagining Ferghana Valley boundary closures," *Political Geography* 25, no. 6, (2006): 622–640. https://doi.org/10.2307/1775498

Müller, Martin. "Text, Discourse, Affect and Things," in *Ashgate Research Companion to Critical Geopolitics*, edited by Merje Kuus and Jo Sharp. Ashgate, 2012.

Newman, David. "Citizenship, Identity, and Location: The Changing Discourse of Israeli Geopolitics," in *Geopolitical Traditions: Critical Histories of a Century of Geopolitical Thought*, edited by K. Dodds and D. Atkinson. London: Routledge, 1998: 302–332.

Ó Tuathail, Gerard. "A Strategic Sign: The Geopolitical Significance of ' "Bosnia ' ":
US Foreign Policy," *Environment and Planning D: Society and Space* 17, no. 5,
(1999): 515–33.

Ó Tuathail, Gerard. *Critical Geopolitics: Writing Global Space*. Routledge , . 1996.

Ó Tuathail , Gerard. "(Dis)placing Geopolitics: Writing on the Maps of Global
Politics," *Environment and Planning D: Society and Society* 12, no. 5, (1994):
525 – -546.

Ó Tuathail , Gerard. "Political Geography of Contemporary Events VII. The
Language and Nature of the ' "New Geopolitics ' " — – The Case of US–El
Salvador Relations," *Political Geography Quarterly* 5 (1), (1996): 73–85.

Ó Tuathail, Gerard , and Agnew, John. "Geopolitics and Discourse: Practical Geopolitical Reasoning in American Foreign Policy," *Political Geography* 11, no. 2,
(1992): 190–204.

Ó Tuathail, Gerard, and Dalby, Simon. "Introduction: Rethinking Geopolitics:
Towards a Critical Geopolitics," in *Rethinking Geopolitics*, edited by Gerard Ó
Tuathail and Simon Dalby. New York: Routledge, 1998.

O'Loughlin, John. *A Dictionary of Geopolitics*. Greenwood, 1994.

Paasi, Anna. "Boundaries as Social Processes: Territoriality in the World of Flows,"
Geopolitics and International Boundaries 1, no. 1, (1998): 69–88.

Routledge, Paul. "Critical Geopolitics and Terrains of Resistance," *Political
Geography* 15, (1996): 509–532.

Routledge, Paul. "Introduction to Part Five: Anti-Geopolitics" in *The Geopolitics
Reader*, edited by G. Toal, S. Dalby, and P. Routledge. Oxford: Routledge, 2006.

Slater, David. *Geopolitics and the Post-colonial*. Wiley-Blackwell, 2004.

Walker, R. B. J. *Inside/Outside: International Relations as Political Theory*. New
York: Cambridge University Press, 1993.

NOTES

1. It is one of the points that can be directly realized that no references to critical geopolitics is given in most of the educational books of International Relations
Theory. Tim Dunne, Milja Kurki, and Steve Smith, *International Relations Theory*,
(Oxford University Press, 2013); Scott Burchill, Andrew Linklater, Richard Devetak,
and Jack Donnelly, *Theories of International Relations*, (Palgrave Macmillan, 2013).

2. Gerard Ó Tuathail and Simon Dalby, "Introduction: Rethinking Geopolitics:
Towards a Critical Geopolitics," in Gerard Ó Tuathail and Simon Dalby (eds.),
Rethinking Geopolitics, (New York: Routledge, 1998).

3. Gerard Ó Tuathail, "(Dis)placing Geopolitics: Writing on the Maps of Global
Politics," *Environment and Planning D: Society and Society* 12, no. 5 (1994):
525–546.

4. For such a theoretical discussion see David Slater, *Geopolitics and the Postcolonial*, (Wiley-Blackwell, 2004).

5. Ó Tuathail and Dalby, "Introduction: Rethinking Geopolitics: Towards a Critical
Geopolitics."

6. Dalby, Simon. *Creating the Second Cold War: The Discourse of Politics*. New York, London: Bloomsbury Academic, 2016.

7. Ó Tuathail, "Displacing Geopolitics," 527.

8. Klaus Dodds, *Geopolitics: A Very Short Introduction*, (Oxford University Press, 2007), 28.

9. Agnew and Corbridge, *Mastering Space: Hegemony.*

10. Agnew and Corbridge, *Mastering Space: Hegemony.*

11. Halford Mackinder, "The Geographical Pivot of History," *The Geographical Journal* 23, no. 4 (April 1904): 421–437.

12. See for a work where the important representatives of classical geopolitics are given, Gerard Ó Tuathail and Simon Dalby, *Geopolitics Reader*, (London and New York: Routledge, 2006).

13. Agnew and Corbridge, *Mastering Space,* 64.

14. Klaus Dodds and David Atkinson (Ed.), *Geopolitical Traditions: A Century of Political Thought*, (London and New York, Routledge, 2000).

15. John Agnew and Luca Muscara, *Making Political Geography*, Second Edition, (Rowman & Littlefield Publishers, 2012).

16. Gerard Ó Tuathail and John Agnew, "Geopolitics and Discourse: Practical Geopolitical Reasoning in American Foreign Policy," *Political Geography* 11, no. 2, (1992): 190–198.

17. Not only the discourse analysis, but critical geopolitics studies also benefit from many of the studies of Foucault. Especially Foucault's *Security, Territory, Population* work is important for the ones studying critical geography.

18. See for a work reviewing in detail the conceptual and theoretical diversity in critical geopolitics, Klaus Dodds, Merje Kuus, and Joanne Sharp, *The Ashgate Research Companion to Critical Geopolitics*, (Ashgate, 2013).

19. Hepple, "Metaphor, Geopolitical Discourse and the Military in South America," in *Writing Worlds: Discourse, Text & Metaphor in the Representation of Landscape*, ed. Barnes and Duncan (Routledge, 1992), 139.

20. Ó Tuathail, *Critical Geopolitics.*

21. Agnew, *Geopolitics.*

22. Dalby, *Creating the Second Cold War.*

23. Different from other critical geopolitical theoreticians, John Agnew says in his many analyses that the approach enriching critical geopolitics theoretically is the World-System Analysis developed by Immanuel Wallerstein. Peter Taylor, who is one of the first editors of one of the most important magazines in human geography today, *Political Geography,* was one of the most vigorous defenders of this view in the early years of the magazine. In fact, Agnew takes the expansion of and formation of different hegemonic orders in different historical periods by capitalism subject to the World-System Analysis as the core of his research in many of his books and articles.

24. Agnew and Corbridge, *Mastering Space,* 15.

25. Agnew and Corbridge, *Mastering Space,* 47.

26. Atkinson, "Geopolitical Imagination."

27. For such a study see David Newman, "Citizenship, Identity and Location: The Changing Discourse of Israeli Geopolitics," in *Geopolitical Traditions: Critical*

Histories of a Century of Geopolitical Thought, ed. K. Dodds and D. Atkinson (London: Routledge, 1998), 302–332; David Atkinson, "Geopolitical Imaginations in Modern Italy," in K. Dodds and D. Atkinson, *Geopolitical Traditions*, 93–118.

28. Gertjan Dijking, *National Identity and Geopolitical Vision: Maps of Pride and Pain*, (Routledge, 1996): 14.

29. Gerard Ó Tuathail, "Political Geography of Contemporary Events VII. The Language and Nature of the 'New Geopolitics'—The Case of US–El Salvador Relations," *Political Geography Quarterly* 5, no. 1 (1996):73–85; Ó Tuathail, *Critical Geopolitics*; Ó Tuathail, "A Strategic Sign: The Geopolitical Significance of 'Bosnia' in US Foreign Policy," *Environment and Planning D: Society and Space* 17, no. 5 (1999): 515–33.

30. Ó Tuathail, *Critical Geopolitics.*

31. Ó Tuathail, *Critical Geopolitics.*

32. Paul Routledge, "Critical Geopolitics and Terrains of Resistance," *Political Geography*, 15, (1996): 509–532.

33. Gerard Ó Tuathail and Simon Dalby (eds.), *Rethinking Geopolitics* (New York: Routledge, 1998).

34. R. B. J. Walker, *Inside/Outside: International Relations as Political Theory*, (New York: Cambridge University Press, 1993): 108–110.

35. Ó Tuathail and Dalby, *Rethinking Geopolitics.*

36. Anna Paasi, "Boundaries as Social Processes: Territoriality in the World of Flows," *Geopolitics and International Boundaries* 1, no. 1 (1998): 69–88.

37. Paul Routledge, "Introduction to Part Five: Anti-Geopolitics," in *The Geopolitics Reader*, ed. G. Toal, S. Dalby, and P. Routledge (Oxford: Routledge, 2006), 234–48.

38. Jacques Derrida, *Of Grammatology*, (Baltimore: Johns Hopkins University Press, 1976); Michael Dear, "The Postmodern Challenge: Reconstructing Human Geography," *Transactions of the Institute of British Geographers* 13, (1988): 262–274.

39. Ó Tuathail, *Critical Geopolitics.*

40. Simon Dalby, "Critical geopolitics: Discourse, difference and dissent," *Environment and Planning D: Society and Space* 9, (1991): 261–283; Ó Tuathail, "(Dis) placing geopolitics."

41. Martin Müller, "Text, Discourse, Affect and Things," in *Ashgate Research Companion to Critical Geopolitics*, ed. Klaus Dodds, Merje Kuus, and Joanne Sharp, (Ashgate, 2012), 49–69.

42. Klaus Dodds and James. D. Sidaway, "Halford Mackinder and the 'Geographical Pivot of History': A Centennial Perspective," *The Geographical Journal* 170, no. 4 (2004): 292297.

43. Barnes and Duncan, "Introduction," in *Writing Worlds: Discourse, Text and Metaphor in the Representation of Landscape*, eds. Trevor J. Barnes and James S. Duncan (London and New York: Routledge, 1992), 2.

44. David Livingtone, *The Geographical Tradition: Episodes in the History of a Contested Enterprise* (Oxford, UK: Blackwell Publishing, 2002), 28–29

45. Critical geopolitics argues that our act of writing about the world should, as it reveals our method of representing the world, at the same time be understood as a condition revealing ourselves. In this regard, the represented world inevitably is related directly to the worldview of the representing person. This renders the act of writing important on its own.

It handles the act of writing of James Clifford in five bases and this is very important regarding the critical space studies. Accordingly, the social context, institutional regulations (audience, intellectual tradition, school of thought), genres that are part of it (schoolbooks, academic studies, newspapers), the political position of the writer maintaining its authority (colonial government), and the historical contexts rendering all these factors logical and meaningful at a certain time and space. Referenced from Clifford by Barnes and Duncan, "Introduction," 3.

46. Trevor J. Barnes and James S. Duncan, "Introduction: Writing Worlds," in *Writing Worlds*, eds. Barnes and Duncan, 1–17.

47. Barnes and Duncan, "Introduction," 2.

48. Dalby, *Creating the Second Cold War*, 180.

49. Ó Tuathail, *Critical Geopolitics*.

50. Richard K. Ashley, "A Double Reading of the Anarchy Problematique," *Millennium*, 17, (1988): 241–242.

51. Dalby, *Creating the Second Cold War*; Ó Tuathail, *Critical Geopolitics*; Klaus Dodds, "Geopolitics in the Foreign Office: British representations of Argentina 1945-1961," *Transactions of the Institute of British Geographers*, 19, (1994): 273–290.

52. Jason Dittmer and T. Sturm, *Mapping the End Times: American Evangelical Geopolitics and Apocalyptic Visions*, (London: Ashgate, 2010).

53. Müller, "Text, Discourse," 5.

54. Agnew and Corbridge, *Mastering Space*; N. Megoran, "For ethnography in political geography: Experiencing and re-imagining Ferghana Valley boundary closures," *Political Geography* 25, no. 6 (2006): 622–640.

55. Ó Tuathail, "Geopolitical Structure and Cultures," 82; Merje Kuus, "Europe's Eastern Expansion and the Reinscription of Otherness in East-Central Europe," *Progress in Human Geography* 28, no. 4 (2004): 472–489; Smith, G., "The masks of Proteus: Russia, geopolitical shift and the new Eurasianism," *Transactions of the Institute of British Geographers*, 24, no. 4 (1999): 481–494; Simon Dalby, "Gender and critical geopolitics: Reading security discourse in the new world disorder," *Environment and Planning D: Society & Space*, 12 (1994): 595–612; Häkli, J., "Discourse in the Production of Political Space: Decolonizing the Symbolism of Provinces in Finland," *Political Geography* 17, no. 3 (1998): 331–363.

56. Ó Tuathail and Agnew, "Geopolitics and Discourse," 190–204.

57. Ó Tuathail and Agnew, "Geopolitics and Discourse," 192.

58. Agnew and Corbridge, *Mastering Space*, 48.

Index

About the Contributors

EDITOR AND CONTRIBUTOR

Tayyar Arı is a professor of International Relations, graduated from Middle East Technical University in 1984 and received his PhD from İstanbul University in 1991. He has been at Bursa Uludag University since 1984. He became an associate professor in 1996 and a professor in 2002. Since then, he has been teaching at the same university and some private universities in Istanbul. Prof. Arı made his postgraduate study at Georgetown University, U.S., and has been to several countries for research and international conference purposes, particularly in the Middle Eastern, European, and Eurasian countries. He has several books and articles published in Turkish and English on the Middle East, Eurasia, Turkish-American Relations, and South Asia. Currently, Prof. Dr. Tayyar Arı is serving as the head of the Department of International Relations at Bursa Uludag University.

CONTRIBUTORS

Yücel Bozdağlıoğlu is a full professor at Aydın Adnan Menderes University, Faculty of Economics, Department of International Relations, Aydın, Turkey. After he got his undergraduate degree from Ankara University, Faculty of Political Science, Department of International Relations in 1991, he attended the University of Kentucky, USA, to pursue his graduate studies. He completed his MA in 1997 in International Relations and his Ph.D. in Transnational Relations in 2001. During his stay at the University of Kentucky, he served as a teaching assistant and also taught courses in International Relations at Northern Kentucky University as a visiting professor. His Ph.D. thesis, *Identity and International Relations: Turkish Foreign Policy in the Post-World War II Era*, was published by the Routledge Press in 2003 as a book titled *Turkish Foreign Policy and Turkish Identity: A*

Constructivist Approach. He writes extensively on Turkey's Foreign Policy, Theories of International Relations, and Turkish Politics.

Muzaffer Ercan Yılmaz is a professor of International Relations, currently at Bursa Uludag University, Turkey. He graduated from Ankara University in 1994, completed his MA in International Politics from The American University, Washington, D.C. in 1998, and earned his PhD in Conflict Analysis and Resolution from George Mason University, Fairfax, Virginia in 2002. His research interests particularly include international conflict resolution and peace building in war-torn societies.

Veysel Ayhan, is currently a Professor in the Department of International Relation at Bolu Abant İzzet Baysal University. Prof. Ayhan, after completing his bachelor's degree at Uludag University, Faculty of Economics and Administrative Sciences, Department of International Relations (1995– 1998), has been in England and UAE during 1998–1999. He started his MA at Uludag University, the Department of International Relations (1999–2002). In 2002, he started his academic life at Uludag University as a Research Assistant. During 2002 and 2005, he completed his PhD in the same department at Uludag University. He has published and edited several books on the Middle East and Political Economy. His main books are *Arab Spring: Uprising, Revolutions and Change*, *Oil and Security: Political Economy of Middle East*, and *Lebanon: War, Peace, Resistance.* Moreover, there are many academic works on the Middle East, forced migration, and conflict resolution.

Murat Yeşiltaş is a Professor in the department of international relations at the Social Sciences University of Ankara. He also holds the position of director of foreign and security studies at SETA Foundation, Ankara, Turkey. Dr. Yesiltas's current researches are on international security, terrorism, military studies, ethnic and religious radicalization, and non-state conflicts. He is currently working on the following research projects: The Politics of Kurdish Geopolitical Space in the Middle East; The Logic of Survival of Non-state Armed Groups. His recent books are *Türkiye Dünyanın Neresinde? Hayali Coğrafyalar, Çarpışan Anlatılar* (editor) (Koç Ünivesitesi Yayınları, 2015), *Jeopolitik Zihniyet ve Türkiye'de Ordu* (Kadim, 2016), *Non-State Military Actors in the Middle East: Geopolitics, Ideology and Strategy* (editor) (Palgrave Macmillan, 2017).

Oktay Bingöl received his doctorate and associate professorship degrees in the field of International Relations. His research interests include Turkish foreign policy, international security, conflict and peace studies, strategy and geopolitics. He has various academic publications in Turkish and English. He is a faculty member of the Department of International Relations (English) at İstanbul Arel University. He is also the director of the International Strategic Studies Application and Research Center of the same university.

Bülent Sarper Ağır is currently working as an associate professor of International Relations (exclusively English) at Aydın Adnan Menderes University, Turkey. He received his BA and MA degrees in the discipline of International Relations from Ege University, and his PhD degree from Ankara University. Bülent Sarper Ağır joined Central European University/Hungary and Paradigm Research Center/Kosovo as a visiting scholar. His main areas of research and expertise are Balkan Studies, Security Studies, and Turkish Foreign Policy. He has published several academic articles and book chapters on international relations. He is the editor of *Kosovo: Past, Present, and Future*, published by Nova Science Publishers, New York, the U.S.

Çiğdem Aydın Koyuncu graduated from Bursa Uludag University, Faculty of Economics and Administrative Sciences, Department of International Relations in 1999. She completed her master's degree at Bursa Uludag University in 2002 and she completed her doctorate in 2008 at the same University. She started her academic life at Bursa Uludag University, Faculty of Economics and Administrative Sciences, Department of International Relations in 2000. She got her associate professor title in 2017 and she is currently working at the same department. Aydın Koyuncu has scientific studies in the field of International Relations. Her areas of interest: International Relations and Women, Feminism, Human Rights, Minorities and the Balkans.

Doğan Şafak Polat completed the International Relations Doctorate Program at Ankara University in 2015. Between 2015 and 2021, he taught undergraduate and graduate/doctorate courses at Istanbul Arel University. His research areas include International Security, Turkish Foreign Policy, and International Organizations. He has various articles, book chapters, and symposium and congress papers published in Turkish and English. He is fluent in English and French.

Zerrin Ayşe Öztürk was graduated from the Department of Journalism, Faculty of Communications, Ege University in 1994. She started to work as a research assistant at Ege University, Faculty of Economics and Administrative Sciences in 1995. She completed her MA in International Relations at the University of Kent, Canterbury in 1997, and received her PhD in Politics from the School of Social Sciences of the University of Manchester in 2007. Between 2002 and 2008, she worked as a lecturer at the same Faculty. Her research interests include critical security studies, normative theory, human security, gender studies, and environmental security. She has advanced levels of English and Spanish. Dr. Öztürk currently works as an Assistant Professor of International Relations at Ege University, Izmir, Turkey. Dr. Öztürk has received a 2022 Taiwan MOFA fellowship and is currently working on her project on human trafficking issues and policies of Taiwan from the human security perspective at the National Taiwan University in Taipei.

Mehmet Ali Ak works as a research assistant at Bursa Uludag University and as a PhD candidate at the same university. He specializes in the Balkans, culture and identity studies, postcolonial discourse, and ontological security. He continues to study these issues, such as book chapters, articles, and congress papers. And he works as a researcher in a project called Euro-Skepticism Analysis in Serbia in the context of ontological security.